TWO HEMISPHERES

Two Hemispheres

Nadine McInnis

Brick Books

Library and Archives Canada Cataloguing in Publication

McInnis, Nadine, 1957–
    Two hemispheres / Nadine McInnis.

Poems.
ISBN 978-1-894078-59-7

I. Title.

PS8575.I54T96 2007   C811'.54   C2007-902765-2

We acknowledge the Canada Council for the Arts, the Government of
Canada through the Book Publishing Industry Development Program
(BPIDP), and the Ontario Arts Council for their support of our publishing
program.

Cover images: The crow is from a photograph by Nadine McInnis; the
image of the hands is used "by kind permission of The Royal Society of
Medicine."

Author photograph by Vivian Tors.

The book is set in Bembo and Figural.

Design and layout by Alan Siu.

Printed and bound by Sunville Printco Inc.

Brick Books
431 Boler Road, Box 20081
London, Ontario N6K 4G6

www.brickbooks.ca

"It is impossible to feel sorry for crazy people since their realities do not coincide with our normal conception of tragedy."

Zelda Fitzgerald, letter written to
F. Scott Fitzgerald when she was an
in-patient at the Phipps Clinic, 1932

Every photograph is a certificate of presence... like the ectoplasm of "what-had-been"; neither image nor reality, a new being, really: a reality one can no longer touch.

Roland Barthes, *Camera Lucida:
Reflections on Photography*

Contents

Illustrations

The 10 photographs which illustrate *Two Hemispheres* were taken by Dr. Hugh W. Diamond, Medical Superintendent of Women at the Surrey County Lunatic Asylum (England), in the 1850s. They are used here "by kind permission of the Royal Society of Medicine" in London.

The photographs are officially identified by the numbers listed below. The titles listed below (and used as captions in the book) link each photo to the poem written in response to it.

A perfect and faithful record

Ten women, long dead, photographed
in the Surrey County Lunatic Asylum.
You could be fooled
by their modest dress, Victorian poses, the
grey sheet behind them
obscuring how they arrived here.

Their doctor crouches behind the camera
hidden beneath a velvet cloak.
He has placed them on chairs,
smoothed their hair, asked them
to hold still—a docility today
attained only by pharmaceuticals.

You would never know
from the faded salt-on-paper portraits
that this asylum was considered modern
and humane: a perfect self-contained world
with its own gasworks, water tower,
laundry and gardens tended by patients
rescued from indigence.

Even knowing this, you still want
to turn away and forget them,
the way you focus
on a red traffic light when the homeless
troll for change between lanes,
or cross streets, darting between cars,
when twitching men lurch towards you.
Let them be faint rings of disturbance

trapped in glass. But for you, they become
negatives, darkly transparent.

Move in more closely,
press your face
against the museum case, and you'll see
that one is pretty, her dark hair
falling into her lap like water.
Another does not raise her eyes.
One grips arms across her chest, defiant.
Her truth cannot be held
by this image; across 150 years
the betrayal in her gaze burns.

Their faces have outlasted
the science of physiognomy
that created them, studies in objectivity,
gradations on a scale used to rank suffering:
distress, sorrow, deep sorrow, grief and
melancholy, anguish and despair—
a perfect and faithful record.

And, you wonder, how is one sorrow
deeper than another?
What is melancholy if not grief?
Although the old-fashioned word *anguish*
feels right to you, timeless, lived timelessly.
That's the problem, the never-ending
sense of it, just like these women
who will sit forever
unknown.

Entertainment: lunatic's ball

A caged bird, a wild party of one.
Yellow feathers curl at his neck
like masquerade finery, his piping voice
sings only for himself.
He dances frenetically from bar to bar
tempting me to be a small part of such abandon
but when he is mine, he goes mad.

The pet-store owner has never heard of such a thing,
but will honour his *singing guarantee*
if I wish: guaranteed
to sing for 30 days, for 21 the canary
is demented with song, stuck
in mania, trilling day and night—
even in the covered cage—before he
pulls out all his fancy feathers and falls

silent, the intricate songs forgotten.
Voiceless, he paces the bar,
flight abandoned, scaled feet clicking as he
follows his shadow on the wall, back
and forth, focusing on the enemy, on himself.

Is it premonition, compassion
or morbid fascination that keeps him here,
in my home, and not banished
as all things are that do not live up
to promises made by someone else?

I know what will happen. No asylum
for deranged birds on this earth.

Even in a safe white cage with a view
to the garden, the worst occurs:
the bird hunches at the cage bottom
eating seeds off cut newspaper,
pecking at details of domestic violence,
one hard bitter seed, then another,
mocks—*enjoys walks in the country,*
tick, tick—*no skid marks in hit-and-run*
—*after a long courageous battle with*—
the usual shame-free diseases, tick, tick
—*blowout sale*—tick, tick—*summer*
madness—yesterday's bad weather
swirling around him—*thunderstorms*—
tick, tick—*risk of hail, high gusts, funnel*
clouds. A relief

when he won't drink and falls
curled and reptilian with long claws,
scaled feet, reversing his evolution.
Reduced to fixed bones, feathers,
and spent primitive rage,

a stone fossil broken open
like an egg at the bottom of the cage.

Miasma theory

The fossil record is incomplete.
Only the skulls are preserved
but *this* is known: the brain exploded
one cubic inch per 100,000 years.
Evolution unprecedented and never repeated
from the mollusk brain, to the reptilian brain,
to two beautiful hemispheres
full of chaotic weather.
All the safety features hard-wired in,
then set loose on ten trillion units of information
stored to negotiate the world we live in now:
a fight or flight reaction
that has nothing to respond to
but the enclosure of a city bus
or the precipice of public speaking, undetectable
venom picked up on fingertips
that must be scrubbed raw,
desire that cannot be satisfied, despair
at the emptiness of the night sky,
bush fires in the nervous system
lit by the tinder of tension,
a fever-bearing fog, lightning strike here,
then there, a miasma severing connections
between thought and feeling, drifting continents
frozen in sinister blue,
or lost in tropical depressions.

10a [Chronic puerperal mania]

Chronic puerperal mania

She remembers the age of restraints.
She remembers the *English camisole*,
delicate name for that most indelicate
of straitjackets,
and how she had to relearn to control
her body's functions, also delicately named
the call of nature.

Nature calls to her now, but gently.
Not shrieking of rookeries
blackening the sky over London, not the
simmering hiss of raptors in her head.

Gently, nature summons her.
She prefers to be outside in the garden
or in the pigeon house with its melancholy
cooing, a slanting light revealing
all the hidden emeralds and glistening purples,
the cloud-white rings around their necks,
their wings throbbing around her face
until that breathless moment
when they perch on the edge of the high window,
push off like swimmers into the sky.
Every time they launch themselves
she holds her breath and can't believe it's true.

She has a silvery ring around her neck too,
cut by broken glass, cut by her own hand

years ago when they untied her,
gave her the trembling buoyancy of limbs,
freed from the desolate yard
where she was chained hour after hour, day
after day, until winter locked her
back into the nightmare shackles of her bed.

Now she can't stand to tie her hat
under her chin, wears the scarf around her neck
loose to hide the open buttons
she cannot bear to fasten.

She agreed to sit here
if she could bring a bird indoors with her,
so she would not be trapped in the doctor's studio.
Of black cages, she's already had too much.
She remembers *the tranquilizer chair*,
strapped in with a box over her head
and a bucket under her open seat.

She remembers the leeches on her neck.
She remembers the blisters on her temples
burning through bone, a funnel
sucking angry voices into her head instead of out.

She doesn't remember the man, his face
so unlined, strangely young, bending over to follow
the blue vein along the pale skin of her forearm
with his soft mouth.
She doesn't remember any of the babies,

or the last one that broke her,
the swaddling too tight, too tight, the tension
in her head snapping,

although there is something haunting about the cloth
she places under the pigeon on her lap.
As if memory can be a sensation, as if
she feels again a baby's warm weight
squirming on damp flannel after a bath,
rosy arms by the rosy light of a low and gentle fire.

Entertainment: a dramatic spectacle

Like nineteenth-century British aristocrats
who paid one shilling on Sunday afternoons
to watch lunatics at the Bethlem Asylum,
or the villagers of the Middle Ages
who sent their own ships of fools
to travel up and down the canals and rivers of Europe
bringing merriment and diversion at every port—
I, too, have used insanity to entertain.

I've held my palms out at parties
and invited people gathered around to look
at the lines and cross-hatchings of a madwoman.
Intersecting my hand at the base of my fingers
the heart line veers disastrously towards
a chained head line, the worst possible sign
of a nervous system lost to static.

I used to embellish an impressive picture
of the woman whose palms
I mysteriously possess, describing her
right down to her mismatched shoes:
her gait, stiff and shuffling, from nights spent
sleeping under the bridge near the off-ramp,
her hair, a tangled nest of leaves and dead grass.

Then I would gleefully explain that she,
in turn, has my hands,
and the next time a homeless woman
thrusts her hand in the car window for spare change
they should check for my life

imprinted there—one strong marriage,
two healthy children, thousands of books read,
all the potential a new century
has given women of my inclination—
and be a little more generous on my account.

Distress

Fire forms and moves and follows
as we leave the ocean behind,
closing down the trails where we hiked
across crackling dry highlands,
sealing off the dusky edges of the park
where coyotes yipped all night
disturbing our sleep.
My neck muscles taut with a growing
and inexplicable vigilance.

Fire follows me home—
flying sparks lick the car's chassis,
wings beat above the burning trees,
after lifting from knotted nests
and homing in on me alone.

Madness as a romantic notion,
a purifying fire, and all that is not
authentic falls away. If only this
could fall away. But each moment is
too real. No past, no future,
only the torturous present.

Vanity long gone, I clench sweaty sheets,
face curled between my knees,
hair a mass of tangles.
My shoes are locked away in the closet,
inaccessible, unnecessary—
weeks since I've felt ground
beneath my feet.

The books I cannot read
smoulder on the bedside table.
A glass sends off fumes
in the darkened room,
only organizes into the balm of water
when tranquilizers need to be swallowed.

Sorrow, then deep sorrow

Fall comes, season of auguries.
I'm desperate for some sign to counteract
the fact that evolution has not perfected
itself in my bloodline.

My father has poisoned himself again.
Flesh of my flesh, toxic
once more. The charcoal burns through him,
followed by a wave of convulsions
breaking against hospital white
in the slow process of purging his brain.
But these details are merely physical.
He suffers, as all suicides do,
in isolation.

Vivid, unbidden as hallucinations,
are the others: his own father
weighed down in a winter coat
breathing in oblivion under the waves;
his grandmother, who succumbed
to *melancholia*, a euphemism for strychnine.
I see her hunched over her agony
in the barn, mourning doves in the rafters
cooing encouragement.

Let these sylphs fade back into the past
where they belong.
Amnesia is the gift of the well,
but for me there is only will power—
that elixir the smug believe in.

I focus my mind on tropical birds
in a magazine open beside his bed,
vivid flashes living all winter
around the hot lights of parking lots,
escaped through open windows,
apertures of light at the end
of darkened rooms. Birds

trapped and then free,
fantastic sea-green, a yellow flickering,
flash of fuchsia drifting from light
to light in the falling snow.
Too close and their feathers melt,
too far, and they fall, frozen
like stones, to the earth.

It's dark again, and his self-hatred
burns, barely contained
by the bars of his hospital bed.
He's tied down by tubes,
sedated, but still emitting
a bright chemical fire
that will burn me if I get too close.

11a [Delusional melancholia precipitated by grief]

Delusional melancholia precipitated by grief

Each day she places the lace handkerchief
on her hair and carries
a cloth bag looped over her right arm, ready
to return home.

But there is no home anymore.
Her husband, too, lost more than he could bear—
lost her as well as the baby
and has fled to a future
made tangible by another woman's body.
Their yeasty combustion has given rise
to new silky curls, moon-coloured fingernails
small as ladybugs, soft skin
so pale it chases away ghosts,
while she stares at the floor of the asylum,
keeps watch, as though her baby
will crawl back out of nothingness
to pull at the hem of her dress.

She's sure that she can feel
her breasts hot and full again
pushed against her baby's feverish face—
but the lure of milk is not enough,
poured out as tears, emptied,
her chest now flat and numb. So empty,
she wandered to the edge of town
followed the cry, now lost down a well, now
hidden in the grasses along the river, now swinging
wildly, snagged and condemned
in the tallest tree. Disconsolate, every night

she woke her husband to come with her,
his strong arms more capable than hers
of carrying the baby home.
But he would not come, and the baby
would not be borne back to its empty cradle.

The string she's tied to her finger loops
back along her lap, leads her out
to neither world. She must fold
and endlessly unfold the baby's clothes
carried everywhere with her, along with
the small Bible he left behind,
knit leggings grimy from her hands,
sweaters and bonnets with moth holes
that mysteriously appear and multiply,
traces of insects that crawl invisibly
through tightly knotted string at night
when her vigilance fails.

At dawn the baby's cry wakes her
and she rises with the exhaustion
of those first nights, unfolds the small
clothes, growing smaller by the day.
She must start again,
prepare to rise from her chair
and resume her life. She's ready.
She'll lift her eyes once she hears
the familiar rhythm of her husband's step.

A trial in mesmerism

In the neurology unit, I'm amazed
at what the complicity of illness
gives this stranger licence to do to me.

He has braided electrodes into my hair.
Hours I have spent smelling the sweet tang
of his underarms. In this dim room
his white coat could be a bathrobe
threatening to swing open and reveal
the dark patch of his dress pants.

The metal contacts he fixes to my skin
are coldly bright, a constellation
lighting up the dome of my skull.
He's held my hand in his precise hands.
Before we are done, he will know my nerves,
my every response, how much it takes
to make me tremble.

He has been gentlemanly in his requests—
turned away as I removed my stockings,
touched my sleeve and waited
as I lifted it further. He observed
the blue pulse in my wrist speed up.
We'll start here, he says
and touches an ankle with the probe.

At first I feel nothing
and he's turned away to watch my brain's
lightning strike harmlessly over the ocean.
Then he's rushing behind me out of the dark

and my legs shake as though
he's pumping me full of pure adrenaline.
But it's only fight or flight,
a chemical reaction, nothing more.

Shock treatment, he says, then laughs.
He can guess what's brought me here
although all I've mentioned
are the unaccountable electric current
down the left leg making my gait
awkward and uncoordinated,
a tingling slipped like a radioactive glove
onto the left hand, and the constant migraine
behind my left eye.

He talks about happiness,
how you must choose to be happy.
And I wonder if he says this
to the sufferers of MS and brain tumours.
Does he know already that he will find
nothing here, nothing most people
would call real?

He tells me we're finished
and my heart pounds hard.
He observes my terror and laughs,
holding the bundle of wires in one hand—
the solid weight of Rapunzel's braid
still warm from resting on my back—
and pulls the male from the female plugs
one by one, as easily as that.

Happiness.
What could he know of my happiness
and what was remembered
as my brain refused to yield
its mysteries to him:

Sunrise, walking the hills with the man
who will be my husband.
Heavy-headed dandelions
thud wet against our legs,
leaving cool snail trails like kisses
on bare skin.
We cast aside our clothes,
hurl them into the blazing yellow morning.
My voice calls across twenty-five years,
"Remember this on the day you die,"
unable to imagine how anything but happiness
could ever claim us.

29a [Epileptic ecstatic mania]

Epileptic ecstatic mania

Her delicate fingers are clenched.
But how could it be prayer
to a god so cruel? Her right knee
braces against the next onslaught,
for there will always be another,
and another after that.
You could snap her bones
like kindling. She's been broken
over and over by the god-fire
that consumes her during the fits.

The dogs know, the wily dogs that roam
the narrow alleyways of Lambeth Marsh
as she wanders home at sundown
from the factory where she sorts paper.
The dogs sense her disorientation
as the orange swirls in the sky
behind the railway bridge that arcs over
the sulphurous crooked streets.
Sundowning, that term still to be invented,
a time of day infamous for agitation
in mental hospitals in the next century.

Dogs only know the language of scent,
the odd smouldering film on her skin,
eerie ringing that kindles a fire-storm
only they can hear.
She draws down her lower lip
as though snarling at the enemy

almost upon her. They snarl back and cower,
fur standing up along their thin spines and then
she falls.

Time and earth are destroyed
and created again, mud thrown on her face
from god's violent fusion,
mud she will not rise from one day.
Dust to dust. Happily, she would be
dust, not dirt to those
who step over her in the alleyway
or squeeze by close to the brick wall,
not glancing down, hurrying away.

She prays fire will never find her
at the factory, but how could it not—
stacks of blank paper of every texture
waiting for some cataclysm
to make it real. She feels heat
when she sorts and folds.
Fire licks at the ends of her fingers.
She is paltry fuel, twisted and stubborn,
unlike the leaping incandescence
gone in a flash, all gone finally:
her independence, her livelihood.

She's safer here, where she is held close
during the fits, where she is given
the gift of dreamless sleep.
So she is startled by the burning line
of powder that lights up the doctor's studio
when the shutter opens.

The familiar smell of scorched rubber,
and burned onto the glass negative
for all time is that split-second recognition
usually denied to mortals, not of fire,
but of the blackness beyond fire,
metal shutter opening and drawing her in
for all time.

Approaches to the clinical gaze

Is it darkness? No. It has none of the gentle
insistence of night pressing in
and opening your senses,
night-blooming *nicotiana*, mock orange
laid low with little lanterns of sweetness,
none of darkness's liquid magnified sound.

Is it a purifying fire? Ask that
of the asylum's inmates chained to their beds
as flames lick the hems of their night clothes.
No metaphor, no flickering reflection
on the wall. You'd climb the walls too,
anyone would, with fire's irresistible incentive.

A veil of tears? *Veil* is too filmy,
too unsubstantial to capture the daily occupation
of crying, enough tears to fill a reservoir.
What could live in such foul salty water?
That creature, eyeless, pitiless,
could be a metaphor.

But this is what comes in a dream,
memory and metaphor both.
This is what it is like:

Standing on a crowded bus in Spain with my husband.
He is carrying the heavier pack as we jostle towards the port
that will take us away from the oppressive heat of the city,
to a cool island, the fresh wind pushing muslin
against my young body. This was years ago.

At first it seems accidental, a weight resting against my hip
but then it starts to move with deliberate purpose
and I know it is a hand. I try to twist away, wedged
tight in the crowded bus. The weight on my back locks me in,
baggage only literal at this point in my life. What I dread most
begins to happen: the hand changes direction. I struggle
to wrench free, pushed up against my husband. Can he
feel the hand moving lower? But he smiles,
thinking I'm perturbed by the heat, the enclosed space,
whispers, "Soon we'll be out of here." I twist away
again but cannot escape the hand, my heart racing, black wave
of the first of a lifetime of anxiety attacks in enclosed
spaces. Desperately looking into the closest faces,
a kerchiefed old woman, a bored teenaged girl,
the glossy back of a man's head, slightly balding,
and my husband smiling. No connection
between what I see and what I feel. I could scream,
or whisper to him, but what could he do to help me?
I'm on my own. I've never been so alone.
I will not tell him about this for years.

6a [Anorexic hysteria]

Anorexic hysteria

An acrid cloud fills the air
as the camera's eye opens, and there again
is the leaping fire burning in a basket
suspended over the canoe's prow.
She's home, across the ocean, ankle-deep
in a lake large enough to be an inland sea.
The men torch for eels at night,
a small crab turns under her foot
burrowing deeper into the silt.

He lunges with the spear, his motion
fluid and beautiful, piercing soundless water,
and a point of fire flickers between her legs.
Caught on his spear is a dark ribbon
writhing, voluptuous shape of pain.
She eases towards the men's gentle cajoling
her body, weightless as the water deepens.
"Hold your skirt up," she hears in a language
she has forgotten, then remembers.
In the pool created by her lifted hem
he places two eels stretched out in death

but dancing again in the cooking pot,
humid, faintly salty. Nudging the sides,
flexing, undulating. The smell drives her out
of the wigwam, away from the spruce boughs
where her mother has lain for months
coughing red from her lungs onto dirt. A sharp cramp
brings her close to the forest floor. Young summer grass
streaked with blood, her mother's blood,
now her own,

hidden. And then there is confusion.
The eels are dead, her mother
is dead. Blood and salty humid smell, rocking
across the ocean with this strange white man
who told her relatives she would pose
beside the Indian bones and quillwork baskets
in the Crystal Palace, but before that happens,
money changes hands on the dock
and he is gone.

At first she likes the way the woman washes
and brushes her dark hair, calls her *green fruit*,
laughs as though fond of her new name.
Here she is, layered and quiet on a bed
trimmed with eyelet lace

until her door is thrown open,
and he's upon her, springy tense and grinning.
She doesn't understand why he's so happy
to see her. And it hurts, and it hurts,
still stinging from the bloody sponge
the woman has pushed inside her.
But too soon his face is red with rage.
He strikes her until all the English words
she's learned flare and go out.

After that, men slip against her open thighs,
white as death, hot and urgent pushing inside her
or warm and damp, spent against her side

or shove her hands along the length or make her
take all of it still writhing into her mouth,
the same smell sickening her as the day
she became a woman. *Elie y ni'niknaq,*★
she screams until she is cast out.

She trembled when the doctor drew close
to tidy her hair. He stepped back then,
offered her a ripe apple to quiet her hands.
She must hold still for 10 beats of her heart
or she will blur, she will not exist. She holds the apple
loosely, for red has given her much pain in life,
and a little relief. During her monthlies,
she could rest, as she rests here,
but without absolution. Touches her pulse
to make sure she's still alive, keeps the apple
within reach should hunger ever happen again.
She'll put it into her mouth only if appetite
arrives in its most innocent form.

★ *I am going home.*

Entertainment: storytelling on a winter's night

Unsettling, the stories that haunt me
during my long hours in bed.

A balcony, grade 11. Not my crowd
but I am carried along somehow
to an apartment furnished with cardboard boxes
and old silver butter knives burned from hash
they're inhaling over the greasy stove,
the element coiled red hot. I want
to be out of there, but the balcony is as far as I can go
without drawing attention to myself.
Far below, a flock of sparrows pecking
in the dead grass, and I cast around for something
that's bound to make them laugh and sweep me
into the drugged hilarity of their circle.
Those birds look just like toads, a flock of toads.
But no one reacts. They look at me blankly.
Then laughter comes from where I least expect it,
from the boy just out of the psych ward, who laughs
and laughs and looks over the railing and laughs again,
catching my eye. I've reached through his fog
without wanting to. Horrified that he's the only one
who sees what I see, I run as if my life depends
on it, taking stairs two at a time, hurl the doors open.
The sparrows fly up in my face, and I'm free of him.

Free of him in a way I'll never be free
of my father, no matter how cunning I am.
Another story surfaces, to be forgotten, quickly—
ten years ago, the father competition,
a table of poets at a restaurant, winding up
into the same hysterical laughter, high on pain.
The champion will be the one with the worst father story—
and I win with my description of his attempted suicide
on my 13th birthday, the poison in the garage at dawn,
my mother's scream up the stairs. The suburban
details, perfect and pitiful. No pink cake for me,
sitting in the hospital lobby as they pump his stomach,
lace his blood with charcoal.
Now I know I could have lost to a woman who knew
the word *rape*. I'm appalled
to think of who didn't enter the game over the Cornish hen,
who might have stopped eating altogether while I
dealt out my little sorcerer's bones, conjuring up this horror
for a laugh and a high five.

18a [Nymphomania]

Nymphomania

She pinned her hair this morning
luxurious around her face.
He doesn't seem to notice.
She knows he's touched some of the others—
placed the religious fanatic's elbow on a table,
handed an apple to the red Indian whore,
but most exasperating of all
she sneaked a look into his studio
just as he pushed back a strand of hair
from the fool who folds and unfolds
and sniffs those filthy baby clothes.
Her hair is greasy as the cloth bag
she drags everywhere with her.
How could he want a photo of that!

She's left undone the top button of her dress.
She knows she has a fine strong throat
and still relishes the memory
of her sister's husband, the way his tongue
rested where her voice-box hums, then
moved down to the hollow of her collarbone.

God, that felt good! Even better
than the priest—so hopeless, he shot it
all over her thigh, weeping on top of her, and
there was Jesus, looking fine up there on his cross
by the flickering red lights of the candles
lit by virgins and widows before the priest
pushed them out into the night
and locked the doors.

Jesus! Supple breast-bone laid bare
and vulnerable, belly stretched with trembling
desire, looking as young as her first man.
The demure legs, folded one over the other,
nailed in place so he's hers to do with whatever
she wants. This body is hers, hairless,
on the verge of slipping free of a knot of linen.
Too bad he's dead. Even so,
maybe she could get him to rise again.
She snorts with laughter under the crying priest.

The doctor's sad-dog eyes are hidden.
He's buried his head under the velvet cloth
and she laughs, imagining him burrowing
like that under his wife's stiff skirts.
That little bird wouldn't know how to peep.
In the hospital laundry, she's checked
the wife's bloomers, never a spot of his juice.

"Keep still," he says, a little impatient,
the way men can be when they want their way,
and it arouses her. She can see his legs
fleshy in dark trousers, and bent over like that,
the fabric pulls against his groin.
But there's nothing but a soft bulge,
small, curled up asleep, making her angry.

She wants to hear him whimper and retch
the way men do. The way he has made her retch
so many times, spitting his poisons into the basin
the attendants hold under her chin,
trying to weaken her, make her limp and helpless.
But it's no use. His mild white life will drop
into her blood red cauldron, diminishing him,
making her stronger.

Stupid man!
If she can't have his flesh one way,
she'll have it another: gouged, licked, stroked,
bitten, stabbed. He doesn't sense the rattling
of her discontent, arms coiled around her ribcage,
ready to strike. He doesn't see her teeth
parting, her mouth readying to open wider
than he can imagine before she swallows him
whole.

Immersion cure

Long ago I bore them, pushed them
before me through dark water, through pain.
They don't exist in this place that claims me.
One or the other stands at the door, saying:
"Mom, how are you?" And I'm thankful
for their perfect manners, the way
they ask permission before drawing close.
Maybe I am as unreal now for them
as they are for me. Time drags, then speeds up,
slows again, elastic and torturous.
And in this extreme relativity I find something
like a reason to hang onto: simultaneous
reincarnation. My father is his grandmother,
surviving each poisoning, living out
the suffering she seemed to elude.
I am my father trying to forego poison,
refuse oblivion, sideline the death wish.
And if I succeed, I am rewarded
with my children's lives—both of them
so eager and sensitive, good swimmers,
strong enough to resist the familial undertow.

Grief and melancholy

On the better days,
my past life flashes before my eyes,
images unreal, yet punishing
in their verisimilitude:
My tiny son gathering crab apples for jelly—
I know the exact resistance of slipping
that blue T-shirt over his head,
can see the fruit he's secreted in his pockets,
the red stain when I run his clothes
through the wash.
A certain waterfall that spills
like a cold sparkler down my daughter's back.
A cove teeming with tadpoles,
the luminous veins of light playing
on the sandy bottom, the lazy way
their blunt heads bump against my legs.
All those nights by the river, watching
an August star-shower, a lunar eclipse,
my children's eyes picking up available light.
A baby between us in bed,
one or the other perfuming the night
with their sweetness, my hand
on my husband's bare shoulder as he sleeps,
our gold rings a protective circle.
I thought it would always be like this,
but these are all just flickerings,
reflections on a cave wall.

12a [Apparent idiocy]

Apparent idiocy

Before the illness there must have been pleasure:
swish of a green dress frayed where it was cut
but never hemmed, slippery on her knees,
and cool as long spring evenings
when she slipped out the upstairs window,
climbing back in when the bats flickered
under the trees, black flames licking darkness
now that daylight couldn't push hunger back.

Someone must have looked into her face at birth
and recognized her, the heart quickening.
But no. One must go back to careless floating
in amniotic fluid to find a human connection.
Silky pool, a warm cocoon, and then the inevitable
time came to pull down and out of the hourglass
of her mother, a rough birth. An outcast.

"Girl" she was called at the baby farm,
once she'd somehow survived her infancy
and language started to multiply like kitchen bugs
in the empty cupboards of her mind.
She was nameless to the eight weakest babies
stashed in the back room. She was nothing
but a finger in the mouth, finger in the dyke
of the fierce power of their sucking, ravenous
as the act that created them.

She moved from crib to crib, reaching across
a dark gulf, fingers in different mouths at once.
When that was not enough to keep them silent,
she poured lime and water into bottles,

put up with thin whining until their bellies filled.
Or she reached under their weak necks to tip
their wobbly, too-large heads forward to the spoon
of dreamless sleep held in suspension in a blue bottle.
After dark, the sound of the shovel near the lilac
had nothing to do with her.

"Girl" was all she could say when they asked
her name, a week after she slipped back from the river
and found the doors of the house hanging open,
wind sucking the curtains out the open windows,
the older woman gone. All week she hid
and watched men dig up the yard,
mud in mounds, glistening wet in the lantern light.

That week, hunger she'd always known
turned on her like a dog, punishing her
with the scent of roses, her stomach growling
with an anger she had never learned how to feel.
"Girl," she said when the man asked her name,
luring her from under a bush with a crust of bread.

She doesn't think of the babies,
their firefly cries burning in the briefest of seasons.
She doesn't mind the noise here, screams echoing
down the hallways. No one needs anything from her.

She likes the way food comes before she is hungry,
varied and jewelled, tart greens, sweet scarlet,
vibrant orange exploding on her taste buds.
She holds food in her cheeks as long as she can,
swallows the last mouthful only when
the next plateful is placed before her.

She's forgotten the babies, is grateful to be fed,
hasn't acquired a name. She misses only the caress
of moist spring air near the river those nights she escaped,
the sweet wild scent of lilacs coming home,
endless crooning of frogs, full and satiated,
the most beautiful sound on earth.

Awakening cures

Lead helmet for light-headedness,
a ring made from the right forefoot of an ass,
immersion in ice, application of fire,
swooning and vomiting in the *Rotary Chair*
turned at high velocity,
long sea voyages, confined naked in a cage,
mandrake, vitriol mixed with quinine,
St. John's Wort *gathered on a Friday*
in the hour of Jupiter, imprisoned
on the treadmill of the *Padded Wheel*,
clitoridectomy, forced marriage,
forced abstinence from men,
a diet of white food,
the healer's hand on the thigh,
the healer's tongue in the mouth,
surgery to remove the *Stone of Madness*
from the head, from the chest, from the belly,
from behind the eye, from the genitals,
an induced coma, induced wakefulness,
icy water dripping for hours
on the immobilized forehead,
the application of leeches, of scabies,
of strong purgatives, *the application*
of living swallows, cut in two and laid
hott reeking unto the shaved Head,
a tape played over and over and over
during drugged sleep.

I would try all of these since the talking
has lost its power, my panicked voice,

small whining wings bumping against
a seething mass of illness.

So I pass through the heartbreak
of the children's ward, enter what was once
called asylum. Nothing feels safe here,
although there is no screaming now,
just puffy docile adolescents
with their shell-shocked parents. I
pass through these doors to see the alchemist,
who prescribes an elaborate ritual
involving cutting open gelatin capsules,
dividing powder on a mirror,
increasing from dust to dust, some at dawn,
some at dusk. He wants me to have faith.

But sometimes it seems that the efficacy of
the hook up the nose,
the scarlet spilled in the basin,
the pick through the eye,
the mercury in the blood,
the push backwards into freezing water,
the purgative to induce vomiting,
the pile of dry sticks
in the village square

equals the efficacy of
Senequin plus Ativan plus Paxil plus
Clonazepam plus Remeron plus Lamictal plus
Elavil plus Desyrel plus Nortriptyline plus Effexor.

There seems to be more sorcery
than science here, sweet, white and blank
on the tongue, the smallest
wafers of the pettiest gods:

one makes you cry for 8 days,
one makes you shake,
one makes you terrified
and burns your skin with a fiery rash,
one makes your head rage with blinding light,
one destroys your appetite, one makes you ravenous,
one gives you violent, exhausting nightmares,
one makes your heartbeat career off the walls,
one leaves you on your knees crawling to the bathroom,
one rings in your ears like angry simmering bees
and one, thankfully, one

offers fleeting interludes of calm.

Your liver is fine, he tells me. Just a genetic variation
makes this so difficult. But my liver
is not on my mind. What I mind is the way
my mind turns and turns in on itself.
If only I could crack the skull and let it all pour out—
the bad humours I've come to believe in
even as I swallow these blank white theories
for lack of any great new ideas.

7a [Paranoid mania]

Paranoid mania

She sees what they're up to, humbugging one another
in the garden. Baggage, bobtails, blowings, bogtrotters, whores!
Two snakes swallowing each other against the garden wall.
She'll keep her bone box shut tight tonight, won't darken
the daylights, won't shut her eyes, a string tied from the
doorknob to her thumb. She won't be ground sweat
tomorrow, no, no. She won't be dead. In the morning
she'll yell in the corridor that they came into her room
and poured poison down her throat, put maggots in her bed.
Weigh me, weigh me, she'll demand. *How much did they
get into me?* She swears her eyes were open all night.
Once they frogmarched her up and down the hallway
and no one came. She was tired, so tired. She follows them,
watching through leaves as they pass secrets from mouth
to mouth. Dastardly plans, never to be spoken out loud,
bug hunters, a dead lurk. They'll get claws for breakfast
when they're lagged. The slaughterhouse—that's the place
for them with their maggots and schemes and poisons.
Dresses come off in the cold, centipedes squirming
in their cast-off bonnets. Lully priggers, so mean
they rob children of their clothes, lully snow priggers.
Mummer, her mill clapper shut, sniffing out their mog.
Pot scum, that's what they are. If she can trick them,
they'll stop putting maggots in her bed. They'll have to be
Resurrection men then, stealing dead bodies from the
churchyard. They tip velvet when they talk to the doctor,
they wheedle, while she is under the screw. Their poison
weakens her. They go on the shallow, half-naked to excite
passion. Fakers, flam artists. The flying stationers
shout it out on street corners for shillings. They have to
keep moving to sell this story, or they would be hunted down
and murdered in their beds. Street patterers know, she knows,
even if the doctor is too stupid to see.

Anguish passing on to despair

I am digging a flowerbed,
but I might as well lie down in the earth
the way I feel. First, the violent
tearing of hair peeled back from the cranium,
crumbling phosphorous and loam,
thoughts fragmenting, falling apart,
even before I think them.

Clouds skid by quickly, darkening the soil,
anti-flashes or the blindness that follows
a bright blaze, as my fingers
rake through soil, searching out grubs.
The lawn is rotten with them, so hardy,
they wintered more easily than I.

Picking them clean as I unearth them,
fat pearls curled blind in the light,
I throw them on the road,
a fast pitch intersected by a crow
gorging itself between sideways skitters
and quick leaps away from passing cars.

When I'm inside, washing my hands,
darkness running from my wrists
onto white porcelain, I notice
my wedding ring is gone. My heart
stops. What I've always feared has happened,
feared since that day 20 years ago,
over eight months pregnant,
when the two of us rushed the purchase
for our rushed wedding,
choosing two rings that didn't match.
Mine has shown every scratch, while his
glows from the inner earth's warmth.

I've wanted to have new rings made,
Celtic knots in serene silver,
one of a kind, the vows given again,
but he's superstitious too,
"Isn't that tempting unhappiness?" he's said.
But tempted or not, here it is, unhappiness
its mildest name, if for me alone.

The clouds have gathered, dropping
a low ceiling as I kneel in the earth again.
The crow on the curb growing more bold, its eye
reflecting the garden, my bent form,
frost-withered, miniaturized,
a blackened crone bent beneath too many griefs.

I dig and seize upon each bright curved shape
with a hunger I haven't felt in months,
knowing I'll feel the precursor to joy
if I find my wedding ring again
but each time it's a grub. Eerie how all of them
are my size, writhing snug around my finger
before I fling them away.

The crow is gorged and will not help now,
flies to the overhead wire for the best view of me
pulling back my hand with all my strength,
bracing my heel against the earth.

Who have I almost forgotten
when the spring light washes through me
smelling like lilacs?
Who is surfacing to claim me
and fill my mouth with voluptuous mud?

Loss of reason

Start with the obvious:
because he poisoned himself on the garage floor
in the driver's seat of the car in the driveway
in his office   in the living room
because it was early morning when he did these things
because he was drunk by nightfall
all the winters of my childhood

No, that's not it:
because no one talked about such self-hatred,
his violence is named here and now
because some words are hooks: *denial, displacement,*
projection, reaction formation, catch in the throat
and others are kites that travel
through the bloodstream carrying oxygen
because I cannot breathe without them

Go further. You might find
what you're looking for:
because I get edgy when the light slants in the fall
because evolution exploded into two hemispheres
of the brain   because consciousness makes us prey
to instinct   because id is the first part of identity

Keep trying:
because of the chained lines on my palms
because of a rotten rung on the double helix
because of heavy metals glittering in the food chain
the moon is dead cold and trapped by gravity,
smell of sweet ash in the forest,
smoke drifting down from the north
made the sun blur wan and pink

where I walked with my newborn daughter
not knowing if I could be a mother in the aftermath
of another of his botched self-deliveries,
because winter is too cold   summer too hot

Don't give up:
because I cannot breathe
and restlessness makes me pace and pace at night
because I try to get away from myself but can't
if only I could sleep   if only I could eat
if only the roaring would stop in my head   if only
the dots on the page could form coherent
sentences   I could escape for a moment
if only love was enough   because I love   I love
I've never stopped   I can't stop
because my son's eyes are black at birth

their depth frightens me
white light poured out of my body for him
light whose bluish undertone can only fill him
temporarily   because his cry is only one of billions

Because reason is lost all the time:
because there is hunger   because I cannot eat
and it arrives in a season of plenty
my husband holds me and it doesn't help
he tells me I'm strong   because individual will
has nothing to do with it   because my children
are almost grown and I'm still lying in bed
because it could get much worse than this

38a [Religious melancholy]

Religious melancholy

I'm damned! A brute with no soul! she cried.
They cut her hair, after finding her
too many times on her knees,
hair wrapped around other patients' feet,
kicked hard, an open stigmata above her eye.

She didn't care about blood or pain,
or the ache like a sword in her side.
She only wanted to hear the words:
Your sins, which are many, are forgiven;
for you have loved much.
                    But she is damned.
Tears came often before her hair was cut, and
she would fall to her knees
to wash the feet of the closest patient,
avoiding the attendants, who firmly lifted her,
supporting her weight, walking her
up and down the gallery until the grey pall
of exhaustion closed down her grief.

If she could, she would pull off shoes
and stockings, run her tear-stained hands
over feet, wrinkled or smooth,
kiss yellow nails, bunions,
then dry them with her hair.
Some seemed not to notice and
could be touched without resistance;
some would panic, lash out, giving her
a bruised jaw, deep cuts,
floating stars she saw when pushed hard,
hitting her head on the stone floor.

She screamed and thrashed,
whipped her hair around her face so hard
it stung her open eyes, but once she heard
the hiss of the scissors against her neck,
she knew the slender threads connecting
her to Heaven were falling to earth,
never to rise again. She was damned.

With her hair gone, the tears stopped,
and those words she craved seemed lost
to her, until the impervious one
calls to her, leads her
to the garden and asks her
to wash her feet.

There are no tears, no hair to dry
the other's feet, pale as milk,
with blue veins like the faint shadow
of an ancient tree cast on long toes,
slender ankles parting innocently,
legs relaxed as a child's,
ribcage so warm under her shaking fingers.

The impervious one's throat is a tunnel
leading to the most temporary
of heavens: up to the warm cave
of her mouth, where their tongues spar
like two knowing serpents. Or down
to what she never knew existed, elusive
taste of pink nipples. How they promise
to satiate but make her grow more

desperate. She will do anything:
take the slender pungent wafer of flesh
between her lips; move her hips against
the other's bony hips, caught on this hard
cruel cross of the other's body. Beg
until she's turned on her back,
her soul released in a cry of agony,
then flying back into her body,
earthbound again.
She doesn't know whether this is
punishment, or whether it is love.

Forgive me, for I know not what I do.
Forgive me, for I know not
what I do. Forgive me. She paces
and prays. But she is damned. She
knows it. She will
not be forgiven.

Ruthlessness

Gardening again, and what I planted
has preserved its greenness, blossomed
into vivid colour—
the red of impatiens.
I am impatient too,
for the full spectrum of feeling,
purples tucked behind perennial reds,
late-blossoming whites opening
like slow fireworks.

That shadow passes overhead again
and I ignore it, let it pass,
as I'm learning to.
It's just a brain trick,
a random off-time firing,
that ragged patch of nothingness
interrupting the blue of the sky.

The cries break through,
a mother robin caught in the beak
of the crow, taken right off her nest,
struggling and calling piteously, pulling
the crow's flight low
with four male robins in pursuit
shrieking, swooping after the crow.

I want to run to the fence
where the crow finally lands
and brandish my gardening fork,
as though my hunger for life

is more insatiable
than this crow's hunger for death.
One peck through the chest
and it's over.

The male robins depart,
the crow carries the limp body
to the roof of the neighbour's house
to feast on a simmering plate of hot
asphalt, grit and feathers pushed aside,
the joy of baring a mother-heart
still quivering. The power of it.

So this, then, is what it will take to live,
stab softness through the heart,
leave a warm nest to cool,
cancel all potential.

I am willing now
to assume this kind of ruthlessness.
Life will be as simple as this:
When you are hungry, you must eat.
When you are pushed, you push back.

Delicacy of heart

But I must learn to cherish too,
like the story a friend told me
as I lay in my darkness,
her voice a thin, beaten line of gold
I followed back into life.

A little story that would have been
snuffed out in a blink just weeks ago.
About an elderly woman she knew
who lived alone with a goldfinch.
This woman gathered each feather
from the bottom of the cage,
each fallen feather that drifted out
on currents of air, and she saved them
in a basket, shimmering, a golden pillow
shifting light, gathered over years.
So beautiful. So grateful was she that
she couldn't let even one feather go.

23a [Royal monomania]

Royal monomania

She told the weeping one
that the blood in her veins ran blue,
same as all royalty. This was when the girl
was her lady-in-waiting, still timid,
washing her feet in the cold garden.

Later, when the girl cries about damnation,
she strokes her shorn hair, tells her that royalty
is allowed certain exceptions
to natural law. Egyptian royal brothers
lie with their sisters, queens have as many lovers
as they wish and women are preferable
for queens to love. She tells her that the purity
of the line assures the purity of the act.

But her gentle maid grows ever more
distraught, cries every time they meet
though, strangely, without tears.
Their assignations take place far away
from others, out of sight of the sick
and the well. Easy enough in this season,
when the garden is tangling, falling
into useless, fibrous overgrowth.

The fruit trees are losing leaves
revealing gnarled branches that begrudge
every season of growth, sour fruit
clenched and dried as mummy hands.
Soon, they will be visible to more than
the stooped madwoman in her bonnet
who follows them, suspicious and muttering.

Soon they will need to be quiet, hidden
away in some corner of the asylum.
Perhaps a nest in the laundry
where lines of dripping sheets are veils
around any royal's bed, where she can
tell her maid that clean-smelling rain
falls gently on the stone floor,
washing away all her sins. She, herself,
as head of church and state
can ordain this at her pleasure.

Her maid's grief starts to convince her
that she only knows part of the story,
so much lost from memory
over the millennia. She never asks
that the crucifix be removed,
lets it lie against her maid's full breasts,
nudging it aside with her mouth,
but respectfully, though she hates
the metallic smell of sanctimony.

Together they make a crown
from leaves of linden and ivy
still thriving on cold autumn rain, gather
dried flowers that rustle in her ears.
She brings a winding sheet,
is Jesus emerging from the tomb, the crown
of thorns still adorning her head.
She brings the skin of a wild animal
from the first and best kingdom where
all living things are under her dominion,
and wraps it around both of them.

She would give her more to soothe her,
would let her royal blood open,
let it flow into her if it would make
a difference. Her own blood is not common
red, not vicious, fallen, but cool
and untroubled and blue, blue as heaven.

The companionable ring of the bonfire

He puts the photo albums away
now that I am able to see my life
in my own mind. I've progressed
from the picture books
I couldn't believe, from the necessity
for him to describe each photo
as though these stories belong to another—
me, standing upright and smiling,
with one of our children in my arms;
then suddenly ten years older, smiling
carrying dessert into the garden;
ten years older again, smiling, with my arm
around my grown daughter at the airport.
Now I want something more complex
than primary colours, the simple censorship
of family happiness.

He reads to me, from the beginning
of Anglo Saxon tradition. He knows
it will take months to prepare me
for *The Wasteland*. First, *Beowulf*
and I'm shocked by how familiar this dark world
is with its severed heads and
angry lizard driven mad by exclusion
from the companionable ring of the bonfire.

A reptile was roused within me,
a misfiring brain stem destroying
the rhythm of my breathing, forcing
my heart to take desperate gulps,
chilled darkness crawling up my spine
late into another sleepless night.
This is a story of courage and endurance.
When Beowulf destroys the monster
with his bare hands, I want to weep
in gratitude for this unknown storyteller
who has brought me fortitude,
a thousand years after death.

A low diet and hard keeping

Stranger. Father. My strange father
goes his own way now.
The way he goes is tangled and rough,
tripping him, the underbrush sizzling
with sparks from which he rises, battered.
Alcohol, suicide attempts, a terrible silence
muffles him until his edges become indistinct,
wavy, as though emitting a great heat
or glimpsed through tears, or both.
Fire and water can coexist in this terrible way.

When I still lived with him,
I often dreamt he had a secret life.
Not his daytime life at the university,
with a real office, students taking down
every word he said, shelves lined with books.
How could the man who lay drunk at night
read books, sit in an ordinary upright chair?

In dreams I caught glimpses of him
by accident from a school bus window.
I saw him stretched out on a park bench,
lifting a crumpled paper bag to his mouth,
or the ridiculous shape of his backside
in frayed plaid pants as he leaned face-first
into a garbage pail. In the evenings,
the whiff of cheap alcohol. My mother
didn't care, the neighbours hadn't guessed,
but I knew and would be burdened forever
with the secret of his wayward days.

Even now, when I see a small fire
flaring under the bridge, unnaturally bright
with the quick hot heat thrown off
by cardboard and river twigs,

I think he must be one of the shapes
shambling black as crooked crows,
boots steaming, face bright and glowing
now that he's lost everything.

I can almost hear him speaking too fast
to the other lost and crazy men who listen
and laugh, rapt with fugitive attention.
May he be given this moment at least—
the warm hearth of a fleeting refuge
before some good citizen calls in to complain.

Visitation by phantoms

The first morning there is a hint of colour,
grey clamps down within the hour
but that hint was there, that first arctic dawn.
The next morning, I watch my face
for a long time, reaching out,
touching with shaking fingers my cheek,
the cold mirror, my cheek again,
differentiating one from another.
I will begin again to exist in the world,
the ice will clear.

Suddenly the clichés become possibilities:
to rise above it, to not be dragged down.
To look down, look back, to look forward
to my own future. A blossoming
of three dimensions instead of the breathless
flat plane that confined me.

The birds will visit me first in dreams,
long before waking
is something to look forward to.
With shimmering feathers, they'll visit—
lime-green, warm as passion fruit, heavenly blue.
Wings softly brushing my cheek,
seeking light, innate, held wavering
throughout the long dark months.

Constitutional for the convalescent

Walking in a field near my house
I find a path never seen before,
enter what I always assumed
was brush, wondering if the path
will straggle into swamp.
But curving gently around brambles
and fallen branches shattered
in last winter's ice storm,
the path grows stronger.

A magical place surrounds me.
Thorn trees, hazy with green,
tangle over my head. Poplar leaves tremble,
still slick, twitchy in the light wind
as leopard-frog skin. Birds call, but lazily.
Their mating is accomplished
and food plentiful.

Only the squirrels are anxious,
walking through the air from tree to tree,
watching my hands with the intensity
of a new lover. I stand amazed
in this place that was always so close,
yet I never knew existed.

Just like a dream where you find
a hidden extension of your house,
a place dank with closed-in air,
but so full of possibility.
Red tapestries and vibrant paintings,

cloudy unused windows
with new and interesting perspectives,
speed up your heart with excitement.

The dog nudges my leg, and grins
as though I am so clever
to have found this place.
But I don't know if it has anything to do
with cleverness, or with a willingness
to change directions on a whim,
or grace, or luck, or the gift of chemistry.

I am happy here, for now.
For the moment, the thorns are hidden
by new leaves. One frog voice
starts up, and another, and another.
Then a chorus surrounds me, blossoming
from the forest floor like the scent
of invisible flowers.

9a [A possible case of catalepsy]

A possible case of catalepsy

There are clues in her posture:
the protective arm across her belly,
thumb touching her breast.
There is room for a baby cradled
against her heart, or perhaps the doll
she left behind in the ward.

The arms are slender but the dress
could hide a matronly figure.
The head scarf knotted under her chin
doesn't reveal the firmness of flesh
so she could be twenty or thirty
or even a childlike forty years of age.

She could be frozen into this pose forever,
she could be singing nonsense songs
to herself all day. She could spend
waking hours rocking
and adding numbers in her head.
She could be frightened
by an hallucination of a fiery lion
floating just to her right,
or an amorphous cluster of lights,
forewarning of a shattering migraine.
She could be remembering a trauma:
house fire, or three generations
of her family dead with cholera.
What could she do, their failing hands
grasping her skirt as she moved
from bed to bed? Or remembering

her mother bloodied and the slow
sway of her father's body
hanging in the barn.

Take your pick. Trauma is an ongoing
theme with endless
variation.

She could have been beaten
or cherished or protected or ignored
or humiliated. She could have felt joy,
hatred, desire, resentment, gratitude,
giddiness, dread, pride, hope,
and an overwhelming transcendent love.
I hope she knew love.

This attention I pay to her
is something like love,
although she will never turn towards
me. The finger she holds at her lip
keeps all she might tell me
held at the brink where everything
rushes away into nothing.

Entertainment: magic-lantern show

Once for science, now for a paying audience,
the women of the Surrey County Lunatic Asylum
have been selected for their visual qualities.
Paupers once, now they are framed in bronze
and hung in the National Gallery.

But they are as delicate in image
as they were in life. Even in death,
they must be protected. They are irreplaceable,
sealed away behind glass from the interplay
of sunlight and incandescence,
the crowd's moist breath and shifting weather.

Halcyon days or intemperate extremes
threaten them equally.
A humidity detector beneath
each sepia-toned portrait registers air quality.
A red-inked pen held by an invisible hand
writes slowly on scrolled paper
in a language that has reverted
to the heartbeat where life begins.

In this exhibit, a retrospective
on photographic perspective,
science meets art. All the fascinations
of science are here: to slow down time,
to speed up time, to capture the smallest detail,
to cast perception beyond distances
that can only be imagined.

But context is everything.
The women are placed close to a photograph
of a speeding bullet passing through a banana,
explosion of white matter light as feathers,
always greeted by laughter.

They are across the room
from swirling distant galaxies
imaged through the recording of gamma waves—
the invisible made visible for the human eye. The women
seem as far away as that,
frozen in their suffering behind glass.

You've paid good money to be here. You,
free to walk away
and contemplate the distance between
you and *Antares the Rho Ophiuci dark cloud*—
cobalt blues, fiery oranges, glorious fuchsia
reminding you of something that is finally
out of your mind.

But in your perfect and faithful record,
this is not possible. You will return
to stand before the women.
You will see your own faint reflection
superimposed on one face, and then another.

Try as you might,
you will never step completely
out of the frame. As you move through the exhibit,
the pen recording your heat, your breath,
it will be your eyes that follow them.

Afterword

I first encountered the photographs of women patients of the Surrey County Lunatic Asylum as part of an exhibit on photography and science at the National Gallery of Canada in 1997. Almost lost amidst the dramatic images from space, the earliest x-rays and playful art shots were ten small sepia figures framed together. Despite their smallness, they were very disturbing. I carried them with me once I left the exhibit: they insinuated themselves into my unconscious. From time to time, one or another of their faces would drift up to the surface.

In 1997, I was in the midst of a decade of healthy years before the re-emergence of my own illness, major depression, in 2001. That long episode of suffering, and I can call it nothing else, lasted two years. During this time, the women's faces became much more insistent. I thought long about how fragile the human mind can be and how these women might have experienced their illnesses before the age of pharmaceuticals, which, at that time, seemed to be causing me more grief than relief. They haunted me until, by exploring the subjective experience of emotional and mental distress, I found a way to listen to them and connect my personal story to theirs. The more I looked at these women's faces, the less disturbing they became. Eventually, they seemed familiar, in all senses of the word.

Although there were other medical photographers in the 1850s in England, I was drawn to the photos of Dr. Hugh W. Diamond, Medical Superintendent of Women at the Surrey County Lunatic Asylum. Other photos, taken at Bethlem Asylum, for instance, seem harsh, exposing more illness than individuality. Dr. Diamond's photos are full body poses, gently lit, allowing the subject's character to shine through. The patients seem remarkably open to the photographer. Some hold objects that must have had personal significance to them—an apple, handiwork, a pigeon. The subjects seem to be full participants in the photographic process rather than examples of illness.

The photographs must have been significant to these women patients as well. It's hard now to imagine how revolutionary photography would have seemed at the time. Paintings preserved the faces of the wealthy and influential, but photography was democratic, capturing the subtle facial expressions of even these indigent women who survive in image only. An essay published at the time by a visitor to the asylum describes how the photographs, hung in the ward for the most severe and volatile cases, had not been damaged in any way.

Dr. Diamond started his photographic study of psychiatric patients in 1850, after the wet collodion process, which required an exposure time of seconds rather than minutes, was developed. This allowed him to photograph patients who, because of their illness, might have been unable to sit still or would have struggled against the restraints necessary for portraits before this time. His stated intentions were primarily scientific in nature: he was most interested in the way photography could provide objective categorization of mental illnesses. But what is obvious from the photographs is that Dr. Diamond was also a skillful photographer whose portraits are as insightful as they are beautiful. As any artist must be, Dr. Diamond was open to mystery. He writes in his article *On the Application of Photography to the Physiognomic and Mental Phenomena of Insanity*, 1856: "The Photographer…needs in many cases no aid from any language of his own, but prefers rather to listen, with the picture before him, to the silent but telling language of nature."

The case notes for the patients have been lost. None of Dr. Diamond's original notes or photographs survive in the Springfield Hospital (formerly the Surrey County Lunatic Asylum) archives. Limited information can be found in an essay by Dr. John Conolly, published in 1858 in the *Medical Times and Gazette*. His focus is primarily on the physical expressions and features that indicate the nature of illness. Three of the women featured in the poems are discussed briefly in his essay, but only the most fleeting discussion of their history is included.

Rather than work from these meager facts, I have engaged with the women in the photographs directly and imaginatively.

One of the great surprises of writing this book was discovering that I harboured misconceptions about the quality of psychiatric care available in mid–nineteenth century England. The images of the mad woman in the attic, women chained and mistreated in dank horrible captivity, or imprisoned because of nonconformity to limited norms, were hard to shake for someone whose creative teeth were cut on the feminist writing of the 1970s and 1980s. Abuses existed before reforms of the mid 1800s, but after that time there was a concerted effort to make the public asylum system humane, providing places of healing for pauper patients who had nowhere else to go.

A number of factors may have contributed to the development of a public system of asylums in England. Understanding mental illness as *illness* rather than *badness/madness* may have been hastened by King George III, who suffered from periodic psychosis through his reign and died insane in 1820. The most important factor, however, was probably the change in social conditions brought about by the Industrial Revolution, which created a crowded and overworked urban working-class population. Whereas formerly ill family members might have been sheltered on the family farm, the new transient reality and stresses of city living left few supports for the mentally fragile.

In 1845, the English Parliament passed a bill requiring all counties to set up public asylums for paupers. This public system would be overseen by the Lunacy Commission, which would ensure asylums offered consistent and ethical medical care. Instead of being detained in jails and workhouses, mentally ill patients would be provided with shelter and treatment. Earlier in the century, a movement in England to abolish restraints had taken hold, and by 1850 physical restraints were no longer used in public asylums.

Asylums endeavoured to provide a healthy environment: good food; occupation in the gardens, workshops and laundries; and entertainment such as dances, plays, choirs and magic-lantern shows. Medication and other forms of physical treatments, such as shower baths, sedatives, exercise and purgatives, were prescribed as required. The average stay in the Surrey asylum at this time was four and half years. Unfortunately, the optimistic view that severe mental illness could be consistently treated was to last only a few decades. By the 1880s, overcrowding in public asylums resulted in the reintroduction of the physical and, eventually, chemical restraints, still evident in psychiatric hospitals today.

Although these photographs are unsettling, it is reassuring to know that these women probably received good care. I hope they passed through their suffering and emerged to experience the full spectrum of emotion, as I myself did, even if no record remains of what followed. Dr. Diamond's photographs nourish this hope.

Bibliography

Ackerman, Diane. *A Slender Thread: Rediscovering Hope at the Heart of Crisis.* New York: Random House, 1997.

Barret-Ducrocq, Françoise. *Love in the Time of Victoria: Sexuality and Desire Among Working-Class Men and Women in Nineteenth-Century London.* (Translated by John Howe.) New York: Penguin Books, 1992.

Barthes, Roland, *Camera Lucida: Reflections on Photography.* (Translated by Richard Howard.) New York: Farrar, Straus and Giroux, 1981.

Berger, Lisa and Alexander Vuckovic. *Under Observation: Life Inside a Psychiatric Hospital.* New York: Ticknor & Fields, 1994.

Burrows, Adrienne and Iwan Schumacher. *Portraits of the Insane: The Case of Dr. Diamond.* London: Quartet Books, 1990.

Donnelly, Michael. *Managing the Mind: A Study of Medical Psychology in Early Nineteenth-Century Britain.* London: Tavistock Publications, 1983.

Flukinger, Roy. *The Formative Decades: Photography in Great Britain, 1839-1920.* Austin: University of Texas Press, 1985.

Foucault, Michel, *Madness and Civilization.* New York, Vintage Books, 1988.

Geller, Jeffrey L. and Maxine Harris. *Women of the Asylum: Voices from Behind the Walls, 1840-1945.* New York: Doubleday, 1994.

Gilman, Sander L. *The Face of Madness: Hugh W. Diamond and the Origin of Psychiatric Photography.* New York: Brunner/Mazel Publishers, 1976.

Gilman, Sander L. *Seeing the Insane.* New York: John Wiley & Sons Inc., 1982.

Greenwood, James. *The Seven Curses of London.* London: Stanley Rivers and Co., 1869.

Haller, Dorothy L. "Bastardy and Baby Farming in Victorian England." *The Student Historical Journal.* New Orleans: Loyola University, 1989–1990 (web: www.loyno.edu/history/journal/1989-0/haller.htm).

Hunter, Richard Alfred, ed. *Three Hundred Years of Psychiatry, 1535-1860: A History Presented in Selected English Texts.* London: Oxford University Press, 1963.

Pearsall, Ronald. *The Worm in the Bud: The World of Victorian Sexuality.* London: Weidenfeld and Nicolson, 1969.

Ramachandran, V.S. and Sandra Blakeslee. *Phantoms in the Brain.* New York: William Morrow and Company, Inc., 1998.

Solomon, Andrew. *The Noonday Demon: An Atlas of Depression.* New York: Simon & Shuster, 2001.

Thomas, Ann. *Beauty of Another Order: Photography in Science.* New Haven/Ottawa: Yale University Press in association with the National Gallery of Canada, 1997.

Winchester, Simon. *The Professor and the Madman: A Tale of Murder, Insanity and the Making of the Oxford English Dictionary.* New York: HarperCollins, 1998.

Acknowledgements

Excerpts from this book first appeared in: *Brick Magazine, The Malahat Review, The Fiddlehead, Descant, Prism, The New Quarterly* and *Ottawater.*

Andrew Solomon's, *The Noonday Demon: An Atlas of Depression* and Michel Foucault's *Madness and Civilization* provided detailed histories of treatment and perceptions of mental illness throughout time. The publication from the National Gallery exhibit, *Beauty of Another Order: Photography and Science* explored the uneasy relationship between subjectivity and objectivity, art and science, which continues to this day.

But most important were two books that focused particularly on Dr. Diamond's photographs: Sander L. Gilman's *The Face of Madness: Hugh W. Diamond and the Origin of Psychiatric Photography*, and Adrienne Burrows' and Iwan Schumacher's *Portraits of the Insane: The Case of Dr. Diamond.* The Royal Society of Medicine in England granted permission to use the photographs.

Thanks to Marnie Parsons for her sensitive editing, Andrée Christensen and Brenda Carr-Vellino for conversations that proved to be the impetus for some of these poems, and to Richard Harrison, Ann-Marie MacDonald, Vivian Tors and Sandra Nicholls for refinements, both editorial and emotional. I'm also deeply indebted to my husband, Tim Fairbairn, and my children, Nadia and Owen, for many years of love and support.

Thanks, as well, to Dr. Marjorie Robb, for helping me delicately balance the objective and the subjective.

I'm indebted, as well, to the City of Ottawa and the Ontario Arts Council for financial support during the writing of this book.

*N*adine McInnis is the author of six other books, including *Quicksilver* (a volume of short stories), *Hand to Hand* (poetry), and *Poetics of Desire*, a book-length study of the love poetry of Dorothy Livesay. Her work has appeared in many anthologies, journals and magazines, including *The Malahat Review*, *The New Quarterly*, *Event*, and *Room of One's Own*. She has taught creative writing at the University of Ottawa and worked as a policy analyst for the federal government, focussing on the publishing industry. She now teaches in the Professional Writing Program at Algonquin College. Nadine McInnis lives in Ottawa.

GW00634470

"The
guidebook
that pays
for itself —
in one day"

VIENNA LEIGH
CHRISTINA PROSTANO

Publisher Information

PUBLISHER

Metropolis International
(UK) Limited
222 Kensal Road
London W10 5BN
England

Telephone:
+44-(0)181-964-4242

Fax:
+44-(0)181-964-4141

E-mail:
metropolis@for-less.com

Web site:
http://www.for-less.com

FOR LESS TITLES

London for less
New York for less
Paris for less

FORTHCOMING

Amsterdam for less
San Francisco for less
Miami for less
Ireland for less

PARIS FOR LESS

First published in Great Britain in 1998 by Metropolis
International (UK) Limited.

Discounts by Metropolis International (UK) Limited.
Text by Vienna Leigh and Christina Prostano
Principal photography by Olivier Prevosto

ISBN 1-901811-15-8

COPYRIGHT

DISCLAIMER

Contents

for less guidebooks . . .

Paris for less is part of a revolutionary new series of guidebooks. Unlike "budget guides", these high quality guidebooks are designed to enable <u>every</u> visitor, however much they anticipate spending, to explore and to save money at the <u>best</u> places.

For less guidebooks cut your costs by providing you with specially negotiated discounts at hundreds of top attractions, tours, restaurants, shops, theatres and other venues.

These unique discounts ensure that, unlike any other guidebook, **for less** guidebooks really do "pay for themselves – in one day".

Over one million people from 30 different

countries have already saved money with **for less** guidebooks. If you look through this book you will quickly understand why **for less** guidebooks are becoming the natural choice for the intelligent traveler.

Customer Response Card

We want your comments so that we can continue to improve this book. On page 287 you will find a customer response card that you can mail back to us (at no postal cost) from anywhere in the world.

. . . *for less* guidebooks

For less guidebooks have been designed to make visiting a city as easy and pleasant as possible.

The simple, attractive, area-by-area format ensures that you can focus on enjoying the city and do not waste time puzzling your way through a complicated guidebook.

The substantial discounts are easy to obtain and can cut the total cost of a stay for an individual, a couple or a family by over 20%.

For example, each of the restaurants offers 20% off the total bill (including <u>all</u> food and beverage costs) at <u>any</u> time.

Uniquely, each **for less** guidebook comes with a fold-out city map, divided by neighbourhood. This large map links to hundreds of mini-maps in the guidebook, enabling you to find exact locations quickly and easily.

How to Use *Paris for less*

Paris for less has been created to enable visitors to save money by obtaining discounts at the best places in Paris. All discounts are applicable for up to four people for up to eight consecutive days. Each page is colour coded as follows:

| Attractions and Museums | Tours |

| Shops | Restaurants |

| Nightlife and Performing Arts |

Before you use the card, you must validate it by following the instructions printed underneath it on the inside front cover. The card should always be presented when you request the bill (check) and before payment is made.

Discounts apply whatever method of payment you choose. However, ***Paris for less*** cannot be used in conjunction with other offers or discounts.

Throughout this book, you will find the *for less* logo. Every time it appears, it indicates that you are entitled to a discount.

Use of the card or vouchers must conform to the instructions on pages 7 and 8 and to the specific instructions set out in each entry.

All organizations offering discounts in this guidebook have a contract with the publisher to give genuine discounts to holders of valid *for less* cards and/or vouchers.

Care has been taken to ensure that discounts are only offered at reputable establishments, however, the publisher and/or its agents cannot accept responsibility for the quality of merchandise or service provided, nor for errors or inaccuracies in this guidebook.

The publisher and/or its agents will not be responsible if any establishment breaches its contract (although it will attempt to secure compliance) or if any establishment changes ownership and the new owners refuse to honour the contract.

For post-publication updates and amendments to the discounts offered, call ☎ 0800-909649.

for less

CREDIT CARD SYMBOLS USED

AM = AMEX
VS = VISA
MC = MASTERCARD
DC = DINERS CLUB

How to Obtain Discounts...

ATTRACTIONS AND MUSEUMS

To obtain discounts at attractions or museums you must either show your card or hand in a voucher which you will find at the back of the book (follow the particular instructions in each entry). When you hand in the voucher you should circle the number of people in your party and also show your **for less** card.

At most attractions, discounts are available off the adult, child, senior and student prices. Children are usually defined as under 12, seniors as over 65. An index of attractions, museums and galleries that offer **Paris for less** discounts is on page 260.

Musée Grevin

TOURS AND TRANSPORTATION

Paris for less offers you discounts of 20% on airport transfers (page 19) and more than 20 tours in and around the city. These include open-top bus tours, evening floodlit tours, trips out of Paris and a walking tour of the Louvre (pages 216-222).

To obtain the discounts, you must book as instructed in each tour's entry. You cannot book through a travel agent, hotel concierge or other intermediary.

Cityrama tours

RESTAURANTS

Paris for less entitles you to a flat 20% off the total bill (check), including food, beverages and service charge (tip), at more than 90 restaurants in Paris. The vouchers on pages 274-286 entitle you to discounts at any Oh!...Poivrier!, L'Amanguier and Poul'd'Or restaurant.

The price indicated is not a fixed or minimum price. It is only a guide to the average cost of a meal. It is based on a typical two-course meal for one person without an alcoholic drink. You are entitled to the discount however much you spend.

To obtain the discount, you should present your **for less** card when you request the bill and before payment is made.

You may return to each restaurant as many times as you wish and receive a discount every time as long as the card is valid.

Dupont-Durand restaurant

SHOPS

Paris for less offers a 20% discount at 65 shops, listed on page 262. To obtain the discount, simply show the card before you pay for the goods. Discounts on goods already reduced in price or on sale are at the discretion of the shop's management.

L'Habilleur

. . . How to Obtain Discounts

PERFORMING ARTS

Paris for less offers you discounts at nightclubs, cabarets, dinner shows, jazz clubs and theatres (see pages 201-212). Unfortunately, we cannot guarantee that you will be able to obtain discounts at particular theatre performances, as shows sometimes sell out.

FOREIGN CURRENCY EXCHANGE

With the vouchers on page 277, you can change money commission-free at UK and US branches of Travelex / Mutual of Omaha listed on page 253. Their rates are competitive and you will save 100% on the transaction charge.

TELEPHONE CALLING CARD

Enjoy savings of up to 70% on your international telephone calls by using your *for less* card as a calling card. Best of all, when you activate your card you will receive £5 (US$8) worth of free calls.

A. To activate your *for less* card as a discount calling card:

When in Paris, dial freephone (toll free) 0800-906-706 and wait about 20 seconds for an operator (ignore the instruction to enter your card number and PIN).

Give the operator the last 8 digits of your *for less* card and your credit card details. You will then be given a secret Personal Identification Number (PIN).

B. To make a telephone call using your *for less* card:

1. Dial freephone (toll free) 0800-906-706
2. Enter your unique card number and PIN
3. Wait for the greeting and then dial the country code + area code + telephone number you require (do not dial the international connection prefix "00")
4. If you have any problems dial * 0 and an operator will assist you at no charge.

Some hotels bar toll-free calls or even charge you for making them. To avoid this, use your calling card at any public telephone.

When you return home you will be sent a permanent Calling Card which you can continue to use to make great savings from home or abroad. Ask the operator for details.

Any questions relating to telephone calls should be referred to Interglobe Telecommunications (International) PLC (☎ *44-(0)171-972-0800)*. Your credit card statement will show a charge from Interglobe for calls you make after using up your free £5.

Opéra-Comique

Théâtre de la Bastille

Public telephone box

DIALLING IN FRANCE

Unless otherwise noted, the telephone numbers in this book are within the (01) Paris area code. This must be dialled even when calling from another Paris number.

Introduction

Introduction to Paris . . .

'Paris is the greatest temple ever built to material joys and the lust of the eyes'
– Henry James

Paris, the City of Light, is one of the world's most romantic places. Although its grand monuments rival those of any other capital city, its unique beauty and charming atmosphere is a combination of thousands of years of history and centuries of artistic and literary heritage.

Arc de Triomphe

The priceless art collections in the **Louvre**, the foreboding **Conciergerie**, the unique and unmistakable **Eiffel Tower** and the legendary towers of **Notre Dame** provide the perfect backdrop for a stroll along the banks of the Seine.

Turn a corner, however, and you are plunged into the winding medieval streets, elegant avenues and everyday bustle of a modern city.

Paris, enclosed completely within the **Boulevard Périphérique**, is both an unspoilt treasure from the past and a showcase for 20th-century urban life and culture. Monuments from past eras stand side by side with innovative modern structures such as the **Pompidou Centre**, the **Opéra Bastille** and the Louvre's new glass **Pyramids**.

Statue of Victor Hugo outside the Sorbonne

Recent developments on the edge of town, such as **La Villette** and **La Défense**, contrast with the well-preserved, historical centre and mark the continuing cultural and financial growth of France's capital city.

Paris is both united and divided by the Seine, which separates the genteel **Right Bank** from the artistic **Left**. The Right Bank, with its smart, bourgeois inhabitants, its elegant buildings and its wide tree-lined avenues, is, to some, the quintessential Paris.

. . . Introduction to Paris . . .

Others see the trendy, bustling Left Bank, the age-old haunt of students and artists, as the true heart of the city.

Evening entertainment

The city is further divided into *arrondissements* which form a spiral around the river. Each of these areas manages to maintain a very individual ambience. **Montmartre**, for example, preserves a village atmosphere coloured by the presence of artists past and present.

Montparnasse, to the south, was the centre of Paris nightlife between the First and Second World Wars. The same cafés which were frequented by Ernest Hemingway and his contemporaries have remained popular to this day.

Palais de Luxembourg

With its chequered past and vibrant present, Paris is a pot-pourri of history, myth and tradition. Today, its residents include distinctive groups from all corners of the world, each contributing their own customs and culture to particular corners of this diverse city.

The wide and graceful avenues around the **Arc de Triomphe** may seem a world apart from bustling **Chinatown**, but the many contrasting areas are linked by the métro system, one of the cleanest and most efficient in the world. Although Paris's most famous attractions are clustered around the

Notre Dame from the Square René Viviani

river within walking distance of each other, many of its overlooked treasures are just a *métro* ride away.

Although it does not have a midtown oasis like Hyde

REFLECTIONS

'To live anywhere else is to exist in the relative sense of the word...to live in Paris is to exist in the absolute sense' - Anon, 14th-century

. . . Introduction to Paris . . .

Park or Central Park, Paris does boast some pleasant green spaces. The **Jardin du Luxembourg**, the **Tuileries** and the **Champ-de-Mars** provide welcome respite in the centre of town, albeit in the formal French "keep-off-the-grass" style.

Place St-Michel

In the outer reaches of the city, expansive areas of green such as the **Parc des Buttes Chaumont** and the **Parc Monceau** are great for picnics or strolls, and offer the odd surprise such as a stunning view or a hidden grotto.

Frequent visitors to Paris will always find new surprises. Even when following the tourist trail on the ancient **Ile de la Cité** or around the delightful **Latin Quarter**, a simple wrong turning can reveal a lovely square, a stunning edifice or a superb restaurant destined to become a well-kept secret.

First-time visitors have their work cut out for them, however, by the sheer number of famous and unmissable attractions in Paris.

Parisian streets

Viewing the world-class collections in the **Musée d'Orsay**, the **Petit Palais**, the **Musée de Cluny** and the **Musée Picasso**, not to mention the **Louvre**, could easily fill a week's holiday.

A view of the Ile de la Cité and Notre Dame

Even without the museums there is plenty to see in the city; indeed, some consider it a living museum in itself. Even eating a meal in one of the charming and very French pavement cafés is an experience, as Parisians have made sitting for hours and watching their fellows go about their business an art form.

The pace in Paris can be as frantic as in any other capital city, but eating and drinking is a serious

. . . Introduction to Paris

business over which true Parisians take their time, and you will never be hurried to finish by one of the waistcoated Parisian waiters.

The clichés about residents of Paris being conceited and rude are unfounded. Although the **Champs-Elysées** is still a catwalk for fashionable Parisians, the majority of them are down-to-earth and genuine, but they all share a deeply instilled pride in their city.

Musée Carnavalet

If shopping is a holiday requirement, you've come to the right place – the fashion capital of the world has an unsurpassed collection of specialist boutiques and department stores, most famously **Galeries Lafayette** and **Bon Marché**.

Those visitors who are more budget conscious can

explore the famous second-hand bookstalls by the Seine, the many fascinating street markets and the original fleamarkets still to be found on the outskirts of the city.

Any visitor to Paris, rich or poor, cannot miss or fail to appreciate its literary and artistic heritage. The memory of James Joyce, Ernest Hemingway, Picasso, Gertrude Stein and

A gendarme

Salvador Dali, to name just a few, lives on. The great buildings and vistas of Paris have inspired writers, artists and filmmakers, and continue to do so to this day.

Paris has an inexhaustible supply of attractions, but should you wish to venture further afield there are plenty of destinations which themselves cherish a precious heritage. For example, **Auvers-sur-Oise** and **Barbizon** preserve the

The colourful Champs-Elysées

artistic legacy of Van Gogh and Rousseau, while the stunning **Palace of Versailles** is just one reminder that France once had a powerful monarchy.

Paris: Area by Area . . .

LOUVRE AND OPÉRA

The Louvre and Opéra area is home to some of the grandest buildings and monuments in Paris. Its opulence is reflected by the presence of financial institutions such as the Bourse (stock exchange) and the Banque de France. Wide boulevards lined with exclusive hotels and designer shops meet at stately squares. Much of the area is composed of the wealthy 1st and 2nd *arrondissements*.

LE MARAIS AND RÉPUBLIQUE

Le Marais, the Jewish Quarter, is one of Paris's oldest existing neighbourhoods. It still boasts many fine examples of 17th-century architecture, and its trendy bars and restaurants make it a popular destination in the evenings. It borders the stretch of the Seine containing Paris's islands, the Ile St-Louis and the Ile de la Cité, home to Notre Dame cathedral.

LATIN QUARTER

The 5th and 6th *arrondissements* make up the intellectual heart of Paris. The multitude of bookshops stand side-by-side with cafés and bars frequented by students and philosophers watching the world go by. The Sorbonne is here, as are the legendary *bouquinnistes*, second-hand booksellers lining the Seine with their wares.

LES INVALIDES AND TOUR EIFFEL

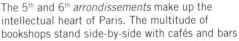

One of the most recognised landmarks in the world, the Eiffel Tower, stands guard over the grand, wealthy 7th *arrondissement*. It is an area of embassies, ministries and wide-open spaces.

CHAMPS-ELYSÉES

The most famous avenue in the city, perhaps in the world, is surrounded by the *haute couture* district. The Arc de Triomphe, central to the 8th *arrondissement*, is home to grand hotels, exclusive boutiques and restaurants and the best-dressed Parisians.

MONTMARTRE AND NORTHWEST PARIS

Montmartre is a village within the city, famous for the artists who first gathered here in the 19th

. . . Paris: Area by Area

century. The grand Basilique de Sacré Coeur overlooks picture-perfect squares, steps and tree-lined streets.

LA VILLETTE AND PARIS EAST

The east of the city is a place of contrasts. The ultra-modern complex of La Villette stands shoulder-to-shoulder with the nostalgic Belleville area, Edith Piaf's birthplace. The atmospheric cemetery of Père-Lachaise is the most famous landmark in the 20th *arrondissement*.

PLACE D'ITALIE AND PARIS SOUTH

This area is best known as the centre of Paris's ancient tapestry industry and the location of its modern-day Chinatown. For the past few decades it has been a target for development, centred around Mitterand's controversial Bibliothèque Nationale. As a contrast, the village-like Butte

aux Cailles retains its cobbled streets and intellectual feel.

MONTPARNASSE

The stomping-ground of American expatriates including Hemingway and Scott Fitzgerald, Montparnasse boasts café culture to rival anywhere in Paris. Traditional art-deco haunts such as La Rotonde and La Coupole are still the places to see and be seen.

PARIS WEST

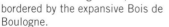

The residential and bourgeois 16th *arrondissement* is the place from which to enjoy the best views of the Eiffel Tower. The area, which still retains elements of its village roots, is

bordered by the expansive Bois de Boulogne.

LA DÉFENSE

La Défense, the 'Parisian Manhattan', is the most ambitious of the city's development projects. The impressive Grande Arche is the centrepiece of this futuristic showcase of architecture.

Before You Go . . .

WHEN TO GO

Paris is thought to be at its most beautiful in the springtime. As a result, attractions and museums can be as crowded at this time as during the height of the summer season.

There are special events nearly every weekend and on holidays throughout the year (see pages 246-247).

Paris's climate is generally mild, with the temperature seldom dropping below 0°C (32°F) in winter or exceeding 30°C (86°F) in summer. The city has less rainfall than the rest of the north of France, but sudden showers do occur.

VISAS AND ENTRY REQUIREMENTS

All visitors require a valid passport to enter France, except European Union (EU) citizens who can show their identity card instead. Visas are not needed by visitors from the EU, the United States, Canada, New Zealand, Switzerland or Norway. Citizens of all other countries should check visa requirements with the local French embassy before they leave home.

Virgin Atlantic Airways

For import restrictions on duty-free goods, see page 250. Animals can be brought into the country when accompanied by documents certifying that vaccinations are up to date.

MONEY

The currency is the *franc* (F). 100 *centimes* equal one *franc*. Major credit cards are widely accepted in Paris, with Visa being the best-known. Many of the automatic teller machines offer cash advances on credit and debit cards.

Travelex foreign currency exchange

If you are also travelling from or through the US or UK, your **for less** card entitles you to commission free (i.e. no transaction charge) currency and travellers cheque exchange at Travelex/Mutual of Omaha branches (see page 254 and the vouchers on page 277).

Paris is by no means as expensive as some other

. . . Before You Go

capital cities. Food and accommodation are relatively cheap, and a careful traveller could manage on as little as 250-300F (£35 / $55) per day.

HEALTH AND INSURANCE

Citizens of EU countries are entitled to take advantage of the French state health service, though they must

provide form E111, available in Britain from post offices and Social Security offices. Citizens of other countries are strongly advised to take out travel insurance.

The French system means that all consultations, hospital visits and

Ambulance

medicines must be paid for, but the health service refunds about 70% of the cost. Pharmacists are highly qualified and can often be consulted instead of a doctor about minor illnesses.

PACKING FOR PARIS

A warm coat is needed in winter and a jacket is advisable in summer, when there are occasional cold, wet days. An umbrella is useful throughout the year.

Electricity is 220 volts (at 50 hz). British travellers will need an adaptor, and travellers from the US will need an electric current converter.

BOOKING A HOTEL ROOM IN ADVANCE

Paris hotels tend to fill up quickly in the spring and summer seasons, and you should therefore book as far ahead as possible. A selection of hotels is listed on pages 31-46, and includes establishments in most parts of Paris suitable for all budgets.

BOOKING THEATRE TICKETS IN ADVANCE

Sheltering from a shower

It is a good idea to book seats well in advance for the more popular Paris shows. With **Paris for less** you can make savings at performances at several venues, including the Opéra-Comique, the Théâtre de la Bastille and the Théâtre de la Cité Internationale (page 208).

Arriving in Paris . . .

CHARLES DE GAULLE AIRPORT

GETTING FROM THE AIRPORT

Most international flights arrive at **Charles de Gaulle (Roissy)** airport, which is 25km (15.5 miles) north-east of the city.

The **Roissybus** will deposit you by the Opéra Garnier in the 1st *arrondissement*. This bus service is run by the Parisian public transport system (*RATP*), and is a cheap method of reaching the heart of the city. Buses run every 15 minutes from 6am to 11pm and take about 45 minutes. The fare is 40F.

Roissybus

An alternative bus service is run by **Air France** and will take you to the Palais des Congrès or into Montparnasse. Buses run every 15-20 minutes from 5.40am to 11pm on the Palais de Congrès route, and every hour from 7am to 9pm on the Montparnasse route. The journey time to both destinations varies from 30 minutes to an hour, depending on traffic. Tickets cost 48F.

Ligne B for the ***RER*** (suburban express train) runs from Terminal 2 straight to Châtelet and the Gare du Nord, where you can easily transfer to the *métro* lines. This is the quickest way of reaching central Paris, with a journey time of about 30 minutes. Trains run every 15 minutes from 5am to 11.45pm, and tickets cost 45F.

A taxi from Charles de Gaulle to the centre of Paris costs about 200-250F and can take up to an hour.

ORLY AIRPORT

Orly Airport is the destination for most domestic flights and several international ones, and is 16km (10 miles) south of Paris.

The *RATP* runs the **Orlybus** which departs every 10-15 minutes for Denfert-Rochereau in the 14th *arrondissement*. The service runs from 6am to 11pm and takes 30 minutes, costing 30F.

Air France runs another bus service, stopping at Les Invalides and Montparnasse, taking 35 minutes at a cost of 48F. Buses run every 15 minutes from 5.30am to 11.10pm.

RER Train

Orly airport has several connections with ***RER*** lines,

. . . Arriving in Paris

with **Orlyval** running every 5-10 minutes to Antony station and costing 52F for the 30-minute trip. The **Orlyrail** courtesy bus takes you to Pont de Rungis RER station, where trains to central Paris cost 30F and take about 40 minutes.

A taxi from Orly airport takes 30 to 40 minutes and costs up to 150F.

For less cardholders arriving at either airport can take advantage of the 20% discount offered by the **Paris Airports Service**. This door-to-door bus service takes you from the airport straight to your hotel. On arrival, call ☎ 01 49 62 78 78 to confirm the meeting point and pick-up time, which is guaranteed to be within a half hour of your call. If you wish to use the service again on departure, arrange a date and time for your pick-up back to the airport now. *(Present voucher on page 283.)*

Eurostar

Getting to Paris from the UK has never been easier. The **Eurostar** train service from London goes all the way to the Gare du Nord.

CHANNEL TUNNEL

GETTING AROUND PARIS

If time is at a premium, you can avoid time-consuming travel and concentrate your sightseeing each day on a particular area. To help you do this, *Paris for less* is organized into areas.

The *métro* - The Paris *métro* is the easiest way to get around the city. Trains run every three to ten minutes, depending on the time of day. The cheapest way to use the system is to buy a *carnet* (book of ten tickets) or a *coupon hebdomadaire*, which offers unlimited travel from Monday to Sunday on *métro* and RER trains and buses within central Paris and the immediate suburbs (see page 258).

A Parisian taxi

RER - Suburban express trains run through the city, with stops more widely spaced than *métro* ones.

Buses - Buses, on which *métro* tickets are valid, are useful for connecting journeys.

Taxis - Parisian taxi journeys are quite reasonably priced. Taxis can be found at ranks or hailed in the street, and a white light indicates that the cab is free.

Planning Your Trip . . .

IF YOU HAVE ONE DAY

Just one day is never enough, but this itinerary will give the first-time visitor a flavour of Paris life.

Sightseeing - A open-top bus tour is the best way to find your bearings, take in as many major sights as possible and travel around the city. For a more luxurious coach tour, take a Cityrama tour (pages 216-222).

(pages 216-222).

Follow this with a walk to appreciate Paris's delights in more detail. Stroll the banks of the Seine alongside the Louvre for the views and cross the river at the Île de la Cité to explore the Latin Quarter, Notre Dame and the Hôtel de Ville area.

An evening boat trip from the Eiffel Tower, after you have scaled Paris's most famous building for a bird's eye view of the city, takes you past all the riverside sights. All the monuments are spectacularly floodlit at night.

Café life - You should allow enough time to join in the famous Parisian café culture, especially in summer

Notre Dame and the Seine

when you can sit outside and people-watch over a leisurely meal or just a drink.

Museums - The most famous, of course, is the Louvre. It's too big to see everything in a day, but you could see the highlights in a couple of hours (see pages 50-52).

Cabaret - Dinner and an evening of traditional Parisian entertainment will round off your day.

IF YOU HAVE TWO DAYS

Spreading the previous itinerary over two days will be far more relaxing. The extra day should allow you to spend an afternoon exploring an area of particular interest such as the Champs-Elysées, Les Halles or Le Marais. You might also like to take in the view from the Eiffel Tower or the Arc de Triomphe, wandering the Champ-de-Mars or the Champs-Elysées afterwards.

IF YOU HAVE THREE OR FOUR DAYS

Spend the first two days as outlined above. On the

. . . Planning Your Trip

third day, make sure you haven't missed any of the
important sights in the central area, such as the gilt-
topped Hôtel des Invalides, the Palais
and Jardin du Luxembourg, the stately
Place des Vosges or the Grand and Petit
Palais.

On the fourth day, venture further afield.
Head north for Montmartre to see the
picturesque streets, steps and squares,
and visit the Sacré Coeur for the views
and a closer look at those wedding-cake
domes.

A bookshop in the Latin Quarter

Alternatively, go eastwards for La Villette
and Père Lachaise cemetery, or westwards for the Bois
de Boulogne and La Défense.

IF YOU HAVE ONE WEEK

A week allows you to go in search of hidden Paris: the
hundreds of smaller museums, historic buildings and
characterful streets that are glossed over by tourist
brochures. Here are some ideas:

DON'T MISS

If shopping is high on your
itinerary, head for the city's
famous *grands magasins*
(department stores) for a
taste of luxury (page 64).

1. The Bois de Vincennes (page 157), just outside the
east of Paris, contains a zoo, a lake, flower gardens
and the imposing, medieval Chateau de Vincennes.

2. The under-rated Butte aux Cailles (page 165) in the
south. This area, largely ignored by tourists, is a haven
of quaint streets and lively cafés.

3. The Musée Rodin (page 116) with its
delightful English rose garden, in which
many of the scuptor's famous works,
including *The Thinker*, are displayed.

4. Escape the formal neatness of
French-style gardens, such as the
Tuileries, by venturing further out to
explore the valleys and copses of the
Parc Montsouris (page 169).

5. Avoid the tourist trails in Montmartre,
around the Sacré-Coeur and the Place
de Tertre, to really appreciate the
architecture there.

6. Visit a museum devoted to a specific
artist, such as Moreau (pages 58-59),
Bourdelle (page 176) and Delacroix (page 96).

Musée Rodin

7. Visit the Orangerie (page 55). It is a treasure trove
of Impressionist painting and less crowded than the
Musée d'Orsay.

If You Do One Thing . . .

These ten ideas may not be the most famous or popular destinations, but they are an honest selection of personal favourites.

If you visit one attraction:

The Eiffel Tower
(page 112)

If you go to one art gallery:

Musée d'Orsay
(page 113)

If you walk in one park:

Parc Montsouris (page 169)

If you go to one jazz club:

Caveau de la Huchette
(page 211)

If you take one tour:

L'Opentour
(page 215)

If you dine at one traditional French restaurant:

Menthe et Basilic
(page 61)

If you go to one store:

Galeries Lafayette
(page 64)

If you make one excursion:

Versailles
(page 224)

If you visit one museum
(apart from the Louvre):

Musée Carnavalet
(page 80)

If you visit one church
(apart from Notre Dame):

Ste-Chapelle
(page 73)

History . . .

Although the confluence of the Seine, Marne and Oise rivers had been home to farming settlers as early as 5000 BC, the first signs of a future city appeared

when a Celtic tribe, the Parisii, established a permanent settlement around 300 BC on what is now known as the Ile de la Cité.

Arriving in 52 BC, the Romans took over the settlement which they renamed Lutetia. The city was rebuilt and expanded across the river to include the area now known as the Latin Quarter.

The collapsing Roman Empire and the constant barbarian attacks left the city

Paris at the time of Henri IV

weakened, and in AD 486 Lutetia was finally conquered by a new group, the Franks.

Their king **Clovis**, the first of the Merovingian dynasty, officially changed the capital's name to Paris and converted to Christianity, an act that would be the catalyst for the Christianization of the country.

REFLECTIONS

'The people of Paris are so sottish, so badot, so foolish and fond by nature' - *Gargantua and Pantagruel*, François Rabelais

The Merovingians were suceeded in turn by the Carolingian dynasty, whose most famous ruler was **Charlemagne**, and the Capetian dynasty. Perhaps the greatest of the Capetian monarchs was **Philippe-Auguste** (1180-1223), founder of the Louvre and Notre Dame Cathedral.

The 11th and 12th centuries were marked by the flourishing of merchant and trade guilds. The founding

of the Sorbonne in the 13th century put Paris at the centre of European academic life.

With the extinction of the Capetian line in 1328, Paris headed for troubled times. The Hundred Years' War with England and the Black Death combined to end the peace and prosperity of the previous centuries.

After years of battling over territories, the French were eventually able to regain their capital, but not before it had fallen under English rule. In 1431 England's **Henry VI** was made King of France.

Louis XIV, the Sun King

The Renaissance spirit infused Paris with a passion for the arts and humanities, but this period of enlightenment was brought to a halt by the Wars of Religion, the pinnacle of which occurred on St. Bartholomew's Day 1572 when over 3,000 Protestants were massacred.

With the conversion to Catholicism of **Henri IV** the

. . . History . . .

Wars of Religion came to an end. Henri and his minister Sully set about re-organizing a dirty, over-crowded Paris. City planning led to the creation of the Pont Neuf and the Luxembourg Palace, while projects begun earlier such as the Louvre's Grand Gallery and the Hôtel de Ville were finally completed.

At the time of the murder of Henri IV, his son **Louis XIII** (1610-1643) was just 8 years old. His mother, **Cathérine de Médicis**, held power until 1617 when the king took control himself, guided by his chief minister, Cardinal Richelieu.

Demolition of the Bastille

It was with the rule of **Louis XIV** (1643-1715), the "Sun King", that absolute monarchy reached its apogee and a series of impressive structures such as the Hôtel des Invalides and the Place Vendôme were created. The ultimate example of ostentation was the building of Versailles. The transfer of the court to its new location annoyed both the aristocracy, who were forced to follow the king, and the majority of the Paris population who were left in poverty. The seeds of the Revolution had been planted.

The Ancien Régime quickly collapsed in 1789 following the storming of the Bastille, a centuries-old prison. This led to the creation of the First Republic and the beheading of Louis XVI and his queen, Marie Antoinette.

The new assembly, headed by **Robespierre**, began the Reign of Terror by executing anyone suspected of treason. The Terror lasted from January 1793 until July 1794, during which time thousands of lives were lost.

In 1800, following a coup, the young general **Napoleon Bonaparte** was named First Consul of the Republic. He went on to create the most efficient, centralized and powerful empire France had ever seen.

Following Napoleon's exile, the monarchy experienced a brief Restoration that ended in the appointment to power of **Napoleon III**. It was he who commissioned Baron Haussmann to transform Paris, clearing entire neighbourhoods to make room for the wide boulevards and open spaces we know today.

The Second Empire came to an end when the

REFLECTIONS

'Paris is as big as Ispahan: the houses there are so tall that one would swear they could only be inhabited by astrologers' - *Lettres Persanes*, Montesquieu

Napoleon I

. . . History . . .

Prussians, provoked by the French army in 1870, laid siege to Paris. Residents suffered through the winter and ate almost every animal in the city in order to survive.

Rue de la Paix, 19th century

To end the siege, the French government signed a peace agreement with Bismarck and retreated to Versailles, leaving behind a betrayed population. In this climate, the populist Paris Commune took over, with an assembly comprised mainly of workers and artists. Inexperience and lack of organization proved to be their downfall, and within 72 days the Commune came to a bloody end.

In the wake of this political upheaval the cultural life of Paris exploded. The Belle Époque was underway and with it a flourishing world of art, music and literature. This was the era of bohemian Montmartre café society, exemplified by the Moulin Rouge and its Can-Can dancers.

In 1889, the first centenary of the Revolution was celebrated with a huge exhibition. A new monument, the Eiffel Tower, was built to commemorate the occasion.

Eleven years later, in 1900, Paris was the location of the World Exhibition that marked the turn of the century and attracted more than 50 million visitors before its close. The same year saw the opening of the first line of the Métropolitain, or *métro* as it came to be known.

The Belle Époque came to a close with the outbreak of the First World War in 1914. Before the return of peace in 1918, the lives of more than a million young Frenchmen had been lost.

The years following the First World War were marked by a visible energy and freedom, as writers and artists such as Picasso and Braque made the city their mecca. Expatriate Americans such as Hemingway whiled away their time in cafés such as La Coupole and La Rotonde on the boulevard Montparnasse.

The grim reality of war struck again in 1939 when Britain and France declared war on Germany. Less than a year later, the Germans occupied Paris, the Nazi flag flying over the Hôtel de Ville while the German army marched down the Champs-Elysées.

By this time, Paris had been nearly emptied as the

REFLECTIONS

'Where shall I begin with the endless delights/ Of this Eden of milliners, monkies and sights-/ This dear busy place, where there's nothing transacting/ But dressing and dinnering, dancing and acting?' - Thomas Moore

. . . History

majority of its residents and government fled to other parts of France and abroad. When they Allies arrived in 1944, they were greeted by a group of Parisians completely prepared for insurrection against the enemy. On August 26th, **General Charles de Gaulle** led his troops on a triumphant march down the Champs-Elysées.

General de Gaulle

Despite, or perhaps because of, the devastation to the country, France experienced an economic boom as jobs were created and industry expanded. De Gaulle was made provisional President and remained so until 1946 when the Fourth Republic began. Political focus turned to the French Empire overseas, which was quickly deteriorating. Riots over political issues such as the colony of Algeria led to more division within the population. De Gaulle was reinstated as President in 1958, a position he held until 1969.

Until the election of socialist **François Mitterand** in 1981, France was ruled by conservative leaders such as Georges Pompidou who is probably best remembered for the innovative Centre Pompidou.

After initial economic failure, Mitterand's socialist government turned out to be quite moderate, and life went on pretty much as usual. Perhaps he is best known for the revitalization of Paris in the form of the Grands Projets that encompassed the Grande Arche de la Défense, the Opéra Bastille and the controversial Louvre project in which huge glass pyramids were added to the courtyard.

REFLECTIONS

'If you are lucky enough to have lived in Paris as a young man, then wherever you go for the rest of your life, it stays with you, for Paris is a moveable feast'
- Ernest Hemingway

In 1995 **Jacques Chirac**, former mayor of Paris, was elected President in a climate of social strife, recession and high unemployment. He and Prime Minister **Alain Juppé** attempted to cut social benefits in order to reduce the national debt and levels of unemployment so that France could qualify for the unified European currency in 1999.

Occupied Paris

The next few years will prove critical to the future of the French state as the millennium rings in to the chimes of radical, controversial ideas about a new Europe.

Timeline . . .

700,000 BC Palaeolithic man inhabits the Paris Basin.

5000 BC Hunter-fishermen settle on the banks of the Seine.

300 BC A Celtic tribe, the Parisii, build a settlement known as Lutetia on the Ile de la Cité.

59 BC The Romans conquer Gaul.

52 BC Lutetia is rebuilt and fortified by the Romans and spreads to the left bank.

250 AD St Denis, bringing Christianity to Lutetia, is executed in Montmartre at the decree of the Roman governor.

285 Barbarians invade the city.

360 Julian, prefect of Gaul, is made Emperor. Lutetia becomes known as Paris.

450 Attila the Hun advances on Paris but is repulsed by an army led by Ste Geneviève.

508 Newly Christian Paris is the capital of Clovis, the Frankish king.

725 Muslims attack Gaul.

756 Pippin the Short is crowned king.

800 Charlemagne becomes the first Holy Roman Emperor. Aix-la-Chapelle becomes the capital in place of Paris.

850 Normans lay siege to Paris.

987 Huguès Capet is crowned the first king of France.

1108 Louis VI "the Fat" begins his reign.

1110 Christians begin to persecute Jews and heretics.

1163 Construction of Notre Dame begins.

1202 A city wall is constructed by Philippe-Auguste to enclose the city on both banks of the Seine.

1226 Reign of Louis XI begins.

1249 Sainte-Chapelle is completed.

1253 The Sorbonne is founded.

1285 Reign of Philippe the Fair begins.

1340 The Hundred Years' War with England begins.

1348 The Black Death spreads through the country.

1358 Etienne Marcel revolts against Charles V.

. . . Timeline . . .

1364 The royal court moves to the Louvre.

1430 Paris is under English rule. Henry VI becomes king of France following Joan of Arc's unsuccessful defence of the city.

1453 End of the Hundred Years' War. The occupying English desert Paris.

RENAISSANCE

1516 Leonardo da Vinci brings the *Mona Lisa* to Paris.

1528 Construction of the new Louvre begins under François I.

1572 St Bartholomew's Day Massacre of 3,000 protestants.

REFORMATION

1593 Henri of Navarre (Henri IV) converts to catholicism, ending the Wars of Religion.

1607 Construction of the Place des Vosges begins.

ANCIEN RÉGIME

1610 Henri IV is assassinated. Louis XIII succeeds him.

1629 Cardinal Richelieu builds the Palais Royal.

1643 Louis XIV (the Sun King) ascends the throne at the age of five.

1648 A civil war, the *Fronde*, begins, as a result of peasants rebelling against taxes.

1662 Manufacture des Gobelins founded.

1682 Louis XIV moves the royal court to Versailles.

1702 Paris is divided into 20 *arrondissements*.

1715 Louis XIV dies.

1755 Construction of the Place de la Concorde is begun.

1763 End of the Seven Years' War. France loses colonies in Canada, India and the West Indies.

FRENCH REVOLUTION

1789 Opposition to Louis XVI culminates in the storming of the Bastille prison. The king flees the city. Adoption of the Declaration of the Rights of Man.

1792 Following the "September Massacres", the monarchy is formally abolished and France becomes a republic.

1793 The Reign of Terror begins. In total more than 60,000 people are executed.

1794 Robespierre, revolutionary zealot, is overthrown and executed.

. . . Timeline

NAPOLEON

1799 Napoleon Bonaparte becomes leader of the post-revolutionary government.

1804 Napoleon is crowned Emperor of France and proceeds to invade Europe.

1806 Arc de Triomphe is commissioned.

1814 Following the unsuccessful invasion of Russia, Napoleon abdicates and flees to Elba. The monarchy is restored.

1815 Napoleon returns, is defeated by the Duke of Wellington at Waterloo and is exiled to St. Helena where he dies in 1821.

SECOND EMPIRE

1848 The Paris Revolution leads to the Second Rebublic.

1852 Haussmann replans large sectors of Paris.

1870 Napoleon III invades Prussia and is captured. The Prussians occupy Paris and the Third Republic begins.

1871 The Paris Commune rules the city for 72 days.

BELLE ÉPOQUE

1889 The Eiffel Tower is built for the Paris Exhibition.

1898 Marie Curie discovers radium.

WORLD WARS

1914 Beginning of the First World War.

1919 The Treaty of Versailles is signed, ending the First World War.

1924 Olympic Games held in Paris.

1940 The Second World War. The German occupation of Paris begins.

DE GAULLE TO THE PRESENT

1944 Paris is liberated. Women get the vote.

1946 Charles de Gaulle falls from power, to return in 1958 with the advent of the Fifth Republic.

1962 A programme of renovation is begun by Culture Minister Malraux.

1968 Student riots break out over the Vietnam war.

1977 Jacques Chirac is elected as mayor of Paris.

1981 François Mitterand becomes President of France.

1995 Jacques Chirac elected President.

1997 Lionel Jospin (Socialist Party) becomes Prime Minister.

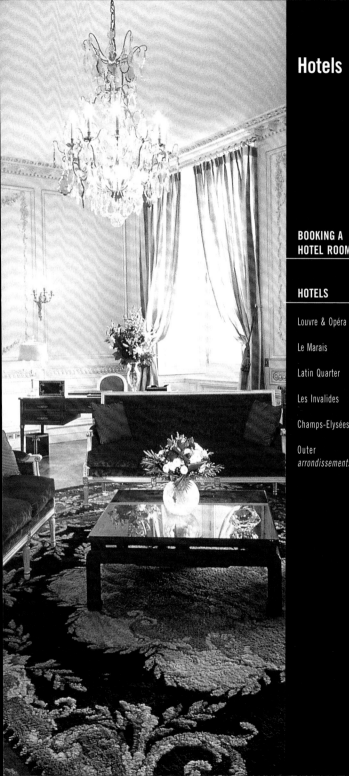

Hotels

Hôtel de Crillon (see opposite)

HOTEL FACILITIES

 Shower

 Bath

 Minibar

 Tea / coffee making

 Room service

 24-hour room service

 Radio

 TV

 Satellite / cable TV

 Direct dial telephone

 Wake-up call

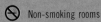 Hairdryer

 Trouser press

 Room safe

 Non-smoking rooms

 Air-conditioned rooms

Laundry service

Babysitting service

Elevator / lift

Disabled facilities

Secretarial services

Fitness centre

Swimming pool

Booking a Hotel Room

Paris has more hotel rooms than almost any other European city, but in spite of this it is still sensible to book well in advance, at least a month ahead, in the tourist season. The busiest months are May, June, September and October, and annual events such as the Tour de France can often lead to an increase in visitors.

To make a booking, telephone the hotel directly, and be prepared to confirm you booking by fax or letter. Alternatively, approach the *Office de Tourisme* (see page 257) which, for a small fee, will find you last-minute accommodation.

The hotels on the following pages are a general selection of those in the central areas of Paris which cater for every price range. They are <u>not</u> recommended by *Paris for less* and you cannot obtain a discount at them. They are grouped according to area in descending price order.

The F symbols by each hotel's entry indicate the standard high season double room rates: F=under 500F, FF=500-1000F, FFF=1000-1500F, FFFF=1500-2000F, FFFFF=over 2000F. (Breakfast is included where mentioned.)

After you have decided how much you would like to spend, you should choose the area in which you would like to stay. Most luxury hotels are located on the Right Bank, and there are more characterful, family-run establishments on the Left Bank. For a summary of Paris's areas see pages 14-15.

The number of stars under each hotel's name indicate its quality:

★ : You will probably have to share a bathroom and there may not be a lift.

★★ : At least half the bedrooms have en suite bath/shower rooms and may also have phones and TVs.

★★★ : Full reception services, more formal restaurant and bar arrangements, bedrooms all have en suite facilities, mostly with baths.

★★★★ : More spacious accommodation offering high standards of comfort and food. The range of services should include porterage, room service, formal reception and often a selection of restaurants.

★★★★★ : "Palace" hotels, frequented by the rich and famous and including a unrivalled range of facilities and quality of service.

Hôtel de Crillon

★★★★★

10 place de la Concorde, 1st
☎ 01 44 71 15 00

The Hôtel de Crillon is the destination of the rich and famous when they visit Paris. Sumptuous interiors and superb views have attracted the likes of Chaplin, Roosevelt and Churchill. *(Louvre and Opéra. 163 rooms)*

PRICE CATEGORY

FFFFF

Hôtel Meurice

★★★★★

228 rue de Rivoli, 1st
☎ 01 44 58 10 10

The so-called "Hotel of Kings" is centrally located with great views of the Tuileries. The rooms are sumptuously and individually decorated, and no detail is overlooked for a stay in the lap of luxury. *(Louvre and Opéra. 152 rooms)*

PRICE CATEGORY

FFFFF

Hôtel Regina

★★★★

2 place des Pyramides, 1st
☎ 01 42 60 31 10

The Hôtel Regina overlooks the Louvre and the Tuileries and has an elegant and refined ambience. It features Art Nouveau décor and has a cosy English-style bar and tea room. *(Louvre and Opéra. 130 rooms)*

PRICE CATEGORY

FFFF

Hôtel Beau Manoir

★★★★

6 rue de l'Arcade, 8th
☎ 01 42 66 03 07

This hotel is close to Ste-Marie Madelaine and the Place de la Concorde. The interior, with its tapestries, stonework, wooden beams and fine fabrics, is both sumptuous and cosy. *(Louvre and Opéra. 32 rooms)*

Villa Fénelon

★★

23 rue Buffalot, 9th
☎ 01 48 78 32 18

This townhouse is a peaceful haven in the 9th *arrondissement*. The service is friendly and the rooms are quiet. There is a delightful garden, and breakfast is included in the rate. *(Louvre and Opéra. 39 rooms)*

Hôtel Favart

★★★

5 rue de Marivaux, 2nd
☎ 01 42 97 59 83

The Hôtel Favart is located close to the Opéra Garnier, and was briefly the home of the painter Goya. The spacious rooms are tranquil, and breakfast is included. *(Louvre and Opéra. 37 rooms)*

Hôtel le Relais du Louvre

★★★

19 rue des Prêtres, 1st
☎ 01 40 41 96 42

The Hôtel le Relais du Louvre is ideally placed between the Louvre museum and La Samaritaine. The peaceful, charming rooms have 18th-century furniture and modern facilities. *(Louvre and Opéra. 21 rooms)*

Hôtel Lido

★★★

4 passage de la Madelaine, 8th
☎ 01 42 66 27 37

The Hôtel Lido's bar opens onto an enclosed garden, and vaulted cellars are the setting for breakfast. The spacious guest rooms feature period furniture and modern facilities. *(Louvre and Opéra. 32 rooms)*

Hôtel Chopin

★★

46 passage Joffroy, 9th
☎ 01 47 70 58 10

The Hôtel Chopin is five minutes from the Opéra and the big department stores, but is nevertheless quiet as none of its rooms face the street. The hotel and the passage Joffroy are listed buildings. *(Louvre and Opéra. 35 rooms)*

Résidence du Pré

★★★

15 rue Pierre Sémard, 9th
☎ 01 48 78 26 72

The newly-renovated Résidence du Pré is ideally situated close to Montmartre and the shopping area of the 9th *arrondissement*. The well-appointed rooms are reasonably priced. *(Louvre and Opéra. 40 rooms)*

Pavillon de la Reine

★★★★

28 place des Vosges, 3rd
☎ 01 40 29 19 19

The Pavillon de la Reine is located in the Place des Vosges. The beamed rooms overlook flowery courtyards, and the breakfast room is decorated with tapestries that evoke the Middle Ages. *(Le Marais. 55 rooms)*

Hôtel Saint-Merry

★★★

78 rue de la Verrerie, 4th
☎ 01 42 75 14 15

The atmospheric, gothic-style rooms in this hotel incorporate the architecture of the neighbouring church. It is ideally situated in Le Marais, close to the Pompidou Centre. *(Le Marais. 11 rooms)*

Hôtel du Jeu de Paume

★★★★

54 rue Saint-Louis en l'Ile, 4th
☎ 01 43 26 14 18

PRICE CATEGORY

FFF

The desirable Île St-Louis is the location of this hotel, housed in the 17th-century elegance of a former *jeu de paume* (real tennis) court. The beamed ceilings and stone walls offer an old-world charm. *(Le Marais. 31 rooms)*

Hôtel Bastille Speria

★★★

1 rue de la Bastille, 4th
☎ 01 42 72 04 01

PRICE CATEGORY

FF

This hotel is located between the Place des Vosges and the Place de la Bastille. It has a modern, spacious feel and offers friendly, attentive staff and every convenience. *(Le Marais. 42 rooms)*

Hôtel Beaubourg

★★★

11 rue Simon Lefranc, 4th
☎ 01 42 74 34 24

PRICE CATEGORY

FF

This hotel opened in 1986 after a major renovation and offers peace and quiet in the centre of the city. It is minutes from the Pomipdou Centre and Les Halles. Breakfast is included in the room rate. *(Le Marais. 28 rooms)*

PRICE CATEGORY

FFFF

PRICE CATEGORY

FFFF

PRICE CATEGORY

FFF

Le Relais Saint-Germain

★★★★

9 carrefour de l'Odéon, 6th
☎ 01 43 29 12 05

Le Relais Saint-Germain is based in a 17th-century house, and the large rooms have many of the original features as well as antiques and fine fabrics. Breakfast is included in the tariff. *(Latin Quarter. 22 rooms)*

Hôtel Relais Christine

★★★★

3 rue Christine, 6th
☎ 01 40 51 60 80

This 16th-century cloister is in the heart of the St-Germain-des-Prés district and has a private courtyard and garden. Its tastefully decorated rooms are finely furnished. *(Latin Quarter. 51 rooms)*

Hôtel Buci Latin

★★★

34 rue de Buci, 6th
☎ 01 43 29 07 20

This unusual hotel displays an inspired taste in interior design. The contemporary, unique and arty feel is enhanced by the use of modern furniture, fabrics and lighting. *(Latin Quarter. 27 rooms)*

Hôtel le Clos Médicis

★★★

56 rue M. de Prince, 6th
☎ 01 43 29 10 80

This superb mansion was built in 1773 for the Medicis family, and is now a Provençale-style hotel with interiors designed by Jean-Philippe Neul. The comfortable rooms are furnished with antiques. *(Latin Quarter. 38 rooms)*

PRICE CATEGORY

FFF

Hôtel de l'Abbaye

★★★

10 rue Cassette, 6th
☎ 01 45 44 38 11

This 18th-century residence incorporates the vaulted cellars of an old convent and has a beautiful, lush garden. All the rooms are furnished with antiques, paintings and fine fabrics. *(Latin Quarter. 46 rooms)*

PRICE CATEGORY

FFF

Hôtel Left Bank St-Germain

★★★

9 rue de
l'Ancien Comédie, 6th
☎ 01 43 54 01 70

This romantic hotel is ideally situated within walking distance of Notre Dame and the Latin Quarter. It features period furniture, Aubusson tapestries and oak beams. *(Latin Quarter. 31 rooms)*

PRICE CATEGORY

FFF

PRICE CATEGORY

FFF

PRICE CATEGORY

FF

PRICE CATEGORY

FF

La Villa

★★★★

29 rue Jacob, 6th
☎ 01 43 26 60 00

La Villa's owners chose the up-and-coming designer
Marie-Christine Dorner to refurbish their little hotel, and
the result is unique: modern curves, vibrant colours and
polished stone surfaces. *(Latin Quarter. 32 rooms)*

Hôtel des Grandes Ecoles

★★★

75 rue du
Cardinal Lemoine, 5th
☎ 01 43 26 79 23

The small and reasonably priced Hôtel des Grandes
Ecoles is located in the Latin Quarter. It has all the charm
of a country cottage, and you can eat breakfast outside
under the trees. *(Latin Quarter. 51 rooms)*

Hôtel de Fleurie

★★★

32-34 rue
Grégoire-de-Tours, 6th
☎ 01 53 73 70 00

This hotel, in the centre of Saint-Germain-des-Prés,
offers 18th-century elegance combined with modern
comfort. The quiet rooms are a stone's throw away from
the bustling nightlife of the area. *(Latin Quarter. 29 rooms)*

Select Hôtel

★★★

1 place de la Sorbonne, 5th
☎ 01 46 34 14 80

The Select Hôtel has an abundance of potted plants and even a fountain in its elegant stone halls. The rooms are atmospheric and peaceful, and food is served in a vaulted lounge. *(Latin Quarter. 68 rooms)*

PRICE CATEGORY

FF

Hôtel Saint-Paul

★★★

43 rue M. le Prince, 6th
☎ 01 43 26 98 64

This hotel is located close to the Jardin du Luxembourg. It is a 17th-century residence with oak beams and stone walls. The English-style décor complements the Haute Epoque furniture. *(Latin Quarter. 31 rooms)*

PRICE CATEGORY

FF

Montalembert

★★★★

3 rue de Montalembert, 7th
☎ 01 45 49 68 68

This hotel, located in an historic building, offers comfort and elegance. The rooms are decorated in Louis-Philippe and modern styles, with period or specially designed furniture. *(Les Invalides and Tour Eiffel. 50 rooms)*

PRICE CATEGORY

FFFF

Hôtel Lutetia

★★★★

45 boulevard Raspail, 6th
☎ 01 49 54 46 46

PRICE CATEGORY

FFFF

The luxury Hôtel Lutetia is where de Gaulle spent part of his honeymoon. Its elegant atmosphere is enhanced by Art Deco furniture, Lalique chandeliers and 1930s leaded windows. *(Les Invalides and Tour Eiffel. 250 rooms)*

Hôtel Le Saint-Gregoire

★★★

43 rue de l'Abbé-Grégoire, 6th
☎ 01 45 48 23 23

PRICE CATEGORY

FF

This small 18th-century mansion has reasonably priced rooms with an intimate, old-fashioned atmosphere. The hotel has period furniture and a private garden. *(Les Invalides and Tour Eiffel. 20 rooms)*

Hôtel Verneuil

★★★

8 rue de Verneuil, 7th
☎ 01 42 60 82 14

PRICE CATEGORY

FF

This hotel calls itself the 'best kept secret in the heart of Paris'. The small, charming establishment is just a short walk from the Louvre, the Latin Quarter and Les Invalides. *(Les Invalides and Tour Eiffel. 26 rooms)*

Hôtel de l'Université

★★★

22 rue de l'Université, 7th
☎ 01 42 61 09 39

The Hôtel de l'Université has individually decorated rooms which transport guests back into the past. The building incorporates an atmospheric crypt. *(Les Invalides and Tour Eiffel. 27 rooms)*

PRICE CATEGORY

FF

Hôtel Royal Monceau

★★★★★

37 avenue Hoche, 8th
☎ 01 42 99 88 77

This luxurious hotel, minutes from the Arc du Triomphe, has welcomed prestigious guests for nearly seventy years. Its well-equipped sports centre makes it the ideal choice for fitness lovers. *(Champs-Elysées. 219 rooms)*

PRICE CATEGORY

FFFFF

Hôtel le Bristol

★★★★

112 rue du Fbg-St-Honoré, 8th
☎ 01 53 43 43 00

This sumptuous hotel has terraces, views and a French-style garden. The rooms are decorated with the finest fabrics, furniture and objets d'art, and it has the most palatial bathrooms in Paris. *(Champs-Elysées. 180 rooms)*

PRICE CATEGORY

FFFFF

L'Astor

★★★★

11 rue d'Astorg, 8th
☎ 01 53 05 05 05

L'Astor boasts a literary ambience combined with Thirties elegance. Some of the rooms have balconies, and the Regency Revival style extends to the restaurant and cosy bar. *(Champs-Elysées. 134 rooms)*

Hôtel Galiléo

★★★

54 rue Galilée, 8th
☎ 01 47 20 66 06

This hotel is minutes from the lively Champs-Elysées and the American Church on Avenue Georges V. Its façade hides a calm, welcoming interior and a peaceful garden. *(Champs-Elysées. 27 rooms)*

Centre Ville Matignon

★★★

3 rue de Ponthieu, 8th
☎ 01 42 25 73 01

The Centre Ville Matignon hotel is ideally located in one of the smartest areas of town, minutes from the Arc de Triomphe and with easy access to the rest of Paris. It has an elegant, Arc Deco interior. *(Champs-Elysées. 25 rooms)*

La Villa Maillot

★★★★

143 avenue de Malakoff, 16th
☎ 01 53 64 52 52

This hotel is minutes from the Arc de Triomphe and the Bois de Boulogne in the select 16th *arrondissement*. The spacious Art Deco interiors have all modern conveniences to hand. *(Paris West. 39 rooms)*

PRICE CATEGORY

FFFF

Saint James Paris

★★★★

43 avenue Bugeaud, 16th
☎ 01 44 05 81 81

This beautiful château-hôtel, built in 1892, has its own private garden. In the luxurious and grandiose surroundings you will find attentive service and modern comforts. *(Paris West. 48 rooms)*

PRICE CATEGORY

FFFF

Hôtel Centre Ville Etoile

★★★

6 rue des Acacias, 17th
☎ 01 43 80 56 18

This hotel combines modern French elegance with neo-Art Deco rooms. It is situated close to the Arc de Triomphe and La Défense, with easy access to the centre. *(Montmartre and Northwest Paris. 20 rooms)*

PRICE CATEGORY

FF

PRICE CATEGORY

FF

PRICE CATEGORY

FF

PRICE CATEGORY

FF

Hôtel de Neuville

★★★

3 rue Verniquet, 17th
☎ 01 43 80 26 30

The Hôtel de Neuville is a former private 19th-century house in an elegant residential district, with easy access to the centre of town. The bar area incorporates a garden. *(Montmartre and Northwest Paris. 28 rooms)*

Hôtel de Banville

★★★

166 boulevard Berthier, 17th
☎ 01 42 67 70 16

Each of the individually decorated rooms at the Hôtel Banville combines old-fashioned charm with modern comfort. It is ideally situated for quick access to the rest of Paris. *(Montmartre and Northwest Paris. 38 rooms)*

Hôtel Istria

★★

29 rue Campagne
Première, 14th
☎ 01 43 20 91 82

This Montparnasse hotel boasts a guest list that has included Man Ray, Marcel Duchamp and Erik Satie. Modern comforts have been added to the old-world atmosphere. *(Montparnasse. 26 rooms)*

Louvre and Opéra

Introduction . . .

The north side of the river **Seine**, which is known as the *Rive Droite* (Right Bank), is as well known for its

Louvre Museum

opulence as the Left Bank is recognized for its slightly eccentric artistic and literary history.

The Louvre and Opéra area is home to some of the grandest buildings and monuments in Paris. The wide boulevards with their exclusive hotels and designer shops meet at huge, stately squares. Much of the area is taken up by the 1st *arrondissement*.

The exclusivity of this *arrondissement* began when it was chosen as the site of the **Louvre** (pages 50-51) by King Philippe-Auguste in the 13th century. The building began life as a fortress, but little evidence of this remains now.

Its purpose has varied over the years. From its foundation until 1682, when Louis XIV moved to Versailles, it was home to the royal family.

Although parts of the building were first opened to the public as a museum in 1703, until the late 1980s it continued to house a number of state officials and government departments.

The Louvre is now the largest and possibly the best known art museum in the world. In addition to the spacious galleries of the Louvre proper, there are also several museums housed within the building, each dedicated to a unique art form. The **Musée des Arts**

INSIDER'S TIP

Avoid the huge queues at the pyramid entrance to the Louvre Museum by going in through the underground shopping centre. There is a second entrance to the museum here.

Décoratifs (page 56) showcases works by many of the best-known figures in the world of decorative arts and traces the history of functional art through to contemporary times.

Inside the Louvre

The **Musée de la Mode et du Textile** (page 56) is a fashion-lover's dream, complete with centuries worth of costume and clothing including ample coverage of modern *haute couture*. The focus of the **Musée de la Publicité** (page 56) is advertising, but the strength of the collection lies in the display of nearly three centuries of posters.

In 1988 the Louvre underwent an extensive restoration project during which the glass **Pyramids** were constructed. At the same time, the **Carrousel du Louvre** was created. This giant subterranean shopping

. . . Introduction

mall also includes an exhibition centre and a food court.

The **Jardin des Tuileries** (page 60), which lies at the western side of the Louvre, was commissioned by Catherine de Médicis in the 1570s. The sculptures from the Château de Marly and Versailles were added by Louis XV. For a pleasant stroll, follow the arcaded walkways along the rue de Rivoli.

At the far end of the garden, the stately **Place de la Concorde** (page 55) was the site of the guillotine during the French Revolution. Between 1793 and 1795, 1300 members of the nobility were executed here. The square commands magnificent vistas down wide avenues leading to the **Arc de Triomphe** (page 128), the Louvre and the **Sainte Marie-Madeleine** (page 56).

Jardin des Tuileries

Continuing along the path of grandeur and luxury, the nearby **Place Vendôme** is a striking example of a more intimate and extremely charming Parisian square. Prime real estate and swank jewellery stores occupy space alongside the **Ministry of Justice** and the famous **Hôtel Ritz** (page 56).

Part of the 2nd *arrondissement* has much the same feel as its southern neighbour, the 1st *arrondissement*. It contains national buildings such as the **Banque de France** and the **Bibliothèque Nationale** (page 59). It is also home to a series of elegant, glass-roofed, Neo-classical arcades built in the 19th century.

The 2nd *arrondissement* is also a place of contrasts: further east is the seedy **Rue St. Denis**, the centre of Paris' sex industry.

The neighbouring 9th *arrondissement* contains some of Paris's liveliest shopping areas, centred around **Boulevard Haussmann**. The boulevard is named after Baron Haussmann, the architect of Paris' reconstruction in the 1860s, and is home to several *grands magasins*, or big department stores (page 64).

The opulent **Opéra Garnier** (page 54) dominates the Place de l'Opéra, while a short walk leads to the more modest **Opéra-Comique** (page 208). Also nearby is the **Musée Grévin** (page 52), Paris's answer to London's Madame Tussaud's wax museum.

The northwest of the area contains the **Gare St-Lazare** train station which provides service to Normandy.

REFLECTIONS

'We passed through Place de Vendôme, a fine square, about as big as hanover Square. Inhabited by the high families'
- Samuel Johnson

The Louvre . . .

The Louvre's collection comprises over 30,000 works of art arranged in seven main groups. These are organised into subcatergories, so it is relatively easy to focus on what interests you most, if time is limited.

The entrance hall, topped by the famous Pyramids, is the place to pick up a map, get your bearings and begin. Each of the four floors has a particular focus, with the second floor devoted entirely to paintings and drawings.

Louvre and Pyramids

The three 'wings' of the building are named Sully, Richelieu and Denon, and each wing is then subdivided into different floors. Although the wings are not solely devoted to one particular collection or type, Sully is where the Egyptian antiquities are mainly to be found, while much of Richelieu's space displays paintings and sculptures.

Perhpas the most popular area of the museum is the vast collection of **paintings** covering European art from the 13th century to the mid-19th century, located in all three wings of the first floor and Richelieu and Sully on the second floor.

The three main groups represented are the French School, with paintings by Watteau, Fragonard and de la Tour; the Italian and Spanish Schools, displaying the work of da Vinci, Raphael and Caravaggio; and the Northern European School, exhibiting paintings of Rubens, Van Dyck and Vermeer.

The most famous single exhibit is undoubtedly Leonardo da Vinci's **Mona Lisa** (La Gioconda). This portrait of the wife of a notable Florentine merchant was painted just after the death of her son, hence the famous wistful expression. Surprisingly small behind its bullet-proof glass, the painting hangs in Denon on the first floor.

The **Oriental Antiquities-Arts of Islam** collection (Sully and Richelieu, ground and mezzanine floors) traces the artistic history of civilizations from 7000 BC onwards, from India to the Mediterranean. Highlights include the Winged Bull from the Palace of Sargon II in Mesopotamia. The

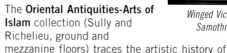

Winged Victory of Samothrace

ADDRESS

Cour Napoléon, place du Carrousel, 1st *arrondissement*
☎ 01 40 20 53 17

GETTING THERE

Métro: Palais Royal, Louvre/Rivoli

HOURS

Mon & Wed: 9am-9.45pm.
Thu-Sun: 9am-6pm.
Tue: closed.

PRICES

Adult 45F (26F after 3pm & Sun)
Child free
Senior 45F (26F after 3pm & Sun)
Student 45F (26F after 3pm & Sun)

. . . The Louvre

Islamic section features works of art from the 7th to the 19th centuries.

The **Egyptian Antiquities** departments (Sully, ground and first floors) illustrate the Ancient Egyptian artistic and cultural heritage both chronologically and thematically. Works from the dawn of the age to the time of Cleopatra are exhibited, and include sarcophagi and the famous Seated Statue of Rameses II. There are further sections devoted to Roman and Coptic Egypt.

Cour Marly

The **Greek, Etruscan and Roman Antiquities** sections (Sully and Denon, ground and first floors) chart the three ancient civilizations from the 3rd millennium BC to the 7th century AD. The ground floor features marble statuary, and the first floor exhibits represent a variety of materials including bronze, silver, glass and terracotta.

European **sculpture** is displayed in the splendid, atmospheric **Cour Marly**, whose glass roof was designed by the architect of the pyramids outside, I.M.Pei. Here you can see examples of French, Spanish, Italian and Northern European sculpture, including the **Marly Horses** which once stood in the Place de la Concorde.

INSIDERS' TIP

Entrance to the museum is free on the first Sunday of every month

The **objets d'art** sections span many different eras, from the Middle Ages to the 19th century. Napoleon's apartments can be seen here, as can furniture, decorative arts, textiles and jewellery.

REFLECTIONS

'I never knew what a palace was until I had a glimpse of the Louvre'
- Nathaniel Hawthorne

The **prints and drawings** section is open only by prior arrangement, although the fragile works are rotated in temporary exhibitions in the main galleries. The collection includes French, German, Italian and Northern European work.

Since 1981 the Louvre and the surrounding area have been the subject of an extensive restoration project, which led to the building of the glass pyramids, the opening of the Richelieu wing and the inauguration of several new rooms.

'Gabrielle d'Estrées et une de ses soeurs au bain'

The programme is ongoing until the end of the century, with plans including a walkway across the Seine to the Musée d'Orsay, the opening of a third entrance and the renovation of the Carrousel gardens. Two rooms in the mezzanine level of the museum present the history and development of the Louvre, including these proposed changes.

ADDRESS

10 boulevard Montmartre,
9th *arrondissement*
☎ 01 47 70 85 05

GETTING THERE

Métro: Richelieu Drouot

HOURS

Mon-Sun: 1pm-7pm
(school holidays 10am-
7pm)

 # Musée Grevin

The Musée Grevin opened its doors in 1882 and since then has received more than 50 million visitors. Famous caricaturist Alfred Grevin gave his name and artistic direction to this wax museum, the Parisian equivalent of Madame Tussaud's.

The sumptuous interior of the Musée Grevin

The extravagantly kitsch **main hall** is the setting for figures from the worlds of sport, cinema and politics.

One or two of the surprisingly lifelike figures may be unknown to non-French visitors, but the big names from Hollywood, sport, entertainment and international politics are also represented.

The figure of French actor Gerard Depardieu, star of *Cyrano de Bergerac*, is especially convincing. Other models include the Pope, Madonna, Bill Clinton and Claudia Schiffer.

An historical display

Downstairs there are tableaux charting the **history of France**, with sound effects and a soundtrack (in French). There are models of such figures as Marie Antoinette and Joan of Arc, and an emotive representation of Charlotte Corday being discovered having just stabbed Revolutionary leader Marat in his bath.

The areas devoted to the **cinema** feature the figures of Laurel and Hardy, Marilyn Monroe and Charlton Heston, among others. Alfred Hitchcock sits in an old-fashioned train carriage opposite the Invisible Man, and Clint Eastwood features in a typical western scene.

PRICES

Adult 55F
Child 36F
Senior 55F
Student 55F

DISCOUNT

50% off admission with
for less card

Upstairs you can walk the galleries, take a closer look at the sumptuous ceiling of the main hall, and visit the spectacular **Palace of Illusions** for a magical sound and light show.

In addition, the museum's **theatre** stages performances in fantasy, magic, mime and juggling every afternoon.

Palais Royal

Richelieu was the first occupant of the Palais Royal, built in the mid-17th century. After his death in 1642 it became Louis XIV's royal palace until the threat of the Fronde (page 29) forced the monarchy away.

From the end of the 17th century to about 1850 the

Palais Royal was owned and put to various uses by the dukes of Orléans, who added further buildings onto the original structure.

Palais Royal

A fire in 1763 destroyed a large part of the palace, and after rebuilding was completed, the galleries surrounding the gardens were rented out as shops for the first time. The palais and its gardens became a popular place to meet, sit or simply stroll and be seen.

After the Revolution, the palace became a gambling house and a meeting place for various political groups, but was reclaimed by Louis-Philippe in 1815. He, however, allowed it to fall into a state of disrepair.

The state took over the building in 1875, and the Ministry of Culture, the Council of State and the Constitutional Council still reside here. This means that the palace itself is not open to the public, but the shops and galleries around the gardens make this a lively centre of activity.

All that remains of Richelieu's original building is the former east wing, the **Gallery of Prows**, which served as

a showcase for maritime trophies. The balcony on this side of the building has also survived.

The adjoining **Comédie Française** (page 203) houses the national theatre company which was established in the 17th century by Molière and his players.

Colonnade and sculpture

Following a fire in 1900, the building itself was replaced by an exact replica, whose foyer contains the armchair in which Molière collapsed and died in 1673.

ADDRESS

Place du Palais Royal, 1st *arrondissement*

GETTING THERE

Métro: Palais Royal

HOURS

Interior of building closed to public. Shops and galleries vary. Comédie Française: see page

PRICES

Free admission to gardens

ADDRESS

Place de l'Opéra, 1st *arrondissement*
☎ 01 40 01 18 58

GETTING THERE

Métro: Opéra

HOURS

Mon-Sun: 10am-5pm
(including auditorium
except during rehearsals)

PRICES

Tours of interior:
Adult 30F
Child 18F
Senior 30F
Student 30F

INSIDER'S TIP

For details of performances
at the Opéra Garnier and
how to book, see page

Opéra Garnier

The building of the Opéra began in 1862, commissioned by Napoleon III. Following the attempted assassination of the Emperor at the old opera house, the architect, Charles Garnier, designed the new one with escape routes.

Garnier's elaborate design and unusual combinations of styles prompted criticism by many observers, including the Empress. He described his cross between Renaissance and Baroque-style architecture as

Opéra Garnier

'Napoleon III style' when called upon to justify his eclecticism.

The building was constructed over an underground water source. This was to be an inspiration for Gaston Leroux, author of *The Phantom of the Opera*, who has his ghost hiding in the damp chambers.

The Opéra was eventually opened in 1875, five years after the abdication of Napoleon III, and soon came to symbolize luxury and leisure in Paris.

For more than 100 years it was the focal point of lyric theatre in the city, but since the opening of the Opéra Bastille (page 204) in 1989, the Opéra Garnier has been used more for dance productions than opera. Guided tours of the interior allow you to see the sumptuous decoration even if you do not have time to see a show.

Poster outside the Opéra

The green copper cupola is the roof of the auditorium, and its interior, repainted by Chagall in 1964, depicts scenes from operas and ballets. The red and gold auditorium has enough room for just over 2,100 spectators and an Italian-style stage.

The most magnificent sight is the Grand Staircase in the Grand Foyer. The staircase, in white, green and red marble, is decorated with torch-bearing statues.

The mosaic ceiling and opulence of the Foyer befits Garnier's plan to make it the 'drawing room for Paris society'.

Other Attractions . . .

The 8-acre (20-hectare) **Place de la Concorde** is the largest of the area's stately squares. It lies at the end of the Jardin des Tuileries, a stopping point on the Grand Axis that leads all the way out of Paris to La Défense.

Place de la Concorde

The construction of the square began in the mid-1700s, the centrepiece at the time being a statue of Louis XV. It was later renamed Place de la Revolution and was the site of the Guillotine during the Reign of Terror when more than 1,000 people, including Marie Antoinette, Louis XVI and Robespierre, were executed.

During the reign of Louis-Philippe in the 19th century, the obelisk from the Luxor temple was made the centrepiece of the square. The statues around the perimeter represent other large cities in France, and it is beautified by the fountains and classical lamp posts.

Place de la Concorde

The **Galerie Nationale du Jeu de Paume** overlooks the Place de la Concorde from the end of the Tuileries. The building was formerly a 'real' tennis court, and has since become an exhibition hall devoted to contemporary art. *(1 place de la Concorde, 8th, ☎ 01 42 60 69 69. Wed-Fri: 12noon-7pm. Tue: until 9.30pm. Sat-Sun: 10am-7pm. Mon: closed. Adult 38F, child 28F (under 13 free), senior 28F, student 28F.)*

Jeu de Paume

The **Orangerie**, on the right side of the Tuileries, is a treasury of Impressionist and later masterpieces. The round gallery at the entrance to the collection is the setting for Utrillo's views of Paris, and the light, airy rooms display familiar and less well-known works by Soutine, Cézanne, Renoir, Matisse, Modigliani, Rousseau and Picasso, among others.

Orangerie

The highlights of the collection are Monet's *Waterlilies* canvases, displayed in the oval rooms downstairs. In addition, there are displays of Monet's letters, photographs of Giverny, his home, and a bust of the artist by Paulin. *(Jardin des Tuileries, place de la Concorde, 8th, ☎ 01 42 97 48 16. Mon & Wed-Sun: 9.45am-5.15pm. Tue: closed. Adult 30F (20F on Sunday), child free, senior 20F, student 20F.)*

. . . Other Attractions . . .

Musée des Arts Decoratifs

Moving east of the Place de la Concorde, the **Musée des Arts Decoratifs** is located in the northwest wing of the Louvre, and houses items charting the rich history of French decorative arts. Exhibits include furniture, toys, ceramics and tapestry. *(107 rue de Rivoli, 1ˢᵗ, ☎ 01 44 55 57 50. Wed-Sun: 12.30pm-6pm. Mon-Tues: closed. Adult 25F, child 16F, senior 16F, student 16F. This museum is currently undergoing refurbishment and only some sections are accessible.)*

Tapestry at the Musée des Arts Decoratifs

The neighbouring **Musée de la Mode et du Textile** is a fascinating collection of costume and fabrics from the 17th century to the present day. *(107 rue de Rivoli, 1st, ☎ 01 44 55 57 50. Tue-Fri: 11am-6pm (until 9pm Wed). Sat-Sun: 10am-6pm. Mon: closed. Adult 30F, child free, senior 20F, student 20F.)*

Musée de la Publicité

The **Musée de la Publicité** is also being refurbished and will open in 1998 as an important exhibition of advertising. The audio-visual, ever-changing displays will feature as many different modes of advertising as possible, including film, sound and poster displays. *(107 rue de Rivoli, 1ˢᵗ, ☎ 01 44 55 58 78. View the website at www.ucad.fr for opening information.)*

Musée de la Mode et du Textile

Moving away from the river, **Place Vendôme** is an outstanding example of 17th-century architecture, and is the location of the luxurious **Ritz** hotel, from where Diana, Princess of Wales made her final ill-fated journey in August 1997. The bronze column in the centre is topped by a figure of Napoleon.

A few streets away, the neo-classical façade of **Sainte Marie Madeleine** dominates Place de la Madeleine. The frieze above the colonnade depicts the Last Judgement, and the interior is richly decorated with coloured marble. It

Sainte Marie Madeleine

Place Vendôme

. . . Other Attractions . . .

is often the setting for celebrity weddings. *(Place de la Madeleine, 8ᵗʰ, ☎ 01 44 51 69 00. Mon-Sun: 8am-7pm.)*

 For a state-of-the-art trip through time, visit **Paristoric**. This thrilling cinematic experience transports visitors back in time to learn about the history of the great city.

Paristoric

The panoramic screen is accompanied by sound and music for an all-encompassing journey into the past. The spectacle is like an audio-visual walk through the centuries to witness key moments in Paris's history.

You will see the city's rise to its position today as one of the greatest cities in the world, and watch the inauguration of its finest buildings and monuments.

The film lasts 45 minutes, and headphones broadcast the commentary in 10 languages. *(11 bis rue Scribe, 9th, ☎ 01 42 66 62 06. Mon-Sun: Apr-Oct: 9am-9pm. Nov-Mar:*

Paristoric

9am-6pm. Shows every hour. Adult 50F, child 30F, senior 30F, student 30F. 2 for the price of 1 with the for less card.)

Musée des Lunettes

 Located above an optician's shop is the unusual **Musée des Lunettes et des Lorgnettes**. It features a fascinating collection of optical aids put together by a Parisian optometrist.

The exhibits include some of the earliest optical instruments, including magnifying lenses which were invented by the Arabs. Medieval corrective lenses and 19th-century monocles can also be seen.

As well as providing a potted history of optometry, the museum has a collection of sunglasses and spectacles which belonged to famous people, Bridget Bardot and Katherine Hepburn included. *(1st floor, 380 rue St-Honoré, 1ˢᵗ, ☎ 01 40 20 06 98. Tue-Sat: 10am-12noon, 2pm-6pm. Sun-Mon: closed. Adult 20F, child free, senior 10F, student 10F. 2 for the price of 1 with the for less card.)*

Musee des Lunettes

The **Gare St-Lazare** is the only mainline railway station in this area and serves Normandy and the northwest.

. . . Other Attractions . . .

St-Trinité

Musée de la Vie Romantique

Musée Gustave Moreau

Outside are two interesting travel-related sculptures by the New Realist artist Arman: a tower of suitcases and a collection of clocks. *(13 rue d'Amsterdam, 8th.)*

Just east of the station stands the church of **St-Trinité**. Although constructed in the 19th-century, the architecture is of a 16th-century Florentine style. It stands in a small churchyard in a busy area of shops, restaurants, kiosks and the Trinité *métro* station. *(Square de la Trinité, 9th.)*

Sculpture outside Gare St-Lazare

The area north of St-Trinité is known as Nouvelle Athènes (New Athens) because of the neo-classical style of some of the buildings. During the 19th-century the area was popular with artists of the Romantic movement, and this is reflected by the **Musée de la Vie Romantique**.

The beautiful, Italian-style shuttered house was once the home of artist Ary Scheffer, some of whose work is displayed here. However, the majority of the museum is devoted to the unconventional author, George Sand (1804-1876), who frequently visited Scheffer here. Her romantic novels were very popular in the 19th century, but she is probably better known today as a result of her eccentric lifestyle and passionate affair with Chopin.

The small museum exhibits her jewellery and other personal items, locks of her hair, watercolours and portraits. The charming house is an attraction in itself, decorated with vines and wisteria and exuding the peace of a country villa. To the left of the quiet garden is Ary Scheffer's studio, which is open to the public, and at the back of the house there is a large conservatory. *(16 rue Chaptal, 9th, ☎ 01 48 74 95 38. Tue-Sun: 10am-5.40pm. Mon: closed. Adult 17,50F, child 9F, senior 9F, student 9F (prices increase during temporary exhibitions).)*

Musée de la Vie Romantique

A few streets away is the **Musée Gustave Moreau**, where every inch of space in the huge studios is taken up with

. . . **Other Attractions**

his paintings. Display cases along the walls contain still more drawings and sketches. The stately rooms are connected by a beautiful spiral staircase, and the small apartment he shared with his parents is also accessible, displaying furniture, letters and personal effects.

Bourse

The Symbolist painter's works had a dreamlike, fantastic quality, mythological scenes being among his most frequent subjects. *Jupiter et Sémélé*, in the first room on the second floor, is a particularly stunning example of his use of brilliant blues and golds. *(14 rue de la Rochefoucauld, 9th, ☎ 01 48 74 38 50. Mon & Wed: 11am-5.15pm. Thu-Sun: 10am-12.45pm, 2pm-5.15pm. Tue: closed. Adult 22F, child 15F, senior 15F, student 15F.)*

Bibliothèque

Bourse

The importance of the area as an administrative and financial district is reflected by the presence of the **Bourse** (Stock Exchange), formerly the corn exchange. The domed hall was remodelled in the late 19th-century. The spectators' gallery allows the public to watch the trading in action. *(2 rue de Viarmes, 1st. Guided tours (30F) Mon-Fri 11.30am and 12noon.)*

The **Banque de France** *(39 rue Croix des Petits Champs, 1st)* is nearby. The 17th-century mansion suffered during the French Revolution, but the luxurious Galerie Dorée, displaying precious works of art and a beautiful painted ceiling, survives. Unfortunately it is only open to the public on *Journées Portes Ouvertes* (page 247).

Banque de France

The old **Bibliothèque Nationale** is also located here. Founded in the 14th century, the huge collection of books and documents is soon to be transferred to a new building in the 13th *arrondissement* (see page 167). Visitors cannot consult the books, but the 19th-century reading room, with its columns, ironwork and glass domes, is accessible. *(58 rue de Richelieu, 1st, ☎ 01 47 03 81 26. Mon-Sat: 9am-4pm.)*

Place des Victoires

Finally, **Place des Victoires** should not be missed. The circle of grand buildings was built in the late 17th century to surround a statue of Louis XIV. The original statue has since been replaced, but the square is still a prestigious address.

Open Spaces

The huge **Jardin des Tuileries** runs from the Louvre to the Place de la Concorde. It is a typical French-style garden, set out with geometric precision.

The gardens were first laid out in the 16th century as the grounds of Catherine de Medici's Palace des Tuileries. The name of both palace and garden derived from the fact that a tile factory (*tuilerie* in French) once stood here.

In 1665 André Le Nôtre, the royal court's head gardener, constructed the wide paths, ponds and parterres which can still be seen today.

Strolling in the Tuileries

During the Paris Commune in the 19th century, the palace was destroyed and the gardens were extended with the creation of the Jardin du Carrousel at the Louvre end. It soon became a popular place for Parisians to stroll, with cafés, benches and kiosks.

Today, the gardens are packed in summer with tourists and Parisians alike, sitting on the seats around the circular ponds or under the neat lines of trees, or strolling along the dazzling, wide gravel avenues. There are refeshment areas, sculptures, games and childrens' rides.

The **Jardin du Palais Royal** is enclosed within the arcades of the Palais Royal, a peaceful oasis in this very busy *quartier* of the city.

It was constructed in the 17th century as a miniature hunting ground for the young Louis XIV. At this time it led into a small wood to the north. After

Jardin du Palais Royal

the building of the surrounding galleries and streets, it became an English-style garden.

It is now laid out in the French style with neat rows of lime trees, a pond, statues, paths and lawns. Chic shops line the surrounding arcades, and the garden is a great place to sit and enjoy the shade of the trees on a hot day.

Eating and Drinking

The most famous restaurant in Paris, **Maxim's** *(3 rue Royale, 8th, ☎ 01 42 65 27 94)* was once popular with the likes of Colette and Cocteau and was the most

The Ritz on Place Vendôme

glamorous and elegant place at which to dine in the city.

Prices these days are still sky-high, although some of Maxim's heyday charm has gone. The Art Nouveau interior is as impressive as ever.

Maxim's

The **Ritz Hôtel** *(15 Place Vendôme, 1st, ☎ 01 43 16 30 30)* has the most stylish hotel bar in the city.

for less **Menthe et Basilic**

French

6 rue Lamartine, 9th
☎ 0148 78 12 20

Average meal: 100-150F
for less discount: 20%
VS/MC

Menthe et Basilic serves delicious French cuisine in a wonderful setting, with the maple tree inside the restaurant providing an unusual centrepiece. Specialities include provincial and traditional dishes.

HOURS

Tue-Sat: 12noon-2.30pm, 7pm-10.30pm.
Sun-Mon: closed

for less **T.G.I. Friday**

American

8 boulevard Montmartre, 9th
☎ 01 47 70 27 20

Average meal: 100-150F
for less discount: 20% with voucher on page 273
AM/VS/MC/DC

T.G.I. Friday's has an informal party atmosphere. The menu is reminiscent of an American diner, with ribs and fries. You can also choose from more than 300 alcoholic and non-alcoholic drinks.

HOURS

Sun-Thu: 11.30am-12midnight. Fri-Sat: 11.30am-1am

Tue-Fri: 12noon-2.30pm,
6.30pm-11.30pm. Sat:
6.30pm-11.30pm. Sun-
Mon: closed

HOURS

Tue-Sat: 10.30am-3pm,
7.15pm-11.30pm. Sun-
Mon: closed

HOURS

Mon-Sun: 12noon-3pm,
7pm-12midnight

La Table d'Alphonse

French

15 rue Lamartine, 9th
☎ 01 42 80 45 01

Average meal: 100-150F
for less discount: 20%
AM/VS/MC

The speciality at this intimate restaurant, located close
to Chopin's house, is cuisine from the south-west of
France. Particularly recommended are the delicious fish
dishes.

Chez Chalomé

Spanish / North African

9 rue de Trévise, 9th
☎ 01 47 70 91 03

Average meal: 100-150F
for less discount: 20%
AM/VS/MC

The recipes here are based on North African cooking.
Try the tajine, a meat stew made with vegetables, fruits,
nuts and spices. The genial atmosphere makes this a
good place for a relaxed meal.

L'Amanguier

French

20 boulevard Montmartre, 9th
☎ 01 47 70 91 35

Average meal: 100-150F
for less discount: 20% with
voucher on pages 279/281
AM/VS/DC

Dishes at L'Amanguier are prepared with the freshest of
ingredients. There are snacks and light or full meals for
any appetite, and the healthy salad starters and classic
desserts are particularly recommended.

Sannine

Lebanese

32 rue du Fbg Montmartre, 9th
☎ 01 48 24 01 32

Average meal: 50-100F
for less discount: 20%
AM/VS/MC

Sannine's atmosphere is authentically Lebanese. The Middle Eastern dishes, which include traditional mezze with *arak*, a Lebanese spirit, are served in welcoming surroundings.

Oh!...Poivrier!

French

2 boulevard Hausmann, 9th
☎ 01 42 46 22 24

Average meal: 50-100F
for less discount: 20%
with voucher on page 279
AM/VS/MC

Oh!...Poivrier! restaurants all have modern, stylish décor. In addition to their reasonably priced, unique dishes, they serve a good range of hot and cold sandwiches with various fillings.

Poul' d'Or

Rotisserie

23 boulevard des Italiens
☎ 01 42 68 00 10

Average meal: 50-100F
for less discount: 20%
with voucher on page 281
AM/VS/MC

Delicious, corn-fed roast chicken dishes are the speciality at Poul' d'Or. You can buy a take-away or have a sit-down meal, with a selection of salads and other accompaniments.

HOURS

Mon-Fri: 12noon-2.30pm,
6pm-11.30pm. Sat-Sun:
6pm-11.30pm

HOURS

Mon-Sun: 11.30am-
12midnight

HOURS

Mon-Thu & Sun: 11am-
12midnight. Fri-Sat:
11am-1am

Shopping

Galeries Lafayette

Boulevard Haussmann (9th *arrondissement*) is the location of two of Paris's biggest and most up-market department stores, **Printemps** *(no. 64)* and **Galeries Lafayette** *(no. 40)*. The interior of Galeries Lafayette, with its exuberant domed ceiling, is especially impressive.

Their gourmet equivalents are located nearby. **Fauchon**, at 24-30 place de la Madeleine, is a veritable museum of food, with mouth-watering displays of the finest groceries in Paris. **Hédiard** *(21 place de la Madeleine)* is almost as luxurious.

Hediard

Closer to the river runs one of the city's main shopping arteries, **rue de Rivoli**. Reasonably-priced clothes shops, museum stores and souvenir shops stand alongside another of Paris's big department stores, **La Samaritaine** *(19 rue de la Monnaie, 1st)*. Founded in 1900, it comprises four large buildings. Its interior is a stunning example of the Art Deco style.

Fauchon

Around the Palais Royal and Bourse area is a maze of delightful glass-enclosed arcades known as **les passages**. These atmospheric 19th-century galleries, often used in films, are lined with chic and unusual shops. *Galeries* **Colbert** and **Vivienne** are especially beautiful, with mosaics and statues.

Café Coton

Men's Clothing

51 rue des Petits Champs, 1st
☎ **01 49 26 04 82**

for less discount: 20%
VS/MC

Café Coton is a well-known French brand of good quality clothes. Menswear in classic styles can be found here. There is also a good selection of accessories such as cufflinks.

American and British Shoes

Shoes

51 blvd des Batignolles, 8th
☎ 01 42 93 29 60

for less discount: 20%
VS/MC

HOURS

Tue-Fri: 12noon-7pm. Sat:
10am-7pm. Sun-Mon:
closed

This shoe shop sells a wide range of footwear for both men and women. There are smart and practical styles for town and country. Brand names stocked include Timberland and Doc Martens.

Josiane Laure

Beauty Salon

255 rue St-Honoré, 1st
☎ 01 42 86 80 02

for less discount: 20%
off services
VS/MC

HOURS

Tue-Fri: 10am-7pm. Sat:
10am-5pm. Sun-Mon:
closed

The practises of this beauty salon are inspired by ancient Chinese methods. The products used are made from natural plant extracts and essential oils. Treat yourself to one of the many pampering services available.

Divine

Women's Clothing

34 rue des Martyrs, 9th
☎ 01 48 78 90 33

for less discount: 20%
VS

HOURS

Mon-Sat: 9.30am-7.30pm.
Sun: 10.30am-1pm

This elegant shop sells a wide range of designer labels. It specialises in smart, business-like clothing and accessories, with brands such as Tiki Tirawa, François Girbaud and Ghost.

HOURS

Mon-Sat: 9.30am-
12.30pm, 2.30pm-
6.30pm. Sat: 2.30pm-
5pm. Sun: closed

Robert

Jewellery

8 rue Rochechouart, 9th
☎ 01 42 80 50 40

for less discount: 20%
No credit cards

Robert sells jewellery in classic and modern styles. You
can see items being made in the adjoining workshop.
Choose from the selection of items on display, or have
something custom-made.

Asphodele

Second-hand designer labels

**44 rue du
Fbg Montmartre, 9th**
☎ 01 42 46 91 88

for less discount: 20%
No credit cards

HOURS

Mon-Fri: 1pm-7pm. Sat:
3pm-7pm. Sun: closed

"*Dépot-vente*" shops like Asphodele sell designer
clothes at cheap prices. As well as clothing you can find
accessories and decorative items, and there is a section
specializing in hats.

Pulcinella

Jewellery / Gifts

10 rue Vignon, 9th
☎ 01 47 42 57 23

for less discount: 20%
AM/VS/MC

HOURS

Tue-Sat: 12noon-7pm.
Sun-Mon: closed

This shop sells reproduction jewellery from the 1930s,
40s and 50s. It also stocks a variety of decorative items
for the home. The cushions, Victorian picture frames and
Art Deco lamps make great gifts.

Le Marais and République

Introduction . . .

Until Roman Times, the city of Paris was confined to an island in the Seine, the **Ile de la Cité**. The site of the very first settlement of Parisii Celts in the 3rd century BC, the town was called Lutetia by the Romans but became known as Paris, after its original settlers, in about AD 212.

On the Ile de la Cité stands the famous cathedral, **Notre Dame de Paris** (pages 70-71). It is believed that there has been a cathedral on this site since the beginnings of

Hotel Dieu

Christianity in France, but the building you see today dates from 1345.

Another of the island's most famous sights is the 13th-century **Sainte-Chapelle** (page 73), located within the courtyard of the **Palais de Justice**. Taking up a large part of the Ile de la Cité, the Palais de Justice houses the judicial offices and law courts of the city. The Gothic towers lining the Seine opposite the right bank mark the part of the building which is the **Conciergerie** (page 75).

The island is also the location of several civic buildings, including the 19th-century **Hôtel Dieu**. Formerly an orphanage, the Hôtel Dieu overlooks the *parvis* in front of Notre Dame and is now the most important hospital for central Paris.

Palais de Justice

A transformation of the island, along with much of the rest of the city, took place under the auspices of Haussmann in the late 19th century. He demolished the medieval buildings in his quest for urban uniformity and space. In the process, he cleared an area in front of Notre Dame which allowed the whole façade to be viewed in comfort.

Upstream from the Ile de la Cité, the Ile St-Louis has no famous monuments or churches, but its streets exude a tranquility seldom found in other parts of Paris. This island was not developed until the 17th century, having been largely ignored as the Ile de la Cité grew.

. . . Introduction

To live here is to live at what Voltaire called one of the best addresses in the world, an honour which has been enjoyed by Daumier, John Dos Passos and the sculptor Camille Claudel, among others.

Ile St Louis

The islands are linked to the left and right banks by several bridges, the oldest of which is the beautiful **Pont Neuf** (page 76). The Pont Neuf leads into the Châtelet area of the Right Bank, where the commercial rue de Rivoli continues into Le Marais. The **Place de Châtelet** is one of the busiest intersections in the city, and is the location of twin theatres designed by Davioud.

Le Marais, the Jewish Quarter, is made up of parts of the 3rd and 4th *arrondissements* and is one of the oldest and most charming areas in Paris. Its name means marsh or swamp, and this is exactly what it was before Paris expanded in the Middle Ages from its beginnings on the Île de la Cité.

The Knights Templar were the first to reclaim some of the land in the 13th century, draining it and making it habitable. The royal family's interest in the area in the 17th century marked the start of its prestigious character, with the building of the stately **Place des Vosges** under Henry IV.

After the French Revolution, Le Marais became a squalid slum and remained so until the 1960s, when talk of demolishing the whole area began. Thankfully, Parisians saw the advantages of preserving the pre-Haussmann buildings and narrow streets, and a clean-up campaign was begun. Today it is a centre of Parisian nightlife, concentrated mainly around the **rue Vielle du Temple** (see page 83) and is also popular area with the gay community.

Bastille, to the east of Le Marais, is one of Paris's most lively *quartiers*. Since the opening of the Opéra Bastille, the previously run-down area has been transformed into a trendy neighborhood filled with bars, restaurants and nightclubs. The name Bastille will, however, always be associated with the French Revolution. It was at the **Place de la Bastille** that, in 1789, the Parisian crowd stormed the royal prison. Today, Bastille Day is still celebrated in great style on July 14 to commemorate the birth of modern France.

INSIDER'S TIP

Le Marais, and especially rue Vielle du Temple, is popular at night. The bars, cafés and restaurants cater for a young crowd, and the area is also the centre of the gay scene of Paris.

Hôtel de Ville

Notre Dame . . .

The Ile de la Cité is thought to have had a cathedral as far back as the 4th century, when the city of Paris was first converted to Christianity after the Romans departed. Just one portal of the original basilica, which was destroyed in 1160 to make way for a new cathedral, survived to be integrated into the new building. The foundation stone was laid in 1163 by Pope Alexander III, and building carried on for centuries.

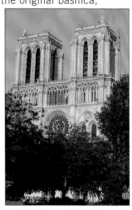

The towers of Notre Dame

The original cathedral did not have the flying buttresses we can see today, as these were added nearly a century after building commenced. Nor did it have side chapels until its final completion, under the last in a long line of architects, in 1330.

Louis XIV renovated the choir in the 18th century, but it was not until the 19th century and the publication of Victor Hugo's famous novel *Notre Dame de Paris* that the city realized the urgent need for full restoration.

Work was directed by Viollet-le-Duc and Lassus, one of the renovators of Sainte-Chapelle (page 73), and continued until 1864. Statues were replaced and the famous gargoyles were restored.

Gargoyles

Its precious examples of 13th-century stained glass and Gothic architecture remain intact. Louis XIV's 18th-century choir and the 19th-century restoration are so faithful to the Gothic style that there is an illusion of uniformity throughout.

There is almost always a queue to visit Notre Dame, so try to go early in the morning, as it becomes very hard to look at the architecture when stuck behind a large group.

Highlights which should not be missed include the rose

ADDRESS

Place du Parvis de Notre Dame, Ile de la Cité
☎ 01 42 34 56 10

GETTING THERE

Métro: Cité

HOURS

Mon-Sun: 8am-6.45pm.
Towers open 9am-5.30pm.

PRICES

Admission to the cathedral is free.
Admission to towers:
Adult 27F
Child 15F
Senior 18F
Student 18F

Admission to crypt and treasury:
Adult 27F
Child 15F
Senior 18F
Student 18F

. . . Notre Dame

windows. The **west window** depicts the Virgin Mary after whom the cathedral is named. The **south window**, which is 42ft (13m) in diameter, depicts Christ and the apostles. The **north window** is a massive 69 feet (21 metres) in diameter, and features figures from the Old Testament.

The view of Paris from the **north tower**, 380 steps up, is impressive. Going up into the tower also allows you a good look at the grotesque and creepy **gargoyles**. The **south tower** contains the cathedral's great bell, **Emmanuel**, immortalized by Victor Hugo in *Notre Dame de Paris*.

Inside there are several examples of the work of

Interior of the cathedral

famous artists and sculptors. Coustou's **Pietà** is behind the altar, and the side chapels contain Le Brun's May paintings, so named because in the 17th and 18th centuries they were presented to the cathedral by the Paris Guilds on May Day. The wooden Louis XIV **choir stalls** are notable for their intricate carvings of the life of the Virgin Mary.

The square or *parvis* in front of the cathedral was cleared by Haussmann as part of his urban replanning, and as well as providing a good place from which to photograph the cathedral, it hides some of Paris's oldest remains. Step underground to the **Archaeological Crypt** for a break from the crowds and an insight into the Gallo-Roman city.

The remains of Roman Empire houses, ramparts and streets are preserved behind glass in dark, low rooms, and dioramas and displays describe the development and growth of Paris.

View of the south tower and rose window

The remains pre-date Notre Dame by several hundred years, and were only discovered during the last thirty years. It is incredible to think that the cellars you can look into belonged to some of the first residents of what was to become Paris.

DON'T MISS

The chimières (gargoyles), the rose windows and the flying buttresses.

INSIDER'S TIP

The rose windows are best viewed from inside at sunset.

Centre Pompidou

ADDRESS

Place Georges-Pompidou,
4th *arrondissement*
☎ 01 44 78 12 33

GETTING THERE

Métro: Rambuteau

HOURS

Mon & Wed-Fri: 12noon-
10pm. Tue: closed. Sat-
Sun: 10am-10pm.

Renovation work will be in
progress until the end of
1999. Only the top floor
temporary exhibitions and
the viewing gallery will
remain open.

PRICES

Admission prices for
temporary exhibitions vary.
Access to the viewing
terrace on the 6th floor is
free.

The **Centre Georges-Pompidou**, or **Beaubourg**, is named after the French president who in 1969 commissioned its construction. An international competition was held to select the designers, but no-one could have guessed what a radical and innovative creation it was to become.

Centre Pompidou

The winning architects were Britain's Richard Rogers, designer of the Lloyd's of London building, and Italian Renzo Piano. The centre was completed in 1977.

The building is unique in that it is 'inside out' - the lifts, escalators, pipes and air ducts are on the outside, so that the inside is as spacious as possible. Even the struts which act as buttresses to hold the building up are outside, like the exoskeleton of an insect.

What's more, the functional pieces are all colour-coded: the ventilation shafts are blue, the water ducts are green, the electricity lines are yellow and the lifts and escalators are red. The most colourful view is of the back, facing rue du Renard.

The 480,000 feet^2 (146,300 metres^2) of space inside has been used in various ways. The **Musée National d'Art Moderne** takes up two floors, and presents art from 1905 to the present day. Artists represented include Braque, Matisse, Chagall and Derain. Of the 30,000 works owned by the museum, about 1,000 are on display at any one time.

Street entertainers fill the Place Georges-Pompidou

The whole of the fifth floor is devoted to the work of contemporary artists, fulfilling President Pompidou's request for a cultural centre which not only exhibited but also encouraged new creations.

The building is also home to a library and design centre, and hosts various shows and meetings throughout the year.

Sainte-Chapelle

Located on the Ile de la Cité, **Sainte-Chapelle** is a treasure of Gothic architecture. Its delicate spire is visible over the roofs of the rather stark **Palais de Justice**, where it stands protected in a stone courtyard.

The chapel was begun in 1242 under the auspices of Louis IX and was intended to house the relics of

Christ's Passion. The Crown of Thorns, purchased for three times as much as the chapel cost, was added by Louis IX.

During the Revolution it was the target of looting and vandalism, and the precious relics were dispersed. Even the organ, rood screen and choir stalls were ripped out, but the chapel was restored to its former glory in the 19th-century by architects Duban, Lassus and Boeswillwald.

Sainte-Chapelle

Security at the Palais de Justice is tight, but once you've passed through the bag checks you enter the **Lower Chapel**. This small, low-vaulted area is dedicated to the Virgin Mary. However, the stars painted on the ceiling, the gilt and the fleur-de-lys designs give it a kitsch rather than holy feel.

The **Upper Chapel** is the real reason to

Detail of stained glass

visit. 6,458 feet^2 (1,968 metres^2) of stunning stained glass lines the walls, depicting the biblical story of mankind from Creation through to Christ's redemption. Each window should be 'read' from left to right from the bottom up.

The dominant colours are red and blue, and the whole chamber seems to glow even when the sun is not shining. The narrow frames seem to fade away to give the illusion

The stained glass windows

of a room made entirely of this magnificent stained glass.

ADDRESS

4 blvd du Palais, 1st *arrondissement*
☎ 01 53 73 78 50

GETTING THERE

Métro: Cité

HOURS

Mon-Sun: Oct-Mar: 10am-5pm. Apr-Sep: 9.30am-6.30pm.

PRICES

Adult 32F
Child 21F
Senior 21F
Student 32F

ADDRESS

Hôtel Salé, 5 rue de Thorigny, 3rd *arrondissement*
☎ 01 42 71 25 21

GETTING THERE

Métro: St-Sébastien Froissart

HOURS

Wed-Mon: 9.30am-5.30pm (6pm in summer). Tue: closed

PRICES

Adult 30F
Child free
Senior 20F
Student 30F

Musée Picasso

Musée Picasso

The **Hôtel Salé**, home of the **Musée Picasso**, almost upstages the collection it contains. The mansion was built for a wealthy salt tax collector, Aubert de Fontenay, who commissioned sculptors to work on the ornate façade and interiors.

It became a literary repository after the Revolution, and then a school: Honoré de Balzac completed his studies here. Its artistic connections date back to the first exhibitions of sculptor Vian's bronze works when the Ecole Centrale des Arts took it over in the 19th century.

The museum contains more than 2,000 works

Much of the interior was redesigned for the establishment of the Picasso museum in 1976. The collection began with pictures given to the French State in payment for death duties after the death of Picasso and his wife in 1973 and 1990 respectively. Today, the collection includes paintings, sculptures, collages, drawings, ceramics and engravings.

Go straight up the magnificent staircase to view the exhibits chronologically, beginning with the formative works he created at the early age of 13 and finishing with those he completed a year before his death.

Some of Picasso's best works were inspired by his stays in Paris. The collection contains examples in every medium and from every stage of his artistic development including Cubism, Surrealism and neo-classicism. His blue period, epitomised by the lugubrious *Self-portrait* (1901), and pink period are also represented.

Les Demoiselles d'Avignon (1907), *The Pipes of Pan* (1923) and *The Kiss* (1969) are some of the most familiar works on show.

Picasso's own art collection can also be seen here. Picasso owned works by Courbet, Cézanne, Renoir, Braque, Miro and Matisse, despite being said to 'collect' his own paintings more avidly than anyone else's. Exhibitions of letters, documents and notebooks give an insight into his remarkable life.

Other Attractions . . .

The grim and striking façade of the **Conciergerie**, on the western side of the Île de la Cité, still dominates the area of river and quay which its chilling towers survey, although its days as a prison are long gone. During the Revolution more than 2,700 people, including Marie Antoinette and Robespierre, were held here before their execution.

Conciergerie

The first port of call for a visit here is the huge **Salle des Gens d'Armes** (Hall of Men-at-Arms), a 209 foot (64 metre) by 90 foot (27 metre) Gothic vaulted room. Throughout its existence it has functioned largely as a dining room, and

Conciergerie

even now it is hired for grand banquets. The old **kitchens**, with their huge fireplaces, are next to this main hall.

The prison area leads off the other side of the hall. The conditions suffered by prisoners here are graphically described. The three types of cell, their standard of comfort and facilities set according to the wealth of their inmates, are reconstructed here. A mock-up of the cell occupied by Marie Antoinette can also be seen, reconstructed on the exact site of the original.

Ile St Louis

The list of names of the thousands executed during the Reign of Terror is particularly moving. The history of the prison is illustrated by documents, artefacts and a video show (in French). *(1 quai de l'Horloge, 1ˢᵗ, ☎ 01 53 73 78 50. Mon-Sun: Apr-Sep: 9.30am-6.30pm. Oct-Mar: 10am-5pm. Adult 28F, child 18F (under 12 free) senior 18F, student 18F.)*

Until the mid-1600s the **Ile St-Louis** was merely pastureland. As most of the houses were built at the same time, the island displays a uniformity of architecture. The neat tree-lined streets are peaceful, with the exception of **rue St-Louis-en-l'Ile**, which is the main thoroughfare. It is lined with exclusive shops, smart restaurants and elegant *hôtels*.

Ile St-Louis

. . . Other Attractions . . .

The **Church of St-Louis-en-l'Ile** has a beautiful Baroque interior and is twinned with Carthage cathedral, Tunisia.

Pont Neuf

The iron steeple clock dates from 1741. *(19 bis rue St-Louis-en-l'Ile, 4th, ☎ 01 46 34 11 60. Tue-Sun: 9am-12noon, 2pm-7pm.)*

Ile St-Louis church

The oldest bridge in Paris is the **Pont Neuf**, completed in 1605. It is decorated with gargoyles depicting Parisian characters, and as a busy meeting place in the 17th century the bridge was a popular site for entertainers, hawkers and even street dentists!

Les Halles

Moving away from the river brings you to the area around Les Halles (see page 86). The **square des Innocents**, formerly a rather primitive cemetery which was little more than a hole in the ground, is the site of the last Renaissance **fountain** to survive in Paris. It dates from 1549 and is the work of Lescot, although the reliefs are by Goujon.

Pont Neuf

The area is home to the delightful **Musée de la Poupée** (Museum of Dolls). There are 60 different displays, some of them featuring exquisite French porcelain-headed dolls from 1850 onwards, and others devoted to dolls from many different parts of the world.

Musée de la Poupée

The museum also offers a doll-restoration service, advice for serious collectors, and runs doll-making workshops for people of all ages. *(Impasse Berthaud, 3rd, ☎ 01 42 72 55 90. Tue-Sun: 10am-6pm. Adult 35F, child 20F, senior 25F, student 25F.)*

Musée de la Poupée

. . . Other Attractions . . .

Nearby stands one of Paris's loveliest churches, **St-Eustache**. It took more than one hundred years to complete this precedent of Renaissance interior

architecture, which combines elements such as pillars, arches and columns. The church also has some magnificent stained glass windows, and a mainly Gothic exterior. *(Rue du Jour, 1st, ☎ 01 40 26 47 99. May-Oct: Mon-Sat: 8am-8pm. Sun: 8am-1pm, 2.30pm-7pm. Nov-Apr: Mon-Sat: 8am-7pm. Sun: 9am-12.30pm, 3pm-8pm.)*

St-Eustache

St-Eustache

Moving into Le Marais along rue de Rivoli, you pass the **Tour St-Jacques**, the only surviving part of the St-Jacques-de-la-Boucherie church, which was attacked by revolutionaries. The 170 foot (52 metre) tower is in the Gothic style and is now used as a meteorological station.

The statue at the bottom is of Pascal, the mathematician who carried out pioneering experiments into meteorology in the 17th century. The tower is not open to the public.

Hôtel de Ville

You can't miss the nearby **Hôtel de Ville**, its stately façade fronted by magnificent fountains. This incarnation of the town hall was completed in the late 19th century, and displays flamboyant stonemasonry and turrets. It is still the home of the city council. *(Place de l'Hôtel de Ville, 4th, ☎ 01 42 76 50 49. Guided tours are available by appointment only.)*

'Les nymphs retirent de l'eau le corps inanimé de Psyché' by Natoire

Le Marais is the location of the **Archives Nationales**, which has been housed in two imposing *hôtels* since 1808. Part of the archives, in the magnificent **Hôtel de Soubise**, is the **Musée de l'Histoire de France**. The permanent display comprises more than 200 documents, including a letter from Joan of Arc and the 1789 Declaration of the Rights of Man.

Musée de l'Histoire de France

. . . Other Attractions . . .

You need to know some French and be interested in history to really appreciate this museum, although the building itself has delightful examples of fine Rococo interiors. *(60 rue des Francs-Bourgeois, 3rd, ☎ 01 40 27 62 18. Mon & Wed-Fri: 12noon-5.45pm, Sat-Sun: 1.45pm-5.45pm. Tue: closed. Adult 15F, child free, senior 12F, Student 12F.)*

Musée de la Chasse et de la Nature

for less The nearby **Musée de la Chasse et de la Nature** is devoted both to hunting and to animal life.

It is housed in the beautiful 17th-century Hôtel de Guénégaud, in the centre of this historic area. The building began life as a private home and became the headquarters of the *Fondation de la Maison de la Chasse et de la Nature* in 1964.

Displays in the museum include an exhibition of hunting artefacts, with a huge range of guns and ammunition.

Musée de la Chasse et de la Nature

There are galleries of hunting and animal-related pictures and prints from many different eras, as well as tapestries, sculptures and ceramics. Exhibitions of taxidermy and wildlife displays may also be seen. *(60 rue des Archives, 3rd ☎ 01 42 72 86 42. Wed-Mon: 10am-12.30pm, 1.30pm-5.30pm. Tue: closed. Adult 30F, Child 5F, Senior 15F, Student 15F. 50% discount on admission with your **for less** card.)*

Musée de la Curiosité

Another fascinating museum in the area is the **Musée de la Curiosité et de la Magie**. From the moment you enter this museum you are plunged into a world of mystery and illusion.

'La Lice et ses Petits' at the Musée de la Chasse

The museum houses a unique collection of magic tricks, ventriloquists' dummies, automatons and conjuring props dating from all eras.

The exhibitions chart the history of conjuring from Egyptian times to the present day, uncovering the secrets of the medieval court jesters and famous magicians such as Houdini.

. . . Other Attractions . . .

There is also a room of optical illusions and a hall of mirrors. The tours around the museum are guided by historians and magicians with a real love of their

subject, and there is a live performance of magic every 30 minutes in the afternoon. *(11 rue St Paul, 4ᵗʰ, ☎ 01 42 72 13 26. Wed, Sat & Sun: 2pm-7pm. Adult 45F, child 30F, senior 30F, student 45F.)*

Musée de la Curiosité

The **Maison Européenne de la Photographie** is in another Marais *hôtel*, with a minimalist extension by Yves Lion.

Maison Européene de la Photographie

Opened in 1996, it has since hosted many important exhibitions of contemporary photography, with both famous and up-and-coming European photographers represented. *(5-7 rue de Fourcy, 4ᵗʰ, ☎ 01 44 78 75 00. Wed-Sat: 11am-8pm. Sun: 2pm-8pm. Adult 30F, child 15F, senior 15F, student 30F.)*

for less The part of Le Marais around the rue des Roisiers is the **Jewish Quarter** of Paris. The **Memorial du Martyr Juif Inconnu** (Memorial for the Unknown Jewish Martyr) is part of the **Centre de Documentation Juive Contemporaine**.

The Centre came into being in 1992 to commemorate the six million Jews who perished without graves as a result of the Nazi regime. The basement crypt has a poignant monument: a black marble Star of David

Memorial du Martyr Juif Inconnu

containing the ashes of Jews from Poland and Austria who perished in the Nazi death camps.

Memorial du Martyr Juif Inconnu

The centre also has a library and archives containing documents and books recording the genocide and oppression. *(17 rue Geoffroy l'Asnier, 4ᵗʰ, ☎ 01 42 77 44 72. Sun-Thu: 10am-1pm, 2pm-6pm (5pm Fri). Sat: closed. Adult 15F, child under 12 free, senior and student 15F. 2 admissions to the Memorial du Martyr Juif Inconnu for the price of 1 with your for less card.)*

. . . Other Attractions . . .

One of the most important museums in this part of Paris is the **Musée Carnavalet**. This huge collection charts the history of Paris from its origins to the

present day. The setting is two mansions, comprising 140 rooms open to the public and surrounded by beautiful, tranquil gardens.

The exhibitions are arranged chronologically, with the entrance halls displaying old shop signs and scale models of Paris. The rest of the ground floor follows the city's history up until the 16th century, with archaeological remnants, paintings, sculptures and furniture.

Musée Carnavalet

There is also an area for temporary exhibitions on the ground floor, one of the most recent having been a display of jewellery and tiaras.

The first floor features room reconstructions from the 17th, 18th and 19th centuries, including Proust's

Musée Carnavalet

bedroom, and the second floor is devoted to the French Revolution. Exhibits here include keys to the Bastille prison.

The street scenes of Paris painted by artists from different eras, including Loir, Utrillo and Lansyer are fascinating, especially if you are familiar with the city. *(23 rue de Sévigné, 3rd, ☎ 01 42 72 21 13. Tue-Sun: 10am-5.40pm. Adult 35F, child 25F, senior 25F, student 25F.)*

Musée Carnavalet

The **Musée Cognacq-Jay** is a more manageable size, displaying mostly 18th-century items collected by the founders of La Samaritaine department store. Follow the stairs up and up to see the ceramics, furniture and paintings by Canaletto, Fragonard and Watteau. The unremarkable garden is open to the public from May to September. *(8 rue*

Musée Cognacq-Jay

Musée Cognacq Jay

. . . Other Attractions

Elzévir, 3ʳᵈ, ☎ 01 40 27 07 21. Tue-Sun: 10am-5.40pm.
Mon: closed. Adult 17.50F, child free, senior 9F, student 9F.)

Moving eastwards, the beautiful **Place des Vosges** is
the location of the **Maison de Victor Hugo**. The writer
lived on the third floor of this mansion from 1832 to
1848.

Maison de Victor Hugo

The staircase is decorated
with theatre posters
advertising the
performances of, among
others, *Les Misérables*. The
first floor, where the
exhibition begins, displays
editions of Hugo's works,
famous illustrations of his
characters by Bayard and
Doré, and some of his own
sketches. There is a bust of
Hugo by Rodin, and the quill
pens he used are also on
display.

Maison de Victor Hugo

The third floor, his apartment, commands tremendous
views over the Place des Vosges and displays the
family's rather startling taste in carpets and curtains.
A collection of portraits, letters, shopping receipts and
holiday photographs can also be seen. *(6 place des
Vosges, 4ᵗʰ, ☎ 01 42 72 10 16. Tue-Sun: 10am-5.40pm.
Mon: closed. Adult 27F, child 19F, senior 19F, student 19F).*

Hôtel de Sully

Nearby, the **Hôtel de Sully** is the most beautiful of all
the Marais mansions. It was built in 1624 for a
gambler, Petit Thomas, who went on to lose it and the
rest of his fortune in the space of just one evening's
gaming.

It is open only occasionally for
temporary exhibitions, but you
can walk in the beautiful
courtyard and look at the
carvings and statues. *(62 rue
st-Antoine, 4th, ☎ 01 44 61 20
00. Mon-Fri: 9am-12noon, 2pm-
5pm.)*

Hôtel de Sully

A few streets away is the
futuristic façade of the **Opéra
Bastille** (page 204) ,
inaugurated in 1989. The new
venue was intended to make opera accessible to the
masses, and its location here has certainly improved
the neighbourhood.

Open Spaces

The **Place des Vosges** is the oldest and one of the most beautiful squares in the city. It began life as Place Royale, but was given its current name in honour of the Vosges region of France, the first to pay its revolutionary taxes. The name has reverted to Place Royale several times throughout history, whenever France ceased to be a republic.

Place des Vosges

It is totally symmetrical, surrounded on each side by a row of nine houses with ground floor arcades. The houses,

Place des Vosges

uniformly red brick and contrasting beautifully with the trees, have dormer windows and slate roofs.

It has always been a very sought-after address, and notable residents have included Victor Hugo, Madame de Sévigné and Cardinal Richelieu.

Duels used to be fought in the square, but it is now a pleasant area to sit and walk, with its neat lawns and gravel paths. There are plenty of benches under the trees, supplying shady respite on a hot day.

The statue in the centre is of Louis XIII, but it is not the original: this was melted down during the Revolution.

The arcades around the square are home to several exclusive shops and restaurants.

The western end of the Ile de la Cité provides the only other real expanse of grass in the area. The **Square du Vert-Galant** (Gay Blade) is so-called in memory of Henri IV, and looks across to the Right Bank where he was assassinated.

It is one of the best places to stand for a truly breathtaking, picture-postcard view of the Seine and the buildings along both banks, including the Louvre.

Square du Vert-Galant

The weeping willow at the tip is said to be the first tree in Paris to bud every spring, and the grassy park is a great place for picnics.

Eating and Drinking . . .

The Ile St-Louis is the location of Paris's most famous ice-cream and sorbet shop, **Berthillon** *(31 rue Saint-Louis-en-Ile, 4ᵗʰ, ☎ 01 43 54 31 61).* Easily identifiable by the long queues, this is the main Berthillon shop, though others are scattered along the Île St-Louis. Many cafés throughout Paris also carry the Berthillon brand which is famous for its incredible array of flavours.

The area around Châtelet and along the Seine has no shortage of outdoor cafés, but the real centres of eating and drinking are the Marais and Bastille areas. In the area around the **rue Vieille du Temple**, Parisians fill the many bars and restaurants from lunch until the early hours of the morning.

Queues outside Berthillon's

Not far from here lie some of Paris' most famous bistros such as **Benoit** *(20 rue Saint-Martin, 4ᵗʰ, ☎ 01 42 72 25 76)* which opened in 1912, and Au Pied de Cochon *(6 rue Coquilliere, 1ˢᵗ, ☎ 01 42 36 11 75).*

At night, the area around the Bastille springs to life fairly early with young trendies who are later joined by a diverse crowd of theatre-goers out for a late-night snack after the opera. A favourite post-opera stop is **Bofinger** *(5 rue de la Bastille, 4ᵗʰ, ☎ 01 42 72 87 82),* a quintessential Paris brasserie and one of the oldest in town.

Bofinger

On the following pages, you can find a selection of traditional French and non-traditional restaurants all of which offer a 20% discount to **for less** cardholders.

for less La Chaumière Normande

French

52 rue de Chabrol, 10ᵗʰ
☎ 01 47 70 30 62

Average meal: 150-200F
for less discount: 20%
VS

HOURS

Mon-Fri: 12noon-3pm.
Sat-Sun: closed

La Chaumière Normande serves traditional French dishes. The speciality is Normandy cuisine such as *pavé boeuf.* Enjoy your meal in the warm and genial atmosphere.

La Petite Adresse

French

13 rue Ste-Anastase, 3rd
☎ 01 42 78 19 90

Average meal: 100-150F
for less discount: 20%
VS/MC

HOURS

Mon-Fri: 12noon-3pm.
Wed-Sat: 7pm-11pm
(call to make reservations).

This restaurant has a friendly, lively atmosphere. It specializes in classic pastries and traditional French home-cooking. It is open in the evening for private parties only.

Le Bois Rouge

French

14 rue de la Fidélité, 10th
☎ 01 45 23 26 26

Average meal: 100-150F
for less discount: 20%
VS

HOURS

Mon-Fri: 12noon-3pm,
7pm-11pm. Sat: 7pm-
11pm.
Sun: closed.

This typically French restaurant has a warm, friendly atmosphere. Specialities include *foie gras* and duck dishes. There is an excellent selection of wines to complement your meal.

Paris Dakar

Senegalese

95 rue du Fbg St-Martin, 10th
☎ 01 42 08 16 64

Average meal: 100-150F
for less discount: 20%
AM/VS/MC

HOURS

Tue-Sun: 12noon-3pm,
7pm-2am (closed
midday on Fri). Mon:
closed.

At this unusual restaurant you can try the traditional cuisine of Senegal. Combine the tropical fish dishes with some African beer or wine. The national dish is *tiep boudienne*, fish with rice and African vegetables.

L'Auberge Nicolas Flamel

French

51 rue de Montmorency, 3rd
☎ 01 42 71 77 78

Average meal: 100-150F
for less discount: 20%
VS/MC

HOURS
Mon-Fri: 12noon-2.30pm,
8pm-11.45pm. Sat: 8pm-
11.45pm. Sun: closed

The chef here has worked with top names such as Chapel and Savoy. The building and décor gives the restaurant a medieval feel. Try one of the traditional dishes such as *gigot des sept heures*.

L'Enchotte

French

11 rue de Chabrol, 10th
☎ 01 48 00 05 25

Average meal: 100-150F
for less discount: 20%
AM/VS/MC

HOURS
Mon-Fri: 12noon-2.30pm,
7.30pm-11.30pm.
Sat-Sun: closed

This lively bistro and bar is popular with locals. Specialities include traditional French dishes such as *blanquette de veau*. The atmosphere is reminiscent of old Paris.

Poul' d'Or

Rotisserie

84 rue Montorgueil, 2nd
☎ 01 42 36 82 54

Average meal: 50-100F
for less discount: 20%
with voucher on page 281
AM/VS/MC

HOURS
Mon-Sun:
10.30am-9pm

The chicken dishes at Poul' d'Or are mouthwatering. Try the delicious vegetable and salad accompaniments. The 20% discount is also available at the Poul' d'Or at 75 rue St. Antoine, 3rd.

BHV

Shopping . . .

The Marais and République areas offer some fantastic shopping opportunities from the inexpensive to sheer luxury.

Providing good value, though lacking in luxury, is **Bazar de l'Hôtel de Ville**, or **BHV** *(52-64 rue de Rivoli, 4th, ☎ 01 42 74 90 00)*. It stocks everything from hardware to car parts to perfume and clothing.

A step up from BHV, but still lacking the class of a store like Galleries Lafayette, **La Samaritaine** *(19 rue de la Monnaie, 1st, ☎ 01 40 41 20 20)* is one of Paris' largest department stores. In addition to household goods and practical items, it carries many of the same clothing brands found at the other big department stores. Prime views over the Seine can be had from the rooftop terrace.

BHV

Le Marais is the best place in Paris for interesting Jewish shops selling books, clothing and other items, especially around **Rue des Rosiers**.

Replacing the covered markets that existed on this site for almost 800 years, the subterranean shopping centre known as **Les Halles** was built in the late 1970s. It contains everything from clothing shops to cinemas, but it never gained the popularity its planners intended and the result is an already shabby shopping mall.

REFLECTIONS

'Everything that exists elsewhere exists in Paris' – *Les Misérables*, Victor Hugo

East of Les Halles, the trendy areas of Marais and Bastille are filled with funky shops, many of which showcase the creations of young designers who may one day figure as the city's *haute couturiers*. If you are looking for an original gift or souvenir from Paris, definitely visit the shops in these areas.

You can buy anything Jewish in this area

La Samaritaine

This is also the place to visit if you are interested in purchasing (or simply viewing) original art from up-and-coming artists. Many open their studios to let visitors watch the art in progress.

. . . Shopping

Many famous designers have shops in this area, including French fashion star **Azzedine Alaia** (*7 rue de Moussy, 4ᵗʰ,* ☎ *01 40 27 85 58*).

Off the Place de la République, the **rue Meslay** is noted for its discount shoe stores. Of these, **Show-Sur** (page 88), **Melbury** (page 89) and **Mary Collins** (page 91) all offer 20% off their merchandise to *for less* cardholders.

For big discounts on chic designer clothing for both

Rue Meslay

Les Halles shopping centre

men and women, visit **L'Habilleur** (page 89).

Along the **rue Paradis**, just about every storefront glitters with the fine crystal, silver and porcelain that make France famous for its *arts de la table*. At number thirteen, **Paradis 13** (below) stocks the best brands and even produces its own line of china.

The most famous crystal-maker in France, **Baccarat** (*30 bis rue de Paradis, 10ᵗʰ,* ☎ *01 47 70 64 30*) has a large showroom and museum here. You will find a wide array of glasses and serving pieces for sale, and some of the crystal commissioned specifically for royal households from around the world is on display.

Baccarat

Paradis 13

China / Gifts

13 rue de Paradis, 10ᵗʰ
☎ **01 47 70 21 94**

for less discount: 20%
AM/VS/MC

HOURS

Tue-Sat: 10am-7pm
Sun-Mon: closed

At Paradis 13 you will find a range of beautiful china and crystal. Famous French brands such as St. Louis and Sèvres are stocked, and Paradis 13 also makes and sells its own special range.

HOURS

Mon-Fri: 10.30am-7.30pm.
Sat: 11am-7.30pm. Sun: closed

HOURS

Mon-Sat: 10am-7pm.
Sun: closed

HOURS

Tue-Sun: 10.30am-9pm.
Mon: closed

Calao

Gifts

95 rue du Fbg St-Denis, 10th
☎ 01 45 23 59 49

for less discount: 20%
VS/MC

This interesting shop stocks items of Asian origin. It has an exotic atmosphere and the entire shop is perfumed with incense. Masks, pipes, ornaments, mirrors and jewellery are sold here.

Show-Sur

Shoes

20 rue Meslay, 3rd
☎ 01 42 74 33 27

for less discount: 20%
VS/MC

Show-Sur sells shoes for both men and women. There is a huge choice of more than 1,000 designs for all occasions. Many famous brands from France and Britain are stocked.

Le Nectar des Bourbons

Wine Shop

37 rue de Turenne, 3rd
☎ 01 40 27 99 12

for less discount: 20%
AM/VS/MC/DC

Le Nectar des Bourbons is located close to the Place des Vosges. The ambiance and surroundings reflect the French passion for wine. It often holds evenings of wine-tasting and music.

L'Habilleur

Men's and Women's Clothing

44 rue du Poitou, 3rd
☎ 01 48 87 77 12

for less discount: 20%
VS/MC

HOURS

Mon-Sat: 11am-8pm
Sun: closed

L'Habilleur has a big range of chic clothing in luxurious fabrics. Designer names sold here include Barbara Bui and Oliver Strelli, and there are items for both men and women.

 # Melbury

Shoes

53 rue Meslay, 3rd
☎ 01 42 74 16 14

for less discount: 20%
AM/VS/MC

HOURS

Mon-Sat: 9am-6.30pm
Sun: closed

This shoe shop sells footwear for men and women. A number of top Italian and French brands are stocked. Melbury specializes in some of the latest, most unusual designs.

 # Café Coton

Men's and Women's Clothing

62 rue de Saintonge, 3rd
☎ 01 48 04 00 86

for less discount: 20%
VS/MC

HOURS

Mon-Sat: 10.30am-7pm
Sun: closed

The Café Coton mark is the sign of a good shirt in France. Men's and women's casual and business items are on sale here. There is also an extensive range of accessories for all occasions.

Optic 2000

Eyewear

**11 place de la
République, 3rd
☎ 01 42 72 88 26**

for less discount: 20%
AM/VS/MC/DC

HOURS

Mon: 3pm-7.30pm. Tue-
Sat: 10am-7.30pm.
Sun: closed

Optic 2000 stocks many different styles of sunglasses.
There is also a great range of frames for optical glasses.
The 20% discount is also available in the shop at 177
avenue Ledru Rollin, 11th.

Franck-Alexandre

Men's and Women's Clothing

**21 rue Beranger, 3rd
☎ 01 42 74 19 73**

for less discount: 20%
VS

HOURS

Mon-Sat: 9.30am-
12.30pm, 1.30pm-
6.30pm.
Sun: closed

Franck-Alexandre is located close to the Place de la
République. It stocks clothing ranges for both men and
women. Special lines include leather goods and
sportswear.

Mary Collins

Shoes

**17 rue Meslay, 3rd
☎ 01 42 74 33 26**

for less discount: 20%
VS/MC

HOURS

Mon-Sat: 10am-7pm
Sun: closed

Mary Collins is the sister shop of Show-Sur (page 88).
The range of shoes sold includes the French brand
Lapidus, and there are also American and British brands
such as Clarks.

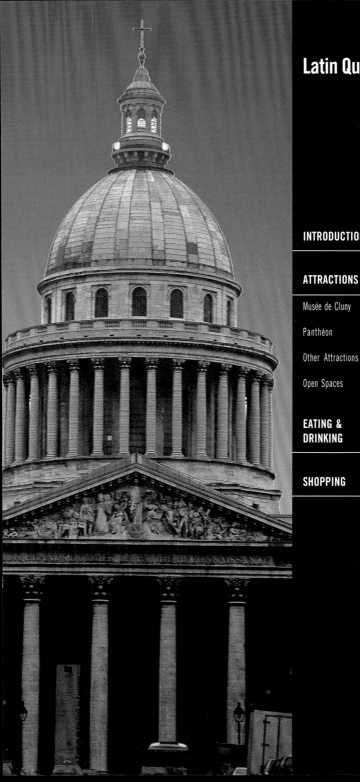

Latin Quarter

Introduction . . .

The Latin Quarter (*Quartier Latin*) is the intellectual heart of Paris and the epitome of everything both trendy and traditional the city has to offer. Students do indeed spend hours sitting in cafés discussing

Latin Quarter streets

philosophy, and the winding streets in the shadow of Notre Dame exude a very Parisian air of romance and style.

Over the centuries this area has been famous as the haunt of intellectuals such as Erasmus, Sartre and Camus.

The Latin Quarter as a whole takes its name from the fact that Latin was the only language allowed to be spoken in the environs of the university, even by the most lowly servants, until Napoleon decreed otherwise at the beginning of the 19th century.

The intellectual theme of the area was reinforced in the 15th century by the establishment of a printing and publishing industry. Much evidence remains of this today: the area contains more bookshops than any other part of Paris.

The hub of this lively area is **boulevard St-Michel**, affectionately known by residents and students as 'Boul-Mich'. The street begins at the **Place St-Michel**, where busy cafés with a riverside view stand side-by-side with shops and cinemas.

The **fountain** in the square is by Davioud and portrays St-Michel slaying a dragon. It was inspired in part by Rome's Trevi fountain.

The boulevard continues past the **Jardin du Luxembourg**, and at night is a ribbon of lights and activity all the way up the hill.

Notre Dame from Square René Viviani

This part of Paris was first settled following the founding of abbeys south of the Seine between the 6th and 11th centuries. Its status as a centre of learning emerged with the establishment of the university in 1253.

The popularity and exclusivity of the Latin Quarter is mainly due to the presence of the **Sorbonne**. Although the university has now spread to other buildings in

. . . Introduction

various parts of Paris, the Sorbonne itself remains the heart of the institution.

The Sorbonne began life as a college for 16 theology students, but over the years many eminent scholars have passed through as both students and teachers, among them Abelard, Aquinas and Foucault.

Abelard was one of the first university tutors, and the subject of one of Paris' greatest tragic love stories. The young logician began an affair with Héloïse, the niece of the Canon of Notre Dame, while he was

teaching her.

The furious Canon had Abelard castrated and Héloïse sent to a convent. The lovers are buried together in Père-Lachaise cemetery (see La Villette and Paris East, pages 149-162).

Despite Haussmann's ruthless town planning in the 19th century, a maze of medieval streets has been

St-Severin

allowed to remain here, especially around the ancient square **René Viviani** by the Seine. This is the location of the oldest tree in Paris, a false acacia planted in 1602. It is now held up by crutches. The Gothic artefacts displayed in the square were found near Notre Dame.

To experience medieval Paris first hand, visit the **Musée de Cluny** (page 94) which has, among impressive artefacts, the remains of the Roman baths that formerly occupied the site.

REFLECTIONS

'St-Germain has never been a real neighbour-hood. You can't find any whores or peanut vendors there' - Jacques Prévert

In complete contrast with the feel of the Latin Quarter is the modern architecture of the **Institut de Monde Arabe** (page 99). Designed by architect Jean Nouvel, the structure incorporates two restaurants and an outdoor terrace with great views of the nearby Seine and the city.

Jardin du Luxembourg

The Latin Quarter has a vibrant nightlife. The outdoor cafés are only part of a variety of night-time entertainment that includes dance clubs, jazz clubs, dinner shows, theatre and more (see Paris by Night, page 201-212).

Musée de Cluny

The **Musée de Cluny**, officially the **Musée Nationale du Moyen Age-Thermes de Cluny**, has one of the most important collections of medieval arts, artefacts and crafts in the world. It is also the location of the ruins of Paris's **Gallo-Roman baths**, which are incorporated into the 1550 mansion.

Musée de Cluny

The collection was installed by Alexandre Sommerard, a state official, and opened in 1844 with his son Edmond as curator.

The museum is approached through a shady courtyard, and the first few rooms display medieval carved furniture, tapestries and artefacts.

The sculpture galleries in the middle of the ground floor include **Romanesque sculpture** from the 13th century, the highlights of which are the series of carved heads of the Kings of Judaea dating from about 1220.

The collection of **stained glass** panels are from famous French cathedrals such as the basilica of St-Denis, Troyes and Ste-Chapelle. The oldest piece dates from the mid-12th century.

Upstairs, the highlight of the whole museum is a series of tapestries, **La Dame à la Licorne** (the Lady and the Unicorn). The six tapestries, reverently displayed in a quiet, dimly lit room, were made in the 15th century as a gift from a nobleman to his intended. Five of the works represent the five senses, and the sixth is named 'To my only desire'.

Musée de Cluny

Not to be missed on the first floor are the exquisite medieval **Books of Hours**, displaying illuminated pages beautifully preserved since the 15th century. Also in the collection are examples of gold and metal work, including the Golden Rose of Basel (1330) and a stunningly decorated bible with a metalwork binding.

ADDRESS

6 place Paul-Painlevé, 5ᵗʰ *arrondissement*
☎ 01 53 73 78 00

GETTING THERE

Métro: Cluny la Sorbonne

HOURS

Wed-Mon: 9.30am-5.45pm (last admission 5pm). Tue: closed

PRICES

Adult: 28F (Sun: 18F)
Child: free
Senior: 18F
Student:
(Separate entrance charge for baths)

Panthéon

The **Panthéon** has long been a familiar landmark on the skyline of Paris, the great neo-classical dome towering like a Greek temple over the Latin Quarter buildings.

It was begun in 1756 as a church to honour Ste-

Geneviève, the patron saint of Paris, after Louis XV recovered from an potentially fatal illness. The architect was Jacques-

The imposing Panthéon

Germain Soufflot, designer of the Manufacture des Gobelins, who died ten years before its completion in 1790.

Following the Revolution, the church became a secularized mausoleum, the resting place of some of France's greatest figures.

Before your visit, take a moment to stand beneath the neo-classical columns and look down **rue Soufflot** for a view of the Tour Eiffel. The pediment relief above the entrance depicts France handing out laurels to her heroes. The dome, which has an iron frame and stone shells, was inspired by that of St. Paul's Cathedral in London.

The interior of the Panthéon is a cool, quiet haven, especially on a hot day. Only a little natural light is allowed into the calm, grey aisles, decorated with

Interior of the Panthéon

19th-century frescoes.

The labyrinthine crypt, downstairs, contains the tombs of many of the great men of France, including Voltaire, Victor Hugo, Emile Zola, Jean-Jacques Rousseau and Louis Braille. The only woman buried here is the wife of scientist Marcelin Berthelot.

ADDRESS

Place du Panthéon, 5th *arrondissement* ☎ 01 43 54 34 51

GETTING THERE

Métro: Cardinal Lemoine

HOURS

Mon-Sun: Apr-Sep: 9.30am-6.30pm. Oct-Mar: 10am-6.15pm

PRICES

Adult 32F
Child 21F
Senior 32F
Student 21F

REFLECTIONS

'Nothing in my early childhood made such an impression on me as seeing the Panthéon between me and the sun' - Jules Michelet

Other Attractions . . .

One of the most famous bridges linking the Latin Quarter with the opposite bank of the Seine is the **Pont des Arts**. This picturesque pedestrian bridge has wonderful views both left and right. It takes its names

from the Palais des Arts, the original name of the Louvre, and dates from the beginning of the 19th century.

Moving away from the river, within the labyrinth of old streets is the **Musée Delacroix**. Across a charming courtyard in a quiet square, this little

Pont des Arts

museum is dedicated to the rebellious artist, with his personal letters and belongings on display alongside his paintings and drawings.

Pont des Arts

Visitors can also enter his studio at the back of the house, which contains studies for his great work *La Mort de Sardanapale*, and walk in the peaceful gravel garden. *(6 rue de Furstenberg, 6th, ☎ 01 43 54 04 87. Wed-Mon:*

Musée Delacroix

9.45am-5pm. Tue: closed. Adult 23F, child free, senior 18F, student 18F.)

for less Another fascinating museum is the **Musée de l'Histoire de la Médecine**. Housed in a magnificent wood-panelled hall in the Université René Descartes, it is part of the medical school of the University of Paris.

Musée Delacroix

The museum charts the history of medicine and health over many centuries, with displays devoted to themes such as surgery, dentistry, the discovery of penicillin, microscopes and the birth of modern medicine.

The collection of medical

Musée de l'Histoire de la Medecine

instruments features items dating from the 17th century onwards, and the displays of glass eyes,

. . . Other Attractions . . .

porcelain dentures and huge syringes are fascinating.
*(12 rue de l'Ecole de Médecine, 6th, ☎ 01 40 46 16 93.
Summer: Mon-Fri: 2pm-5.30pm. Sat-Sun: closed. Winter:
Mon-Wed, Fri-Sat: 2pm-5.30pm. Thu and Sun: closed.*

Sorbonne

*Adult 20F, Child
20F, Senior 20F,
Student 20F. 50%
discount on
admission with your
for less card.)*

The most famous
of the university
buildings is **La
Sorbonne** *(47 rue
des Ecoles, 5th)*. The
institution was founded in 1253, but the building you
see today was built in the 19th century. The courtyard
is open to the public.

Musée de l'Histoire de la
Medecine

There are several impressive churches in
the area, dating from different eras and
displaying a variety of architectural
styles. **St- Severin** *(1 rue-des-Prêtres-St-
Séverin, 5th)*, completed at the beginning
of the 16th century,   is an example of
the Flamboyant Gothic style. **St-Sulpice**
(Place St. Sulpice, 6th) was built between
1646 and 1778 in the neo-classical
style. Medieval **St-Germain-des-Prés** *(3
place St-Germain-des-Prés, 6th)* is the oldest

St-Sulpice

church in Paris, dating from the 11th century, and **St-
Etienne-du-Mont** *(place Ste-Geneviève, 5th)*, an example

St-Germain-des Prés

of Renaissance
architecture, has a
magnificent Gothic rood
screen.

Round the corner from
St-Etienne is the **Musée
de la Préfecture de la
Police**. This free museum
follows the history of law
enforcement in the city
from the Middle Ages
onwards.

The displays comprise
warrants, weapons,
handcuffs and other
crime-related artefacts,
and exhibits focus on particular events such as the
resistance of the police during the Second World War.

Musée de la Préfecture de
la Police

. . . Other Attractions . . .

(1 bis rue des Carmes, 5th, ☎ 01 44 41 52 50. Mon-Fri: 9am-5pm. Sat: 10am-5pm. Sun: closed. Admission free.)

Centre de la Mer et des Eaux

for less An altogether more lighthearted museum is the **Centre de la Mer et des Eaux**. This aquarium is part of the Paris Oceanographic Institute and is educational as well as fun.

Themed exhibition areas include displays about the different oceans of the world, the mysteries of the deep and the survival strategies of marine animals.

There are tanks devoted to all sorts of aquatic life, including reef dwellers, miniature fish and fish indigenous to the coastal areas of France.

Centre de la Mer et des Eaux

There is also a film theatre, where visitors are shown documentaries and videos. The Pacific, Amazonian and

Palais de Luxembourg

Antarctic adventures of sea explorer and photographer Cousteau and his team are among the subjects covered. *(195 rue St-Jacques, 5th, ☎ 01 44 32 10 90. Tue-Fri: 10am-12.30pm, 1.15pm-5.30pm. Sat-Sun: 10am-5.30pm. Mon: closed. Adult 30F, Child 12F, Senior 30F, Student 18F. 2 for the price of 1 with your **for less** card.)*

Musee Zadkine

The **Palais de Luxembourg** and its gardens (see page 100) dominate the south of the Latin Quarter. This 17th century palace was built in the Italianate style for Marie de Médicis and now houses the French Senate. It is not open to the public.

Nearby, the **Musée Zadkine** displays the work of Russian sculptor Ossip Zadkine, who lived here until his death in 1967.

Musée Zadkine

His Cubist, Expressionist and Abstract works are a

. . . Other Attractions

good representation of his use of a range of materials
and his interest in diverse subjects. *(100 bis rue d'Assas,
6th, ☎ 01 43 26 91 90. Tue-Sun: 10am-5.30pm. Mon:
closed. Adult 27F, child free, senior 19F, student 19F.)*

for less The **Institut du Monde Arabe** is housed in a
striking glass and steel building that first opened
its doors in 1988. The seven floors of exhibits are
devoted to the history, craft and culture of the Arab
World.

Institut du Monde Arabe

Institut du Monde Arabe

The collection includes old
coins, manuscripts,
ceramics, textiles, carpets,
scientific instruments and
miniatures which originate
from many eras and
several parts of the globe.

The museum is well laid
out, making thoughtful use
of space and light. In
addition there is an
exhibition of contemporary
Arab art, a vast library and
a sound-and-image centre.

*(1 rue des Fossés St-Bernard, 5th, ☎ 01 40 51 38 38. Tue-
Sun: 10am-6pm. Mon: closed. Adult 45F, Child free, Senior
35F, Student 35F. 2 for the price of 1 with voucher on page
273.)*

Institut Musulman

The **Institut Musulman** introduces visitors to the
Muslim World, and you can visit the beautiful **Paris
Mosque**. *(Place de Puits de l'Ermite, 5th, ☎ 01 45 35 97 33.
Thu-Tue: 9am-12noon, 2pm-6pm. Wed and Muslim holidays:
closed.)*

The highlight of the **Muséum
National d'Histoire Naturelle**,
located in the nearby Jardin des
Plantes, is the recently
rejuvenated **Grande Galerie de
l'Évolution**.

The glass and iron structure is
the perfect setting for this state-
of-the-art journey into the
natural world, displaying a
magnificent collection of
taxidermy, and using sound and

Muséum Nationale d'Histoire Naturelle

light exhibits to trace the development of hundreds of
species. *(36 rue Geoffroy-Saint-Hilaire, 5th, ☎ 01 40 79 30
00. Wed-Mon: 10am-6pm (until 10pm on Thu). Tue: closed.
Adult 40F, child 30F, senior 30F, student 30F.)*

Open Spaces

The largest green area in this part of Paris is the **Jardin du Luxembourg**, the grounds of the Palace (see page 98). The French-style gardens were laid out in the 17th century, although many of the statues were added later, and include works by Antoine Bourdelle and Cain.

Jardin du Luxembourg

The most impressive of the fountains to be seen here is the **Medici fountain**, in the style of an Italian grotto. Another, by Dalou, is dedicated to the artist Delacroix.

Arènes de Lutèce

Arènes de Lutèce

The gardens are very popular with residents and tourists alike. Although the grass is out of bounds there are plenty of seats along the elegant terraces, around the central pond and under the trees, where Frenchmen traditionally congregate to play chess and cards.

The remains of a Roman arena provide an unusual area to relax in nearby. Uncovered in the 19th century, the **Arènes de Lutèce** originally had a seating capacity of 15,000 and would have been used for gladiator fights. Today, the Arène is popular with *boules* and football players.

Jardin des Plantes

As its name suggests, the nearby **Jardin des Plantes** is a botanical garden. It was established in 1625 as a royal herb garden and opened to the public in 1640.

As well as the Muséum National d'Histoire Naturelle (see page 99), the Jardin des Plantes contains a zoo, a school of botany, glasshouses, an alpine garden and a maze.

Jardin des Plantes

There are more than 10,000 species of plants in the gardens, including a 250-year old Cedar of Lebanon originally sent over from Kew Gardens in London, and a slice of 2,000-year old North American sequoia.

Eating and Drinking

The cafés of the Latin Quarter are legendary. Two of the most famous literary haunts visited by Hemingway and his cohorts are **Café aux Deux-Magots** *(170 boulevard Saint-Germain, 6ᵗʰ, ☎ 01 45 48 55 25)* and the **Café de Flore** *(172 boulevard Saint-Germain, 6ᵗʰ, ☎ 01 45 48 55 26)*.

Follow the cobbled **rue Mouffetard** past *traiteurs* serving up the Greek specialties for which this area is known. At the foot of the road, the Mouffetard market is filled with all kinds of delicacies and becomes a sort of street festival at weekends.

Latin Quarter restaurants

Savannah Café

International

27 rue Descartes, 5ᵗʰ
☎ 01 43 29 45 77

Average meal: 100-150F
***for less* discount: 20%**
VS/MC

HOURS

Tue-Sat: 12noon-2.30pm, 7pm-11pm. Mon: 7pm-11pm. Sun: closed

Savannah Café offers a range of meals from all over the world. There are hot and cold dishes from Italy, Lebanon and France. Finish your meal with a delicious dessert such as ice-cream or sorbet.

Coolin

Irish Pub

15 rue Clément, 6ᵗʰ
☎ 01 44 07 00 92

Average meal: 100-150F
***for less* discount: 20%**
VS/MC

HOURS

Mon-Sun: 10am-2am

Coolin is a lively Irish-style pub in the Marché St-Germain. It serves Irish seafood specialities, delicious sandwiches and a range of mouth-watering homemade desserts.

Mon-Sat: 12noon-11pm.
Sun: closed

La Crêpe Dauphine

Crêperie

15 rue Dauphine, 6th
☎ 01 43 25 05 43

Average meal: 50-100F
for less discount: 20%
VS/MC

La Crêpe Dauphine serves traditional French crêpes with a variety of fillings. You can choose sweet or savoury dishes. The range of drinks includes traditional Breton cider.

Mon-Sun:
11.30am-12midnight

Oh!...Poivrier!

French

25 quai des
Grands Augustins, 6th
☎ 01 43 29 41 77

Average meal: 50-100F
for less discount: 20%
with voucher on page 279
AM/VS/MC

Oh!...Poivrier! serves a good range of meals for any appetite. The selection of gourmet dishes is especially tempting. The discount is also available at the branch at 143 boulevard Raspail.

Mon-Sat: 12noon-11pm.
Sun: closed

Bruschetteria

Italian

15 rue Dauphine, 6th
☎ 01 43 25 05 43

Average meal: 50-100F
for less discount: 20%
VS/MC

Bruschetta is a dish which originated in central Italy in the 16th century, where specially prepared and seasoned bread is served with a variety of toppings. Bruschetteria is well known for its range of delicious ice-creams.

. . . Shopping

The Latin Quarter has more bookshops than any other part of Paris. A great favourite with English-speaking visitors is **Shakespeare and Company** *(37 rue de la Bûcherie, 5ᵗʰ, ☎ 01 43 26 96 50).* The original shop in St-Germain was the haunt of James Joyce and Ernest Hemingway. Today's shop is run by the grandson of Walt Whitman, and is an Aladdin's cave of English-language second-hand fiction and non-fiction.

The bouquinistes

The *bouquinistes* along the banks of the Seine are an unmissable Paris tradition. Rain or shine, their stalls line the *quais* with rare masterpieces of French literature hidden among less valuable but equally interesting prints, paperbacks and magazines.

 Emaldi

Women's Clothing

3 rue de Tournon, 3ʳᵈ
☎ **01 40 46 02 90**

for less discount: 20%
AM/VS/MC

HOURS

Mon-Sat: 11am-7pm
Sun: closed

Eléonore Emaldi is a young Italian designer who has worked for Dior. She personally creates all the elegant and timeless clothes in the shop, which include formal and casual items for any occasion.

 Unio

Glassware

17 rue des Quatre Vents, 6ᵗʰ
☎ **01 44 07 33 49**

for less discount: 20%
AM/VS/MC

HOURS

Tue-Sat: 10.30am-7pm
Sun-Mon: closed

Unio sells beautiful and original glass items in all shapes and colours. There are decorative ornaments as well as useful items like vases, and the works of famous glass-sculptors are also on sale.

La Perlotte

Accessories

12 rue Vavin, 6th
☎ 01 43 54 87 09

for less discount: 20%
AM/VS/MC

HOURS

Mon: 1pm-7.15pm. Tue-
Sat: 11am-7.15pm.
Sun: closed

La Perlotte makes and sells an exclusive range of accessories and jewellery. Its specialities are pearl necklaces and bracelets, and there is also a selection of scarves, belts and bags.

Marianne Gray

Hairdressing

52 rue St-André des Arts, 6th
☎ 01 43 26 58 21

for less discount: 20%
AM/VS/MC

HOURS

Mon-Sat: 9.30am-7.30pm
(until 9pm on Fri).
Sun: closed.

Marianne Gray is in the heart of the medieval area of the *quartier*. Have a relaxing haircut in these atmospheric surroundings. The stylists pride themselves on matching haircuts to personalities.

Josiane Laure

Beauty Salon

27 rue des
Grands-Augustins, 6th
☎ 01 46 33 72 32

for less discount: 20%
AM/VS/MC

HOURS

Mon-Sat: 10am-6.30pm
(until 8pm on Fri).
Sun: closed.

This salon is located in the same building as Marianne Gray (see above). Josiane Laure is well-known for her beauty treatments. Essential oils revive the spirit as well as the body.

Ane Kenssen

Women's Clothing

13 rue des Quatre Vents, 6ᵗʰ
☎ 01 43 25 87 83

for less discount: 20%
AM/VS/MC

Ane Kenssen is a well-known German designer who creates fluid styles in natural colours. The shop also stocks her coordinated range of bags, hats and jewellery.

HOURS

Mon-Sat: 10.30am-7pm
Sun: closed

Stege

Shoes

19 rue Guisarde, 6ᵗʰ
☎ 01 46 34 67 70

for less discount: 20%
VS/DC

Stege stocks shoes for men and, to a lesser extent, for women. British and American brands as well as French ones are stocked, and there is an exclusive line of Polish slippers in leather and felt.

HOURS

Mon-Sat: 10.30am-8pm
Sun: closed

François Paultre

Jewellery

13 rue Saint-Sulpice, 6ᵗʰ
☎ 01 43 25 63 90

for less discount: 20%
AM/VS/MC

François Paultre has been creating jewellery for over 12 years. He mixes classic and modern designs to great effect. There are rare and precious stones in an astounding range of colours.

HOURS

Tue-Sat: 11am-1pm,
2pm-7pm.
Sun-Mon: closed

HOURS

Mon: 2pm-7pm. Tue-Sat: 10.30am-7pm.
Sun: closed.

Anne Marie Beretta

Clothing / Tableware

24 rue St-Sulpice, 6th
☎ 01 43 26 99 30

for less discount: 20%
AM/VS/MC

Anne Marie Beretta designs formal but comfortable clothes. Elegant leisure and businesswear is available for women and men. There is also a range of her porcelain and china tableware and glasses.

Parfumerie Lamsel

Perfume / Beauty Shop

14 rue Clement, 6th
☎ 01 43 29 25 60

for less discount: 20%
AM/VS/MC/DC

The Parfumerie Lamsel is located in the Marché St-Germain. It stocks more than 100 brands of beauty supplies. Famous make-up and perfume brands include Clinique, Chanel and Lancome.

HOURS

Tue-Sat: 10.30am-7.30pm.
Sun-Mon: closed.

Cerfvolissime

Toys

29 rue Berthollet, 6th
☎ 01 43 31 65 65

for less discount: 20%
VS/MC

This colourful shop has an extensive collection of toys and games. There are kites of all shapes, juggling equipment and boomerangs. You will also find magic kits, puppets, dolls and spinning tops.

Huilerie Artisanale Leblanc

Oils

6 rue Jacob, 6th
☎ 01 46 34 61 55

for less discount: 20%
No credit cards

HOURS

Mon: 3pm-7pm. Tue-Sat:
11am-7pm.
Sun: closed.

The Leblanc family have been making cooking oils for generations. The range includes walnut, olive, pistachio and almond oils. You can also buy the stoneware jars recommended for storing the oils.

T'cha

Teas / Gifts

6 rue du Pont de Lodi, 6th
☎ 01 46 29 61 31

for less discount: 20%
VS/MC

HOURS

Tue-Sun: 11am-7.30pm.
Mon: closed.

As well as more than 40 types of tea, Tch'a sells gifts and paintings. The Chinese teas are all selected for their quality and distinctive flavours. The handmade teapots and Asian pottery items are ideal gifts.

Création Sylvanie

Housewares / Gifts

28 rue Berthollet, 5th
☎ 01 43 36 30 40

for less discount: 20%
AM/VS/MC

HOURS

Mon-Sat: 10.30am-7pm.
Sun: closed.

Création Sylvanie stocks a selection of gifts and items for the home. Candles, music boxes, teapots and handmade jewellery may be found here. They have a special range of decorative items with a cat theme.

HOURS

Mon-Sat: 10.30am-
7.30pm.
Sun: closed.

Le Monde en Marche

Toys

34 rue Dauphine, 6th
☎ 01 43 29 09 49

for less discount: 20%
VS/MC

Re-live your childhood in this delightful toyshop.
Traditional-style toys include music boxes, wooden boats
and puppets. Fancy dress costumes and educational toys
are also sold.

HOURS

Mon-Sat: 1.30pm-7.30pm.
Sun: closed

Sarah Boutique

Antiques

25 rue Berthollet, 5th
☎ 01 43 37 22 22

for less discount: 20%
AM/VS/MC

This antique shop sells items dating from the time of
Napoleon III. As well as beautiful household items, there
are antique toys and books. Limoges enamels, Murano
glass and Christofle silver may be found.

HOURS

Mon-Sat: 9.30am-7.30pm.
Sun: 9.30am-1.30pm.

Nikita

Lingerie

132 rue Mouffetard, 5th
☎ 01 45 35 11 64

for less discount: 20%
VS/MC

Paris is the perfect place to buy high-quality lingerie.
This little shop is located on the busy rue Mouffetard,
and famous brand names to be found here include
Lejaby, Boléro and Lou.

Les Invalides
and Tour
Eiffel

Introduction . . .

The area around the Eiffel Tower and Les Invalides is the 7th *arrondissement*. This has long been an elegant area of Paris, and today it is the location of a number of government offices as well as being a popular tourist centre.

The tone of the area reflects its importance to the country, both historically and politically. The monuments and state offices are interspersed with elegant townhouses and

This is an area of elegant façades

expensive shops. The broad avenues and immaculate grassy stretches lend it an air of spacious opulence.

The dominant building is, of course, the **Eiffel Tower** (page 112), 'Tour Eiffel' to the French. Designed by Gustave Eiffel, it was completed in 1889 for the *Exposition Universelle* (World Fair), and at the time Parisians protested, calling it an eyesore and a waste of money. It was supposed to stand for only 20 years, but a decision was made in 1909 to keep it for use in radiotelegraphy experiments.

Since then, Paris has come to terms with its most famous landmark. The 1050 foot (320 metre) structure has received 120 million visitors since it opened and is the symbol by which the city is recognized all over the world.

The Eiffel Tower at dusk

The tower has also been the scene of daredevil stunts: several people have attempted to test their home-made parachutes over the years, with varying degrees of success.

The World Fair at which the tower was inaugurated was one of a series inspired by the 1851 Great Exhibition in London. Paris needed a boost, particularly following the Commune and the Franco Prussian War, and the 7th *arrondissement* became the stage for the city's celebrations of its scientific and industrial future. Balloon rides, shows and demonstrations drew visitors from all over Europe.

The 7th *arrondissement* also has a military history. It was the location of the **Ecole Militaire** (page 115),

. . . Introduction

founded in 1751, which trained cadets in the late 18th century but now functions as an institute of military and defence studies.

The **Hôtel des Invalides** (page 114), a former hospital and home for disabled veterans, is nearby. It was the building from which the Revolutionaries stole 28,000

guns immediately before the storming of the Bastille prison in 1789. Today, it houses several museums, all of which have a military theme. The largest is the **Musée de l'Armée** (page 114) which is a must-see for military history buffs.

The eastern sector of the 7th *arrondissement* is known as **Faubourg St-Germain**. It was Paris's most fashionable neighbourhood in the 18th century, and its high-walled and gated mansions remain to be admired today. The

A view of the Tour Eiffel and Les Invalides

residence of the prime minister, the **Hôtel Matignon**, is here.

INSIDER'S TIP

The view from the second rather than the top floor of this Tour Eiffel is better for picking out landmarks. The highest viewing platform is almost *too* high.

Along the river stands the impressive **Musée d'Orsay** (page 113), one of Paris's best museums. Housed in a former railway station along the Seine, the museum is flooded with natural light from the glass roof, showcasing its works of art in an ideal manner.

Another popular Parisian museum is dedicated to the sculptor Rodin. In addition to displaying his own works and items from his private collection, the **Musée Rodin** (page 116) boasts a lovely sculpture-filled garden with a pond and views of the dome of Les Invalides.

Inside the Dôme Church, Hôtel des Invalides

Another pleasant place to relax and a wonderful place to bring children is the vast expanse of open space surrounding the Eiffel Tower, known as the **Champ-de-Mars** (page 117). From here, it is possible to get a real sense of the tower's huge size. Children will also love the **Marionettes des Champ-de-Mars**, the *guignol* theatre whose puppet shows provide entertainment in the grand French tradition.

Tour Eiffel

ADDRESS

Champ de Mars, 7th
arrondissement
☎ 01 44 11 23 11

GETTING THERE

Métro: Bir-Hakeim

HOURS

Mon-Sun: Summer: 9am-
12midnight. Winter: 9am-
11pm

PRICES

1st floor:
Adult 20F
Child 10F
Senior 20F
Student 20F

2nd floor:
Adult 42F
Child 21F
Senior 42F
Student 42F

3rd floor:
Adult 56F
Child 28F
Senior 56F
Student 56F

INSIDER'S TIP

You can take the stairs up
to the 1st and 2nd floors
only for 12F.

The **Eiffel Tower** (*Tour Eiffel* to the French) was designed by engineer Gustave Eiffel as the centrepiece for the 1889 *Exposition Universelle*, which was based on the Great Exhibition in London. It was the world's tallest building until the construction of New York's Empire State Building in 1931.

Eiffel Tower

It took less than two years to build, with an incredible 2.5 million rivets used to hold the 18,000 sections of iron together.

The 1050 foot (320 metre) structure drew complaints at first, but its symmetrical design was soon accepted. Instead of being dismantled as planned at the end of the century, it was saved and used for research into radiotelegraphy, and later as a television station.

It attracted other types of experiments too. In 1912 a Parisian tailor named Reisfeldt made himself some canvas wings and attempted to fly from the first level. Unfortunately, he plunged to his death.

It is now perhaps the most recognized landmark in the world, and has welcomed more than 120 million visitors since its inauguration. It is repainted every four years and has recently been improved with inside lamps which cast a yellow glow from within the framework.

A view of the Jardins du Trocadéro from the Eiffel Tower

There are 1,700 steps to the top, but most visitors take the lift. A film show on the first level tells the story of the building of the Tower, and the second floor houses the famous (and expensive) Jules Verne restaurant.

Musée d'Orsay

The **Musée d'Orsay** is second only to the Louvre Museum as a must-see for visitors to Paris, with its priceless collection of paintings, sculpture and *objets d'art*.

It is housed in the former Gare d'Orsay, a beautiful 19th-century glass and iron railway station, which was reopened as a museum in 1986.

Musée d'Orsay

It is devoted to art, sculpture and decorative arts from 1848 to 1914, filling the chronological gap between the collections of the Louvre and the modern art galleries in the city.

A helpful, colour-coded map identifies the areas of the huge museum according to genre and period. Follow the room numbers for a chronological tour of the whole museum if you have time.

The most popular rooms are those devoted to the **Impressionists**, taking up most of the upper floor. Here you can see countless famous works by, among others, Degas, Manet, Monet and Renoir.

Don't neglect the less familiar areas, however. The **architecture** section at the back of the ground floor displays fascinating scale models of Paris buildings, a pre-Eiffel Tower view of the city by Navlet and a glass-covered walk-over model of the Opéra area.

The **sculpture** galleries include works by Daumier, Gauguin and Rodin, and the **decorative arts** are represented by furniture and

Railway clock

other items by William Morris and Art Nouveau designers.

As you walk through, don't forget to look up at the embellished ceiling and huge, original railway clocks. The flamboyant **Salle des Fêtes**, previously the railway hotel, is a surprising contrast to the cool marble lines of the rest of the interior.

ADDRESS

1 rue de Bellechasse, 7ᵗʰ *arrondissement*
☎ 01 40 49 48 14

GETTING THERE

Métro: Solférino

HOURS

Tue-Wed, Fri-Sat: 10am-6pm. Thu: 10am-9.45pm. Sun: 9am-6pm. Mon: closed

PRICES

Adult 39F
Child free
Senior 27F
Student 27F

DON'T MISS

Manet's *Le Déjeuner sur l'Herbe*, Gauguin's *Arearea*, Van Gogh's *The Church at Auvers-sur-Oise*, Courbet's *Courbet with Black Dog*

GETTING THERE

Métro: Latour Maubourg,
Varenne

Les Invalides

The **Hôtel des Invalides** was established by Louis XIV in 1674 as a home for wounded soldiers. The huge, Classical building is now primarily a hospital, although substantial parts of the complex are still devoted to all things military.

The adjoining **Dôme Church**, whose glittering cupola is a familiar sight on the Paris skyline, should be the first port of call for a visitor to the complex.

Hôtel des Invalides

It was completed at the beginning of the 18th century, and Napoleon's remains were moved here in 1841. His rather unimpressive tomb in the crypt is visible from the ground floor. Marshal Foch, Napoleon's brother Joseph and Louis XIV's military architect, Vauban, are also buried here.

The wings of the complex which surround the courtyard contain three museums, the largest being the **Musée de l'Armée**. It comprises an important collection of arms and armour from various countries and periods, including some frightening military outfits and swords from the Orient.

Dôme Church

Several small courtyards display rows and rows of cannons, and some of the most interesting displays are those devoted to the First and Second World Wars. Documents, posters, letters and clothing provide a poignant reminder of day-to-day life in occupied Paris. The uniform of a front-line soldier is on display, still caked in mud, and the efforts of the brave members of the Resistance are charted.

The **Musée de l'Ordre de la Liberation** is in another part of the building, and is concerned with the triumphant liberation of the occupied city in 1944. However, a moving section about concentration camps and the victims of persecution keeps in mind the horror of war.

On the fourth floor of the east wing, in the atmospheric **Musée des Plans-Reliefs**, you can see a collection of models of fortified French towns.

HOURS

Mon-Sun: Apr-Sep: 10am-6pm. Oct-Mar: 10am-5pm.

PRICES

Adult 37F
Child 29F
(under 12 free)
Senior 29F
Student 29F
(Tickets valid for two days)

Other Attractions . . .

The military theme of the area is reinforced by the presence of the **Ecole Militaire** *(1 place Joffre, 7*th*).* The

academy which taught Napoleon was established in 1751 by Louis XV.

The building, which is not open to the

Ecole Militaire

Ecole Militaire

public, was designed by Jacques-Ange Gabriel in the French classical style. The Champ-de-Mars, which stretches from the academy to the Eiffel Tower, once functioned as the cadets' parade ground (see page 117).

Opposite the Ecole Militaire is the headquarters of the United Nations Educational, Scientific and Cultural Organisation (**UNESCO**). The Y-shaped building was built in 1958, and visitors can enter the lobbies to see the sculptures by Picasso, Calder and Henry Moore. *(7 place de Fontenoy, 7*th*. Mon-Fri: 9.30am-6pm.)*

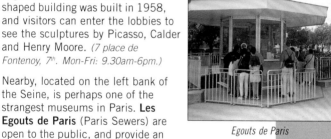

Nearby, located on the left bank of the Seine, is perhaps one of the strangest museums in Paris. **Les Egouts de Paris** (Paris Sewers) are open to the public, and provide an

Egouts de Paris

unusual insight into this important part of any living city.

The present sewerage system was designed in 1850 by Haussmann with the help of engineer Belgrand, who pioneered the idea of discharging waste water well outside the city.

Some will find a tour of the sewers as unpleasant as it sounds, but ignoring the smell, the dripping pipes and suspicious-looking puddles, the so-called "galleries" feature interesting displays about the history and principles of the system. All in all, Paris seems quite proud of what it calls its 'city beneath a city'. *(Pont de l'Alma, opposite 93 quai d'Orsay, 7*th*, ☎ 01 53 68 27 81. Sat-Wed: May-Sep: 11am-5pm. Oct-Apr: 11am-4pm. Adult 25F, child 20F, senior 20F, student 20F.)*

Egouts de Paris

. . . Other Attractions . . .

19th-century pipe

for less The **Musée-Galerie de la Seita** charts the history of smoking in France, beginning in 1560 when Jean Nicot introduced tobacco to the country for the first time.

Artefacts in the collection include pipes, cigarette holders and smoking pouches from all over the world, early and rare cigar and cigarette packets, and smoking items with literary and artistic connections.

There is also a gallery in which temporary art exhibitions are held. *(12 rue Surcouf, 7ʰ, ☎ 01 45 56 60 17. Tue-Sat: 11am-7pm. Sun-Mon: closed. Adult 25F, Child 15F, Senior 25F, Student 15F. 2 for the price of 1 with your **for less** card.)*

Musée-Galerie de la Seita

Moving further westwards along the riverbank you will come across the Hôtel de Salm, housing the **Musée Nationale de la Légion d'Honneur**. The Legion of Honour was a decoration established by Napoleon, and this museum displays it and other French and foreign medals alongside military paintings. *(2 rue de Bellechasse, 7th, ☎ 01 40 62 84 00. Mon-Sun: 2pm-5pm. Adult 35F, child 20F, senior 20F, student 20F.)*

Musée Rodin

One of the best-loved museums in the area is the **Musée Rodin**. Although most of his works are housed in the beautiful Hôtel Biron, the main attraction is the incredible garden.

Légion d'Honneur

The Thinker, *Balzac* and the *Burghers of Calais* are just a few examples of the sculptor's familiar creations standing peacefully among the trees, with the glittering cupola of the Dôme Church in the background (see page 114).

Musée Rodin

Visitors can walk among the roses and the pools and lounge on the grass. Don't miss *The Gates of Hell*, an outlandish sculpture which incorporates several of Rodin's other subjects.

The house contains more than 500 works, including *The Kiss*, and there is a room devoted to the work of Rodin's pupil, Camille Claudel. Some of the Impressionist paintings from his private collection are also on display. *(77 rue de*

. . . Other Attractions

*Varenne, 7ᵗʰ, ☎ 01 44 18 61 10. Tue-Sun: 9.30am-5.45pm
(4.45pm in winter). Adult 28F, child 18F, senior 18F, student
18F. Garden only: 5F.)*

The sculptor Aristide Maillol (1861-1944) is
similarly immortalised in the **Musée Maillol**, which
was founded by his principal model, Dina Vierny. As well
as his sculptures, this beautiful 18th-century house
contains a great number of
his drawings, pastels,
paintings and engravings.

There are also works by his
contemporaries, including
Matisse, Dufy and Picasso.
Gauguin and Degas are
represented by some of
their finest works too. More

Musée Maillol

Musée Maillol

unusual exhibits include the examples of naïve art,
Surrealist sculpture and 1970s Soviet Installation art.
*(59-61 rue de Grenelle, 7ᵗʰ, ☎ 01 42 22 59 58. Wed-Mon:
11am-6pm. Tue: closed. Adult 40F, Child free, Senior 26F,
Student 26F. 2 for the price of 1 with your for less card.)*

Open Spaces

The **Champ-de-Mars** is popular among Parisians and
tourists as a picnicking and resting area. It is one of
the best places to take a photograph of the Eiffel
Tower.

Guignol is the French
equivalent of Punch and Judy,
and at **Marionnettes des Champ-de-
Mars** you can enjoy all the fun of the
show whatever the weather.

The *guignol* theatre at Champ-de-
Mars is covered and heated all year
round, and there are afternoon
shows every day during the school
holidays.

Marionnettes des Champ-de-Mars

The puppeteers perform favourite
fairy tales from all over the world,
so there is a chance to enjoy both familiar and less
well-known tales.

The puppet shows are largely improvised to include the
audience, and a *guignol* is introduced into every
performance, whether in the original tale or not! *(Jardin
du Champ-de-Mars, ☎ 01 48 56 01 44. Wed, Sat-Sun &
school holidays: shows at 3.15pm & 4.15pm. Adult, child,
senior, student 16F. 2 for the price of 1 with for less card.)*

Rue Cler

Eating and Drinking

Not far from the *métro* stop *Ecole-Militaire* is the up-market **rue Cler**. Food shops here sell only products of the best quality. At number 47, marvel at the intricate marzipan creations at **Le Lutin Gourmand**. Another well-known rue Cler shop is **Davoli** *(34 rue Cler, 7th, ☎ 01 45 51 23 41)* where you can find just about every type of ham imaginable, many imported from around the world.

Although there are many expensive restaurants in the 7th *arrondissement*, there are still some good values to be found. Popular French food chains such as **Poul' d'Or** (page 119) and **Oh!...Poivrier!** (page 119) are represented here. Besides providing exceptional value, they also give a discount to *for less* cardholders.

Restaurant Tortue

French

66 rue du Cherche-Midi, 6th
☎ 01 42 84 39 26

Average meal: 150-200F
for less discount: 20%
VS/MC

HOURS

Mon-Sat: 12noon-3pm,
7.30pm-11pm.
Sun: closed.

Tortue's specialities are dishes prepared with fresh market produce. The menu changes according to the vegetable season, and the restaurant is decorated with old-fashioned sepia photographs.

Marie Thé

Tea Room

102 rue du Cherche-Midi, 6th
☎ 01 42 22 50 40

Average meal: 50-100F
for less discount: 20%
AM/VS/MC

HOURS

Mon-Sun:
9.30am-7pm

Marie Thé serves brunch, salads, light meals and delicious desserts. The pastry chef used to teach at the Ritz cookery school. You can choose from 30 different types of tea to have with your cake.

Poul' d'Or

Rotisserie

6 rue St-Placide, 6th
☎ 01 42 84 31 01

Average meal: 50-100F
for less discount: 20%
with voucher on page 281
AM/VS/MC

with voucher on page 281

Poul' d'Or specializes in mouth-watering roast chicken meals and take-aways. The corn-fed chicken has a delicious texture and taste. There are spicy or provençale dishes with salad or vegetables.

Oh!...Poivrier!

French

61 avenue de la
Motte Piquet, 15th
☎ 01 40 65 99 96

Average meal: 50-100F
for less discount: 20%
with voucher on page 279
AM/VS/MC

with voucher on page 279

Oh!...Poivrier! serves good food in stylish surroundings. The salads, sandwiches and hot meals are made from the freshest ingredients. To drink, there are fresh fruit juices, wines and cocktails.

San Francisco Muffin Company

American

35 rue du Dragon, 6th
☎ 01 45 48 45 55

Average meal: up to 50F
for less discount: 20%
No credit cards

San Francisco Muffin Company is an American-style bakery. It serves light meals such as sandwiches, salads and delicious desserts. The cheesecakes, cookies and brownies are particularly recommended.

HOURS

Mon-Sun:
10.30am-9pm

HOURS

Mon-Sun:
11.30am-12midnight

HOURS

Mon-Sat: 8.30am-7.30pm.
Sun: closed

Shopping

Housed in an impressive iron structure, the Parisian department store **Bon Marché** *(38 rue de Sevres, 7th, ☎ 01 44 39 80 00)* can be found here. The name means

Bon Marché

‘good bargain’, but this is no discount store. All the best fashion designers are represented and the store has a much less touristy feel than its Right Bank competitors.

The Conran Shop

Next door, there is a branch of Sir Terence Conran's home furnishings shop. **The Conran Shop** sells a wide variety of unique and cleverly designed furniture and accessories that are as big a hit with Parisians as they were with Londoners when Conran set up shop in his home country.

Bon Marche

In addition to a staggering amount of expensive boutiques, the 7th *arrondissement* also contains some discount shops providing second-hand designer labels at a fraction of their original prices. One of these, **7e Divine** (page 124) offers a discount to *for less* cardholders.

Other interesting shops in the area include original jewellery makers **Rosset-Gaulejac** (page 123) and **Synthetic** (page 121), Parisian master of millinery **Corinne Zaquine** (page 122) and a branch of the fashionable accessories shop **Richard Gampel** (page 121).

Terre de Bruyère

Leather Goods

55 boulevard Raspail, 6th
☎ 01 53 63 30 30

HOURS

Mon-Fri: 11am-7pm. Sat:
10.30am-7pm.
Sun: closed.

for less discount: 20%
VS/MC

Terre de Bruyère stocks high-quality canvas and leather items. Bags, backpacks and briefcases are among the items to be found here. Most items come in autumnal colours to continue the natural theme.

Synthetic

Jewellery

**11 rue
Bernard Palissy, 6th**
☎ 01 45 48 65 40

for less discount: 20%
AM/VS/MC

Synthetic sells jewellery made from many different materials. It specializes in promoting the work of young designers. There are pieces made from crystal, metals, glass and even plastic.

HOURS

Mon-Sat: 11am-7.30pm.
Sun: closed

 # Richard Gampel

Accessories

**55 bis rue des
Saints Pères, 6th**
☎ 01 45 49 26 90

for less discount: 20%
AM/VS/DC

Richard Gampel sells fashionable accessories for men and women. You will find belts, wallets, bags and even mobile phone cases here. The materials used range from leather to crocodile skin.

HOURS

Mon-Fri: 10.30am-2pm,
2.30pm-7pm.
Sat: 10.30am-7pm.
Sun: closed

 # You and Me

Men's and Women's Clothing

75 rue St-Dominique, 7th
☎ 01 47 05 03 71

for less discount: 20%
AM/VS/MC

You and Me stocks a variety of garments for men and women. Natural, luxurious fibres such as mohair and cashmere are in abundance. Designers represented include Armani, Versace and Lacroix.

HOURS

Mon: 12.30pm-7pm.
Tue-Sat: 10.30am-
7.30pm. Sun: closed

Corinne Zaquine

Hats

38 rue de Grenelle, 7ᵗʰ
☎ 01 45 48 93 03

for less discount: 20%
AM/VS/MC

HOURS

Tue-Sat: 11am-7pm.
Sun-Mon: closed.

Corinne Zaquine is hatmaker to brides and princesses. Choose from headwear in velvet, felt, straw, feathers and lace. Hats and veils to all specifications can be made to order.

L'Ibis Rouge

Jewellery / Clothing

35 boulevard Raspail, 7ᵗʰ
☎ 01 45 48 98 21

for less discount: 20%
VS

HOURS

Tue-Sat: 12noon-7pm.
Sun-Mon: closed

To step into L'Ibis Rouge is like entering a Hollywood dressing room. Classic jewellery, evening dresses, pearls and lace are some of the items available. L'Ibis Rouge also specializes in wedding dresses and accessories.

L'Ephemere

Ethnic Gifts

20 rue de la Chaise, 7ᵗʰ
☎ 01 45 44 17 87

for less discount: 20%
VS/MC

HOURS

Tue-Sat: 10.30am-7pm.
Sun-Mon: closed

This shop has a fascinating range of arts and crafts from all over the world. The owner travels the globe looking for interesting native objects. You will find Moroccan pottery, Kenyan cutlery and Indian fruitbowls.

Rosset-Gaulejac

Jewellery

6 rue de Lille, 7th
☎ 01 42 61 10 36

for less discount: 20%
AM/VS

HOURS

Mon-Sat: 9am-6pm.
Sun: closed

Rosset-Gaulejac produces handmade jewellery in quaint surroundings. Traditional skills are used to make beautiful, original pieces, and the shop's specialities are unusual and intricate cufflinks.

 # Only You

Men's Clothing

26 avenue Bosquet, 7th
☎ 01 47 05 06 33

for less discount: 20%
AM/VS/MC

HOURS

Mon: 1pm-7pm. Tue-Sat:
10am-7pm. Sun: closed

Only You sells high quality designer fashion for men. There are ranges of casual, formal and sportswear, all in fine fabrics. Accessories include silk ties and cashmere scarves from Dior.

 # Marie-Liesse

Gifts / Housewares

25 rue Augureau, 7th
☎ 0145 55 55 14

for less discount: 20%
VS/MC

HOURS

Mon: 2.30pm-7pm.
Tue-Fri: 10.30am-7pm.
Sat: 10.30am-12.30pm,
2.30pm-7pm. Sun: closed

Marie-Liesse sells a beautiful range of items for the home. There are candlesticks, hand-painted dinner sets, teapots and vases. Many of the unique items make perfect gifts.

HOURS

Tue-Sat: 10.30am-7pm.
Mon: 12.30pm-7pm.
Sun: closed

HOURS

Tue-Sat: 11am-7pm.
Sun-Mon: closed

HOURS

Mon-Fri: 9am-7.30pm.
Sat-Sun: closed

Etienne Brunel

Women's Clothing

70 rue des Saints Pères, 7th
☎ 01 45 44 41 14

for less discount: 20%
AM/VS/MC

The designer here makes her range from unusual materials. Fabrics used include satin, raw silk, feathers and even foam, and the styles range from classic to avant-garde.

7e Divine

Second-hand Designer Labels

23 rue Malar, 7th
☎ 01 47 53 70 55

for less discount: 20%
AM/VS/MC

7e Divine sells designer labels at affordable prices, and here you can find Max Mara or Givenchy at a fraction of the normal cost. There are also bags by Chanel and Hermès scarves.

Yvie

Jewellery / Gifts

95 rue de Grenelle, 7th
☎ 01 47 05 10 20

for less discount: 20%
AM/VS/MC/DC

Yvie specializes in unusual pieces and ornaments. Here you will find beautiful miniature bottles, boxes and brooches. There is also a unique collection of hand-painted eggs.

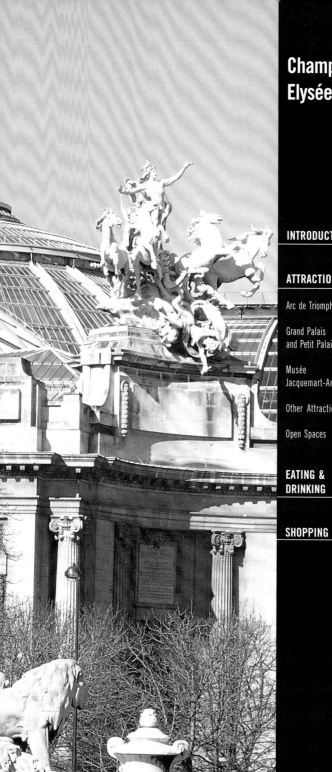

Champs-
Elysées

Introduction . . .

Much of this area, which encircles the **Arc de Triomphe** (page 128), is the smart 8th *arrondissement*. It is perhaps the prime example of Haussmann's almost obsessive attention to geometry and symmetry in the planning of his new Paris; the main avenues are strategically placed to afford spectacular and far-ranging views.

Arc de Triomphe

REFLECTIONS

'From the Arc de Triomphe de l'Etoile/
raise yourself all the way to the heavens, portal of victory/
That the giant of our glory/ Might pass without bending down' - Victor Hugo

The area contains some of the most select and sought-after housing in the city, and **Avenue Montaigne** (page 136), just north of the river, is the most expensive residential street in Paris, even over the Ile St-Louis.

The **avenue des Champs-Elysées** is one of the most famous streets in the world. It began life as a tree-lined extension of the Jardin des Tuileries, and became a distinct street in the early 19th century.

It was at its finest during the Belle Époque at the end of the 19th century, when it was lined with the splendid façades of luxury hotels and apartment buildings.

It has been called the 'pathway of national pride', the backdrop to celebrations of victories, processions and state funerals. Nowadays, it is the focal point of national events such as the last leg of the *Tour de France*, and is still popular with strolling Parisians and tourists alike.

Petit Palais

The northern end of the avenue leads into the **Place Charles de Gaulle**, often thought of as the axis of the city. It is the point at which twelve avenues meet, and the starting point of the 'backbone' of Paris which comprises the Champs-Elysées, the Tuileries and the streets running parallel to the Seine.

This is also the site of the **Arc de Triomphe** (page 128), one of Paris's most famous landmarks. Commissioned by Napoleon in 1806 as a commemoration of his own wartime successes, the

. . . Introduction

neo-classical arch was not completed until after his death. It is 164 feet (50 metres) tall and is decorated with a frieze of battle scenes. Several of the avenues which radiate from the **Place Charles de Gaulle** are named after Napoleon's victories.

Like the area around the Eiffel Tower, this section of Paris also saw some changes as a result of the World Fairs at the turn of the century. The **Grand Palais** and **Petit Palais** (page 129) were built in 1900 for that year's *Exposition Universelle* and were, like the Tower itself, considered an eyesore, too ostentatious and pompous for Paris. Their style of architecture is florid and eclectic, but today they are recognized as unique monuments.

In addition to being architectural attractions, the **Grand Palais** and **Petit Palais** also house the **Palais de la Découverte** (page 129) science museum, the **Musée des Beaux-Arts de la Ville de Paris** (page 129) and host a wide range of temporary exhibitions.

Paris's most ornate bridge, **Pont Alexandre** (page 131), joins the Right Bank to the end of the Esplanade des Invalides across the Seine.

Nearby, the crowd that gathers around the gilt **Flamme de la Liberté** on the Right Bank side of the **Pont de l'Alma** are no longer commemorating the Crimean War - the statue has been reinvented as a shrine to

Musée Jacquemart-André

Princess Diana, whose fatal car-crash happened under this bridge in 1997.

From this spot you can't fail to miss the stark **Palais de Tokyo** (page 131), its white wings softened by sculpture and a Bourdelle bronze. Crossing the courtyard is hazardous when dozens of skateboard fanatics use the smooth slopes for practice.

The **Musée Jacquemart-André** (page 130), on the boulevard Haussmann, is a true gem. It is a fine example of the type of home lived in by the *haute bourgeoisie* during the late 19th century. Today, a visitor can view important works of art within the context of the lavish mansion for which they were collected.

Arc de Triomphe

The **Arc de Triomphe** was commissioned in 1806 by Napoleon, who wanted a monument to commemorate his victory at the Battle of Austerlitz. However, Napoleon's fall from power meant that the Arc was not completed until 1836, fifteen years after his death.

Napoleon's determination to pass through an arch on the way to the Louvre on his wedding day in 1810 led to the construction of a full-size canvas mock-up on the same site, 26 years before the completion of the monument itself.

Arc de Triomphe

The Arc is decorated with friezes and sculptures depicting the battles and victories of Napoleon and the French people. More than 20 artists worked on the decoration of the monument, and Rude's *Marseillaise* relief, showing the departure of citizens on the way to battle, has proved the most popular. The eternal flame underneath the arches burns in honour of the Unknown Soldier of the First World War, buried on this spot.

The Arc stands at the hub of twelve avenues, one of which is the Champs-Elysées, and is ideally placed for tremendous views down the long, straight boulevards.

284 steps (there's no lift) take you up to the displays inside the monument, where pictures and photographs chart its history and the famous events for which it has been the centrepiece.

From the exhibition, follow the signs reading 'Terrasse' to reach the viewing platform at the top. From here you can fully appreciate Baron Haussmann's geometric town-planning and pick out landmarks in all directions.

The Eiffel Tower appears close enough to touch, and the Sacré Coeur perches on top of the highest of several hills surrounding the city. The parks and forests appear as seas of green among the houses, and from the northwestern side you can appreciate the close

The friezes are illuminated at night

proximity and vastness of the complex of La Défense (pages 195-198). Look out, too, for the Opéra, the Centre Pompidou, Notre Dame and the Panthéon.

ADDRESS

Place Charles de Gaulle,
8th *arrondissement*
☎ 01 43 80 31 31

GETTING THERE

Métro: Charles de Gaulle Étoile

HOURS

Tue-Sat: 10.30am-10.30pm. Sun-Mon: 10.30am-6.30pm.

PRICES

Adult 32F
Child 15F
Senior 21F
Student 21F

Grand Palais and Petit Palais

The inauguration of the **Grand Palais** at the *Exposition Universelle* in 1900 raised eyebrows because it broke architectural rules. The huge building, part-palace and part-glasshouse, hid its metal supports behind stone colonnades and statues.

The **Petit Palais**, no less ostentatious, was constructed at the same time, and the pair replaced the 1855 Exhibition's Palace of Industry. Once ridiculed, now revered, the palaces' mixture of Art Nouveau and classical styles have lasted better than many thought possible.

Grand Palais

The Grand Palais lives up to its name: it is 790 feet (241 metres) long. The interior, incorporating glass, iron and foliage, is an excellent example of Art Nouveau interior design. Looking up, you can almost believe yourself to be inside a great 19th-century conservatory.

The natural light makes the palace an ideal exhibition hall, and it has hosted major shows of art, sculpture and design. These have included the 1925 International Exhibition of Decorative Arts, at which Art Deco was introduced to the world, and some revolutionary exhibitions of what was then a radical, misunderstood art form, Impressionism. Currently, however, most of the building is closed for a major overhaul. It is expected to re-open before the end of the century.

One wing of the palace houses the **Palais de la Découverte**, a science museum. The hands-on exhibition has been rather overshadowed by the huge Cité des Sciences (page 152), but this collection is in a more convenient setting.

The Petit Palais houses a permanent collection, the **Musée des Beaux-Arts de la Ville de Paris**. The wings of the building surround a garden and courtyard, and the exhibits include 18th-century art, furniture and busts, Renaissance works and 19th-century French painting.

Petit Palais

ADDRESS

Avenue Winston Churchill,
8th *arrondissement*
☎ 01 44 13 17 30

GETTING THERE

Métro: Champs-Elysées
Clemenceau

HOURS

Grand Palais:
Thu-Mon: 10am-8pm.
Wed: 10am-10pm.

Petit Palais:
Tue-Sun: 10am-5.40pm.
Mon: closed

PRICES

Admission prices vary
according to exhibitions

ADDRESS

158 boulevard
Haussmann, 8ᵗʰ
arrondissement
☎ 01 42 89 04 91

GETTING THERE

Métro: Miromesnil

HOURS

Mon-Sun: 10am-6pm.

PRICES

Adult 47F
Child 35F
Senior 47F
Student 35F

DISCOUNT

2 for the price of 1 adult
with *for less* card

The **Musée Jacquemart-André**'s outstanding art collection is housed in a sumptuous and atmospheric mansion dating from the end of the 1800s.

The collection was the life's work of Edouard André and his wife Nélie Jacquemart in the 19th century when, united by their love of fine art, they toured Italy to find beautiful examples of Renaissance painting.

Musée Jacquemart-André

As well as Italian art, the collection contains 18th-century French and Flemish paintings and drawings, collected by André before his marriage.

The mansion itself is home to a monumental staircase, exuberant state rooms, and a **Winter Garden**. The couple lived in part of the building and used their artistic talents and educated taste to decorate the rest, creating an **Italian Museum** within the classical-style architecture of the beautiful house.

The **Smoking Room** recalls Nélie Jacquemart's travels in the East, and also displays some of her collection of English paintings by Gainsborough and Reynolds. The **Tapestry Room** displays tapestries from the royal workshop at Beauvais.

The small size of their private apartments illustrates the Jacquemart-Andrés' devotion to transforming the mansion into an exhibition area for the public to enjoy. These private rooms offer an insight into daily 19th-century life.

The luxurious interior of the museum

Artists represented in the glorious surroundings include the 18th-century French school, such as David and Fragonard, Flemish masters including Rembrandt, Van Dyck and Hals and the Italian Renaissance leaders Uccello and Carpaccio. The collection is an essential complement to the exhibitions of the Louvre.

Other Attractions . . .

Built at the turn of the century for the *Exposition Universelle*, the flamboyant **Pont Alexandre** spans the

Pont Alexander

Seine between the Esplanade des Invalides and the Grand and Petit Palaises. It features Art Nouveau statues and lamps and is invariably thronging with tourists taking pictures of each other by a lamp, the Eiffel Tower looming in the background. *(Joining the avenue Winston Churchill on the Right Bank to the avenue du M. Gallieni on the Left Bank.)*

The East Wing of the **Palais de Tokyo** contains the **Musée d'Art Moderne de la Ville de Paris**. The collection picks up the history of art where the Musée d'Orsay (page 113) leaves off, displaying 20th-century works by Modigliani, Chagall, Braque and Buren, among others. The highlights of these large, spacious galleries include Matisse's *La Danse de Paris* and Raoul Dufy's *La Fée Électricité*, commissioned in 1937

Pont Alexandre

Palais de Tokyo

by the French Electricity Board.

While the **Palais de Tokyo** undergoes an extensive renovation, the **Centre National de la Photographie** has been temporarily

Palais de Tokyo

relocated to a former mansion at number 11 rue Berryer. Its exhibitions are mostly devoted to contemporary, international talent, photojournalism and up-and-coming new photographers. *(11 ave du Président Wilson, 16th, ☎ 01 53 67 40 00. Tue-Sun: 10am-5.30pm. Mon: closed. Adult 45F, child 35F, senior 35F, student 35F.)*

The **Musée de la Mode et du Costume** is located in a beautiful Renaissance-style palace built in 1892. It consists of thousands of examples of fashion, including clothing, shoes and accessories, from the

Musée de la Mode et du Costume

. . . Other Attractions . . .

18th century onwards. Exhibitions change twice-yearly and are themed according to categories, such as sportswear or evening dress, and historical period.

Items in the 100,000-strong collection include outfits and accessories donated by famous people and renowned designers. *(10 av Pierre 1ᵉʳ de Serbie, 16ᵗʰ, ☎ 01 47 20 85 23. Tue-Sun: 10am-5.40pm. Adult 35F, child 25F, senior 25F, student 25F.)*

Musée Guimet

The **Musée National des Arts Asiatiques-Guimet** is undergoing extensive renovations until the middle of 1999. This important collection of the art treasures of Asia was founded by Emile Guimet in 1889, and comprises items from China, Japan, Tibet, Nepal and Indonesia, among them statues, ceramics, jewellery, fabrics and an unrivalled collection of Buddha figurines. *(6 place d'Iéna, 16ᵗʰ, ☎ 01 47 23 61 65. Wed-Mon: 9.45am-5.15pm. Adult 16F, child free, senior 12F, student 12F. During renovations parts of the exhibition are on display at 19 avenue d'Iéna.)*

A similiar theme can be found further north at the **Musée Cernushi**.

Musée de la Mode et du Costume

The atmospheric museum by the Parc Monceau contains the fruit of explorer Enrico Cernushi's 19th-century Far Eastern travels. His route is mapped out on the wall at the top of the stairs at the beginning of the tour.

The museum has plenty of unusual and quirky items including rabbit teapots, Chinese dragon figures, exquisitely illustrated Japanese books and the massive bronze Meguro Buddha from Tokyo. *(7 avenue Vélasquez, 8ᵗʰ, ☎ 01 45 63 50 75. Tue-Sun: 10am-5.40pm. Mon: closed. Adult 30F, child 20F, senior 20F, student 20F.)*

Musée Cernushi

This salubrious area of Paris, with its smart townhouses, embassies and leafy gardens, is an appropriate location for the **Musée Nissim de Camondo**. Daily life of the past comes alive in this stunning 18th-century-style mansion, surrounded by neat gardens, chestnut trees and quiet streets.

. . . Other Attractions

The collection of tapestries, furniture, paintings and china is carefully displayed in luxurious rooms. Be sure to feast your eyes on the beautiful spiral staircases, the cosy Petit Bureau, the well-stocked library and the

Musée Nissim de Camondo

covetable tiled bathroom.

The museum is named after the son of the founder, who was killed in the First World War.

Musée Nissim de Camondo

Letters and documents illustrate the history of the well-to-do de Camondo family, the last of whom died at Auschwitz in 1943. *(63 rue de Monceau, 8ᵗʰ, ☎ 01 53 89 06 40. Wed-Sun: 10am-5pm. Mon-Tue: closed. Adult 27F, child 18F, senior 18f, student 18F.)*

Open Spaces

The peaceful **Parc Monceau** was the one of the first in Paris to be planned in the Picturesque or *anglo-chinoise* style. It began life as a folly built by Carmontelle in 1787 and takes its name from the village of Monceau which was once located here.

In the 18th century the park was very popular among the gentry, who would parade here among the streams, rock gardens and leafy grottos.

Parc Monceau

Other decorative buildings were added, of which the Egyptian tomb and the rotunda designed by Ledoux remain today.

The park used to be much bigger. Before Haussmann's remodelling of Paris it covered an extra 20 acres (8 hectares). At this time, too, the decorative gates and iron railings were constructed to contain the park.

Today, the Parc Monceau is a pleasant contrast with the formal French gardens found in other parts of Paris. Around almost every shady corner is a surprise, be it a pool, a Greek-style statue or a fairy-tale grotto.

Parc Monceau

Eating and Drinking

There are plenty of restaurants and cafés along the Champs-Elysées, though most are touristy, crowded and overpriced. Opt for a walk along the side streets to discover some out-of-the-way treasures.

In addition to cosy French bistros, you can find some good ethnic restaurants in this area as well. One of Paris's most famous Lebanese restaurants is **Fakhr el Dine** (page 134).

Ledoyen

Its reputation is built on years of serving delicious food in an elegant atmosphere by an attentive staff. Your *for less* card entitles you to a discount of 20%.

Savoy restaurant

The bright and colourful **Restaurant Acropolis** (page 135) serves up traditional Greek fare in a lively setting.

Savoy

For fine Italian food, try **Piccola Roma** (page 135) where the speciality is the many varieties of *antipasti*. For more casual dining, try **Pizzeria Sylvano** (page 135).

The area also contains several high-profile restaurants whose star chefs have a reputation that travels far and wide. **Guy Savoy** (*18 rue Troyon, 17th, ☎ 01 43 80 40 61*), **Ledoyen** (*1 avenue Dutuit, 8th, ☎ 01 47 42 35 98*) and **Taillevent** (*15 rue Lamennais, 8th, ☎ 01 45 61 12 90*) are among the best known.

Fakhr el Dine

Lebanese

30 rue de Longchamp, 16th
☎ 01 47 27 90 00

Average meal: 150-200F
for less discount: 20%
AM/VS/MC/DC

HOURS

Mon-Sun: 11.30am-3.30pm, 7.30pm-12midnight

Choose one of the spicy Lebanese dishes at this restaurant. The authentic décor is magnificent and the ambiance is welcoming. The discount is also available at the other branch, 3 rue Q. Bauchart, 8th.

Restaurant Acropolis

Greek

12 rue de Longchamp, 16th
☎ 01 44 05 03 93

Average meal: 150-200F
for less discount: 20%
AM/VS/MC/DC

HOURS

Mon-Sat: 10.30am-7pm
Sun: closed

Greek music sets the scene in the Restaurant Acropolis. Typical dishes on offer include *moussaka* and suckling pig. The décor is blue and white, evocative of a Greek island scene.

Piccola Roma

Italian

10 rue Saint-Didier, 16th
☎ 01 47 27 22 27

Average meal: 100-150F
for less discount: 20%
VS/DC

HOURS

Mon-Sat: 12.45pm-
2.30pm, 7pm-11.15pm.
Sun: closed

Try the delicious Italian dishes at this authentic restaurant, such as a dish from the wide selection of traditional *antipasta*. The décor is welcoming, and there are Italian frescos on the walls.

Pizzeria Sylvano

Italian

54 rue des Acacias, 17th
☎ 01 43 80 47 29

Average meal: 100-150F
for less discount: 20%
VS

HOURS

Mon-Sat: 10am-3pm,
6pm-11.30pm. Sun:
12noon-2.30pm, 7pm-
11.30pm

This restaurant serves pizza, pasta and other Italian specialities. The pizzas are generously topped with almost anything you wish. Try the delicious tiramisu, a traditional Italian dessert.

Shopping

The stretch of luxurious boutiques along the rue du Faubourg Saint-Honoré continues into this area. Many of the shops here bear names that are recognized the world over - **Hermès** (no. 24), **Yves Saint-Laurent** (no. 38) and **Gianni Versace** (no. 62) are just a few.

Not far from the rue Saint-Honoré lies another deluxe shopping area known as the **Golden Triangle**. Bounded by the Champs-Elysées, avenue George V and the **avenue Montaigne**, the triangle is home to clothing and jewellery shops like **Givenchy** (*3 avenue George V, 8th, ☎ 01 44 31 50 06*) and **Cartier** (*51 rue Francois I, 8th, ☎ 01 40 74 61 84*). On the avenue Montaigne alone, you can find **Louis Vuitton** (no. 54), **Prada** (no. 10) and **Valentino** (nos. 17-19) among many others.

Avenue Montaigne

L'Eventail

Second-hand Designer Labels

65 bis rue Lauriston, 16th
☎ 01 47 04 58 68

for less discount: 20%
No credit cards

This *dépôt-vente* sells designer clothes at knock-down prices. Women's coats, skirts, and suits by YSL and Laroche are all reduced in price. In addition there are selections of jewellery, accessories and antiques.

Café Coton

Men's Clothing

19 rue Marbeuf, 8th
☎ 01 47 20 17 98

for less discount: 20%
VS/MC

Café Coton sells high-quality clothing for men. There are ranges for both work and weekend wear, and the timeless styles are complemented by the range of classic accessories.

Montmartre and North-west Paris

Introduction . . .

This area of Paris was largely rural until the end of the 19th century. Village-like Montmartre, the area best known to visitors, is located on a 426 foot (130 metre) hill which overlooks the city.

High on top of this hill, visible throughout most of Paris, is the dream-like **Basilique du Sacré Coeur** (page140). Not only is the church worth a visit, but the views from here are alone worth the trip.

There are flights of steps just about everywhere in Montmartre, but you can also enjoy a ride on the funicular from the Place Saint Pierre up to the Sacré Coeur.

Montmartre highlife immortalized by Toulouse-Lautrec

Despite being very much a part of Paris now, Montmartre still retains a village atmosphere. It began as a commune of just over 600 people during the Revolution.

Towards the end of the 19th century a new band of settlers were attracted by the reasonable rents and clean air. Many of these were amateur artists, composers and writers, the 'bohemians' who gave the area its arty ambience.

A picturesque Montmartre street

The list of artists who either struggled to make a living or enjoyed their successes here reads like a history of 20th-century art: Renoir, Toulouse-Lautrec, Dufy, Dali, Utrillo and Van Gogh, among many others, spent time in Montmartre.

Various schools of painting were founded by artists living in the area, perhaps the most famous being Cubism.

The **Bateau Lavoir** (page 143), a former piano factory in the Place Emile Goudeau, was a house divided into studios and cheap living quarters that was home to such artists as Braque and Picasso. It was here that the romantic notion of struggling artists starving in garrets began. The original building

. . . Introduction

no longer exists, but its replacement is still rented out to art students.

Among the composers associated with Montmartre were Berlioz and Satie; the latter was granted his request to be buried in the peaceful **Montmartre Cemetery** (page 143), where he rests alongside Degas, Stendhal and Zola.

Montmartre Vineyard

Montmartre life has always centred around the pretty **Place du Tertre** (page 142). Despite being somewhat touristy, it has managed to retain its picturesque atmosphere.

Another pretty square is the nearby **Place des Abbesses**, a haven of relative peace.

The area south of Montmartre is well-known for cabaret. The **Moulin Rouge**, instantly recognizable by its windmill, is almost as famous a symbol of Paris as the Eiffel Tower.

It was here that the Can-Can dance was born at the end of the 19th century, and where Toulouse-Lautrec sketched the performers and pleasure-seekers.

Salvador Dali

The Moulin Rouge is still a popular venue, but the **Pigalle** area and the Boulevard de Clichy display a rather sleazy side of modern Paris.

For a great overview of the Montmartre area, board the **Petit Train Montmartre** (page 141) at the Place Blanche or Place du Tertre and enjoy the sights without having to endure the arduous hills and flights of steps.

To the west is the 17th *arrondissement*. The Eastern part, **Batignolles**, has managed to retain some of its village atmosphere, partly as a result of the founding of a society for its preservation.

Halle Sainte Pierre and the Sacré Coeur

Sacré Coeur

ADDRESS

35 rue de Chevalier, 18ᵗʰ
arrondissement
☎ 01 53 41 89 00

GETTING THERE

Métro: Abbesses, Anvers

HOURS

Basilica:
Mon-Sun: 7am-11pm

Dome / Crypt:
Mon-Sun: 9am-6pm

PRICES

Entrance to the basilica is free.

Dome or Crypt:
Adult 15F
Child 10F
Senior 15F
Students 10F

Combined entrance to the Dome and Crypt:
Adult 25F
Child 15F
Senior 25F
Student 15F

You will often glimpse the **Basilique du Sacré Coeur** from other parts of Paris. Its location, on the highest hill in the city, and the reflected light from the pure white marble of its façade gives it an ethereal look.

It came into being following a solemn vow by two well-to-do Catholics at the outbreak of the Franco-Prussian

Sacré Coeur

war. They swore to build a Catholic church in atonement if France lost the war.

It was finally completed in 1914, though its consecration was delayed until 1919 due to the outbreak of the First World War.

The rather incongruous Romano-Byzantine style is valued by visitors and tourists for its kitsch appeal more than anything else, with more postcards of the basilica being sold every year than pictures of the Eiffel Tower.

Entry into the basilica is free. The **bronze doors** depict the Last Supper and other scenes from the life of Christ, and the portico is flanked by statues of Joan of Arc and Saint Louis.

The ceiling of the chancel has a huge mosaic depicting Christ, with Joan of Arc and others kneeling around him. It was created by Luc Merson and completed in 1922.

Constant prayers remembering the dead of the Franco-Prussian war are held here by priests working in shifts. The **dome** and the **crypt** are

Luc Merson's chancel mosaic

accessible to the public, with the dome offering the second farthest view in the city.

The steps outside the Sacré Coeur are almost as good a spot from which to view Paris, and in the evenings the area throngs with young people busking on the hillside and the ever-present pilgrims paying their respects at the basilica.

Other Attractions . . .

for less For the best introduction to the area, take the **Petit Train de Montmartre** from outside the Moulin Rouge and enjoy a tour around Montmartre with music and a commentary.

Petit Train de Montmartre

The 40-minute round-trip is a godsend for tired feet and takes you past most of the famous sights described in the folowing

pages. *(Place Blanche / Place du Tertre, 18th, ☎ 01 42 62 24 00. Mon-Sun: 10am-7pm (midnight at weekends and in summer). Trips every 30 minutes. Adult 30F, child 18F, senior 18F, student 30F. 50% discount with voucher on page 275.)*

Petit Train de Montmartre

The **Eglise St-Pierre** has to compete with the next-door Sacré Coeur for vistors, but this little church is one of the oldest in Paris. It is the surviving part of a Benedictine convent and is an eclectic mix of architectural styles, even incorporating some Roman columns. *(2 rue de Mont-Cenis, 18th, ☎ 01 46 06 57 63. Mon-Sun: 8.30am-7pm.)*

Halle St Pierre Musée d'Art Naïf Max Fourny

for less The **Musée d'Art Naïf Max Fourny** is located in the Halle Saint Pierre, a former 19th-century market building which is now a cultural centre in the south of Montmartre.

The permanent collection comprises more than 500 contemporary paintings and 80 sculptures from all over the world, representing every technique of naive art.

Musée de Montmartre

Halle St Pierre Musée d'Art Naïf Max Fourny

The temporary exhibitions, which change regularly, are dedicated to native, outsider, folk and "raw" art. They have recently covered such areas as glass painting in Europe, cows in Swiss folk art and naive art from Taiwan. *(2 rue Ronsard, 18th, ☎ 01 42 58 72 89. Mon-Sun: 10am-6pm. Gallery free; entrance price for exhibitions. Adult 40F, child 30F, senior 30F, student 30F. 2 for the price of 1 with your for less card.)*

The **Musée de Montmartre** is devoted to the history of the area. The charming house has in the past provided studio space for painters such as

Musée de Montmartre

. . . Other Attractions . . .

Utrillo, Dufy and Renoir, and once belonged to one of Molière's leading actors.

Place du Tertre

The museum emphasizes Montmartre's Bohemian past. Utrillo's favourite café is reconstructed here in careful detail, and some of Toulouse-Lautrec's original posters can be seen among the other drawings, documents and artefacts. *(12 rue Cortot, 18th, ☎ 01 46 06 61 11. Tue-Sun: 11am-5.30pm. Adult 25F, child 20F, senior 20F, student 20F.)*

Place du Tertre

The **Place du Tertre** began hosting open-air art exhibitions during the 19th century, and the tradition lives on today with the multitude of hopeful artists who set up their easels outside the lively cafés. You can have your portrait painted while amused bystanders look on.

Espace Montmartre - Salvador Dali

for less Nearby is the **Espace Montmartre - Salvador Dali**. This museum was opened in 1991 as a lasting memorial to the eccentric artist Salvador Dali, who had a studio in Montmartre for a time.

Espace Montmartre - Salvador Dali

In the atmospheric underground rooms, painted black and echoing with eerie music befitting Dali's surrealist style, you can see more than 300 of his works.

Included in the collection are some of his bronze sculptures. Though less familiar than his popular paintings, they are prime examples of his mastery of Surrealism.

In addition, there is a complete collection of rare and original signed etchings and lithographs illustrating works of literature, mythology, history and religion, including an edition of La Fontaine's *Fables*. *(11 rue Poulbot, 18th, ☎ 01 42 64 40 10. Mon-Sun: 10am-6pm. Adult 35F, Child 25F, Senior 25F, Student 25F. 2 for the price of 1 with your for less card.)*

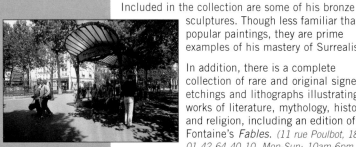

Place des Abbesses

. . . Other Attractions

The **Place des Abbesses** features one of the few
original Art Nouveau *métro* entrances to remain in
Paris. Note the curving green ironwork and the amber
lights, hallmarks of Guimard's design. The square is
also the site of the unusual concrete church of **St-
Jean de Montmartre**

Place des Abbesses

The nearby **Bateau Lavoir** is yet another memento of
Montmartre's artistic past. In 1890 an old piano
factory became a haven for the struggling painters of
the day.

Picasso, Modigliani, Degas and
Cézanne, among others, were
grateful for the squalid shelter
and cramped studio space
offered at this ramshackle
construction, named after the
laundry boats of the Seine.
The original building burnt
down in 1970, but its
replacement still houses art

Bateau Lavoir

students. *(13 place Emile Goudeau, 18ᵗʰ.)*

Open Spaces

In the west of Montmartre is the **cemetery** *(20 ave
Rachel)*. Tucked away in an old quarry below street
level, it is intimate and peaceful. Permanent residents
of the 11 hectares (27 acres) include Stendhal,
director François Truffaut and the original *Dame aux
Camélias*, Marguerite Gautier. The composer Satie
expressed a particular wish to be buried here after he
lived in the area
for a time.

One of
Montmartre's
most famous
sons, Utrillo, is
not buried here
but in the little St.
Vincent cemetery
*(Square Roland-
Dorgelès, 18ᵗʰ)*.

Vineyard

Montmartre cemetery

The only **vineyard** left in Paris is here, and is where the
start of the grape harvest is celebrated on the first
Saturday in October. This site was formerly the garden
of Aristide Bruant, the French singer-songwriter
immortalized in his red scarf, black hat and cape in
cabaret posters by Toulouse-Lautrec.

Eating and Drinking

In warm weather, the streets around the **Place du Tertre** and the **Place des Abbesses** teem with café-goers jockeying for prime positions at the outdoor tables.

A Montmartre restaurant

In winter, the crowds are forced indoors to the cosy warmth of these tiny Montmartre establishments, most of which serve middle-of-the-road, often overpriced, fare.

To avoid these tourist traps, head east to the 17th *arrondissement* where the crowds dissipate and the culinary offerings are more diverse and less aimed at the tourist market.

In addition to traditional French restaurants such as **La Chiffonade** (page 144) and **L'Ecrin d'Or** (page 145), the 17th *arrondissement* has plenty of ethnic options. **A la Grande Bleue** (page 146) serves Algerian cuisine in an art-filled setting, while **Jardin du Kashmir** (page 145) dishes out high-quality Indian fare at very reasonable prices. **La Tour de Pizz** (page 146) is a kosher pizza and fish restaurant.

Lively cafés

La Chiffonade

French

111 rue Legendre, 17th
☎ **01 46 27 08 82**

Average meal: 100-150F
for less discount: 20%
AM/VS/MC/DC

HOURS

Mon-Sun: 12noon-2.30pm, 6pm-11pm (until midnight on Sat)

Although this is a French restaurant, one of the specialities is *paella*. Traditional French dishes include *fruits de mer* cooked in whisky. The restaurant has a fun and friendly atmosphere.

Jardin du Kashmir

Indian

60 rue Legendre, 17th
☎ 01 42 12 94 88

Average meal: 100-150F
for less discount: 20%
AM/VS/MC

HOURS

Mon-Sat: 12noon-2.30pm,
7.30pm-11.30pm. Sun:
12noon-3.30pm

Jardin du Kashmir is situated in the Batignolles area. Specialities include traditional Indian and Pakistani curries. There are lamb, chicken and fish dishes, as well as choices for vegetarians.

L'Ecrin d'Or

French

35 rue Legendre, 17th
☎ 01 47 63 83 08

Average meal: 100-150F
for less discount: 20%
AM/VS/MC

HOURS

Tue-Fri & Sun: 12noon-
2.30pm, 7pm-11pm. Sat:
7pm-11pm. Mon: closed

L'Ecrin d'Or is charming and comfortable. The traditional dishes on offer include *escalope de saumon poêlée* and *foie gras*. The wide range of meals are based around meat, fish and duck recipes.

No Problemo

Italian / American

21 rue André del Sartre, 18th
☎ 01 42 54 39 38

Average meal: 100-150F
for less discount: 20%
VS/MC

HOURS

Mon-Sun:
12noon-2am

No Problemo is a friendly restaurant in the heart of the old Montmartre area. It serves traditional Italian / American dishes, and on warm summer evenings you can dine outside.

HOURS

Sun-Thu: 12noon-2.45pm,
7.15pm-11.30pm.
Sat: 7.30pm-11.30pm. Fri:
closed.

La Tour de Pizz

Kosher

51 rue Bayen, 17th
☏ 01 45 72 07 06

Average meal: 50-100F
for less discount: 20%
AM/VS/MC

This kosher restaurant specializes in fish dishes, with a
range of delicious salads which make great starters.
Alternatively, try a wood-smoked pizza with fish or
vegetarian toppings.

A la Grand Bleue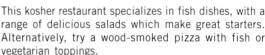

Algerian

4 rue Lantiez, 17th
☏ 01 42 28 04 26

Average meal: 50-100F
for less discount: 20%
AM/VS/MC

HOURS

Mon-Fri: 12noon-3pm,
7.30pm-12midnight.
Sat: 7.30pm-12midnight.
Sun: closed.

Á la Grande Bleue doubles as an exhibition gallery of
paintings. Its unusual specialities originate from Kabyle,
an area of Algeria. Try the berber crêpes and special
couscous.

Oh!...Poivrier!

French

121 blvd Malesherbes, 8th
☏ 01 42 25 24 94

Average meal: 50-100F
for less discount: 20%
with voucher on page 281
AM/VS/MC

HOURS

Mon-Sun: 11.30am-
12midnight

Oh!...Poivrier! offers fresh, good value food in modern
surroundings. It is a great place for a light meal or a
delicious sandwich. There is a also a selection of mouth-
watering, fruit-based desserts.

Shopping

Paris's largest fleamarket, **Saint-Ouen**, takes place at the Porte de Clignancourt. It contains miles of stalls, specializing in antiques of all price ranges. The market also incorporates the antique shops of the **rue des Rosiers**.

The **rue des Levis**, just off the **boulevard des Batignolles**, is one big street market. There are plenty of food shops, regional cheeses being a speciality here, but you can find everything from lingerie to hardware.

Rue des Levis

There is good shopping to be found along the boulevard des Batignolles, the **boulevard de Courcelles** and in the **Palais de Congrès** shopping mall at Porte Maillot.

Les Plaisirs du Palais

Wine Shop

2 place de la
Porte-Maillot, 17th
☎ 01 40 68 22 47

for less discount: 20%
AM/VS/MC/DC

Les Plaisirs du Palais is located in the Palais de Congrès. It stocks a good range of wines, spirits and festive foods. Champagne and caviar are great presents to bring back from Paris.

HOURS

Mon-Sat: 10am-8pm
Sun: 1pm-7pm

La Diligence

Leather Goods

102 blvd des
Batignolles, 17th
☎ 01 43 87 28 04

for less discount: 20%
AM/VS/MC/DC

La Diligence specializes in high-quality luggage in leather and canvas. Classic designs by Nina Ricci and Samsonite, among others, can be found here. The wide range of accessories includes bags and scarves.

HOURS

Mon: 12noon-7pm.
Tue-Sat: 10am-7pm.
Sun: Apr-Jul: 10.30am-
1pm

HOURS

Mon-Fri: 11am-7pm.
Sat: 10.30am-7pm.
Sun: closed

HOURS

Mon-Sat: 9.30am-7.30pm.
Sun: closed

HOURS

Mon-Sat: 10am-7pm.
Sun: closed

Terre de Bruyère

Leather Goods

112 blvd de Courcelles, 17th
☎ **01 42 27 86 87**

for less discount: 20%
VS/MC

Leather goods sold here are made according to old saddlery traditions. There are luggage sets and bags as well as items for the home. The natural materials used include canvas, suede and raffia.

Caillou

Jewellery

10 avenue de Clichy, 18th
☎ **01 45 22 36 00**

for less discount: 20%
AM/VS/MC

This jewellery shop is close to the Place de Clichy. Caillou stocks a large range of rings, necklaces and precious stones. In addition, there is a good selection of watches of all types.

Le Preau de Ferdinand

Toys

22 rue Saint-Ferdinand, 17th
☎ **01 40 68 91 35**

for less discount: 20%
VS/MC

This delightful shop sells classic and modern toys. There are dolls, teddies, construction toys and wooden horses. There is also a selection of party items such as garlands and streamers.

La Villette and Paris East

Introduction . . .

The suburbs of Paris have long been associated with the *cinéma verité* movement of films: agonizing, intellectual comments on the ennui of life. Once, the centre of Paris was completely blind to the goings-on in these outer reaches, but now the suburbs are being included in plans for the future of the city as an all-encompassing cultural and tourist mecca.

Belleville

In Paris East, for example, a new and major attraction is the complex of **La Villette** (pages 152-3), already able to call itself one of the top attractions in Paris. It has received around five million visitors a year since it opened in 1986.

Prior to its renovation, the area consisted largely of slaughterhouses and stockyards. La Villette had the largest slaughterhouses in the world, but these were built in the years immediately preceding the advent of refrigeration technology; they were therefore obsolete almost as soon as they were finished. The buildings stood idle until the government decided that the site was ripe for redevelopment.

The area is now home to a huge complex devoted to culture, science and leisure, thoughtfully incorporating green areas with the latest architecture and innovative structures.

The **Canal de l'Ourcq** leads up to the complex like a miniature mirror image of the Vie Triomphale which leads to La Défense on the other side of Paris. It was opened in 1808 to provide a trade route for the city.

Parc des Buttes Chaumont

This area is home to the **Cimetière du Père Lachaise** (page 156), Paris's largest cemetery and perhaps the most famous in France. It is named after Louis XIV's confessor, who had once owned the land which

. . . Introduction

Napoleon I decreed should become a much needed cemetery.

Where the 19th *arrondissement* meets the 20th is **Belleville**, an area of Paris which has managed to retain its separate village identity, though without the charm of Montmartre.

Bois de Vincennes

It was the weekend retreat for 18th- and 19th-century Parisians wishing to escape the bustle of the centre of town, but was incorporated into Paris as the city expanded, becoming, for a time, the most notorious of slums.

Belleville is bordered by the **Canal St-Martin**, which was built in 1825 as a short-cut for Seine traffic and leads into the **Canal de l'Ourcq** in the vicinity of La Villette.

Belleville's neighbour is **Menilmontant**, a multi-racial area which is somewhat more genteel than Belleville. It is now becoming an alternative centre of nightlife and the ultimate in cool for young Parisians, with numerous bars, cafés and clubs.

What this area lacks in cultural attractions, it more than makes up for in parks and open spaces. The **Parc des Buttes Chaumont** (page 155) is a favourite amongst Parisians who adore its sloping hills and sweeping vistas.

Parc de Bercy

Bordering Paris to the east lies the immense **Bois de Vincennes** (page 157). Once a royal forest ('bois' means 'woods' in French), it now contains woodlands, lakes, flower gardens, a zoo, playground, racetrack, the impressive **Château de Vincennes** and even a Buddhist temple. Throughout the Bois de Vincennes there are plenty of pathways for strolling and cycling.

ADDRESS

Avenue Corentin-Cariou,
19th *arrondissement*
☎ 01 40 03 75 00

GETTING THERE

Métro: Porte de la Villette

HOURS

Mon-Sun: 6am-1am.
Separate attractions have
differing opening hours

PRICES

Entry to the complex is
free, with separate
admission prices for
attractions. Various ticket
packages last all day and
allow entry to several
attractions

INSIDER'S TIP

For an unusual journey to
or from La Villette, take a
canal boat from Place
Stalingrad (call ☎ 08 03
30 63 06 for details)

La Villette . . .

The **Cité des Sciences et de l'Industrie** is the top
attraction in the futuristic La Villette complex. The
huge building itself is a converted abbatoir, with solar
panels in the roof supplying power to the main
concourse.

The museum aims to popularize science and to help
people understand the world in which we live. Almost
all the exhibits are interactive, the 'hands-on' concept
allowing
visitors to
make science
actually
happen before
their eyes.

The museum
comprises
permanent and
temporary
exhibitions,

Cité des Sciences

covering 98,400 feet^2 (30,000 metres$^{2)}$) of floor-
space, and is arranged according to theme.

Level 1 consists of the **southern gallery**, its huge
windows overlooking the rest of the park, where the
exhibitions of Aeronautics, Space, the Ocean, Energy
and the Environment are located. One of the highlights
is the Mirage IV jet plane, the centrepiece of the
Aeronautics display.

The **northern gallery** comprises a range of amusing
interactive exhibits to illustrate the themes of Sound,

Images, Expression and
Behaviour, Mathematics
(not quite as amusing) and
Computer Science. The
Images exhibition is
especially fun, with dozens
of optical illusions to test.

Level 2 features the
Planetarium, which stages
audio-visual presentations
about all aspects of
astronomy, and has
displays devoted to Rocks
and Volcanoes, Biology,
Medecine, and Life and
Health.

Futuristic architecture

Knowledge of French helps with some of the exhibits,
although the main ones have instructions and

. . . La Villette

explanations in English and other languages, and there are guides available in English from the reception desk.

Most of the exhibits are suitable for adults and older children, but the **Cité des Enfants** on the ground floor comprises two innovative playcentres for children aged 3-5 and 5-12.

La Géode

Sessions last 1½ hours, and children learn skills such as teamwork and communication with the toys and games provided. Children aged 3-5 can observe animals, build a house and learn about how bread is made. Those aged 5-12 can explore an ant hill, produce a TV programme and listen to languages from all over the world.

You can't miss what appears to be a huge steel ball in a pond outside the building. This is the **Géode**, a cinema with a hemispherical screen which literally wraps around the audience. Other theatres in the complex are the **Louis Lumière** cinema, where 3D films are shown, and the **Cinaxe** theatre, a venue in which the seats move to accompany the movement on screen.

Cité de la Musique

At the other end of the park is the **Cité de la Musique**, which comprises a concert hall, a *conservatoire* of dance, and a museum that charts the history of music from the 16th century to the present day.

Among the 900 instruments on display you can see Stradivarius violins and Beethoven's own clavichord.

The **Grande Halle**, in the centre of the park, is a masterpiece of 19th century architecture. The glass and metal structure, originally a cattle hall, can house more than 15,000 people and is used for trade shows, festivals, meetings, exhibitions and shows.

Other buildings in the complex include the polyester **Zénithe** concert hall, the **Hot Brass** jazz club and a riding centre. For more information about the park itself, see page 155.

DON'T MISS

The *Argonaute*, a real submarine, built in 1957. With your Cité de la Sciences ticket you can go on board to see the cramped conditions endured by the crew, the advanced operational equipment and the huge torpedoes which the submarine never had cause to use in its active lifetime.

Other Attractions

L'Atelier du Cuivre

The copper workshops of **L'Atelier du Cuivre** have been open to the public since 1986, thanks to an money-raising initiative to display traditional industries to tourists.

At L'Atelier du Cuivre visitors can discover the history of copper and its many uses in our society for both decorative and practical purposes.

Displays cover such aspects as the mining of copper, the effects of this on the environment and economy, and the different uses of the metal throughout history.

L'Atelier du Cuivre

Showcases display the work of the artisans based here, and you can also learn about both the new and traditionally based processes used today. *(113 av. Daumesnil, 12th, ☎ 01 43 40 20 20. Mon-Sat: 10am-12noon, 2pm-5pm. Sun: closed, except holidays. Adult 22F, Child 15F. 50% discount with **for less** card.)*

Musée des Arts d'Afrique et d'Océanie

The **Musée des Arts d'Afrique et d'Océanie** resides behind the stunning bas-relief façade of a 1930s building, with palm trees contributing to the colonial feel.

The collection comprises artefacts, jewellery, statues, carvings, fabrics and masks, with items originating from Morocco, Algeria, Ghana, the Congo, Cameroon, Australia and Polynesia.

The basement is an **Aquarium**, home to tropical fish, turtles and even crocodiles, which is a particular favourite with younger visitors. *(293 avenue Daumesnil, 12th, ☎ 01 44 74 84 80. Mon & Wed-Fri: 10am-12noon, 1.30pm-5.30pm. Sat-Sun: 12.30pm-6pm. Tue: closed. Adult 30F, child 20F, senior 20F, student 20F.)*

Musée Piaf

The Belleville area, home to Edith Piaf, keeps her memory alive at the **Musée Edith Piaf**. This private museum is open by appointment only and run by Piaf fans. The collection of clothes, letters, posters, records and photographs is lovingly presented. *(5 rue Crespin-du-Gast, 11th, ☎ 01 43 55 52 72. Mon-Thu: 1pm-6pm. Call ahead to visit. Voluntary donation.)*

Open Spaces . . .

The **Parc de la Villette**, dating from 1987, comprises 74 acres (30 hectares) and forms the setting for the rest of the Villette complex. There are landscaped lawns, shady paths, and dotted all over are Swiss architect Tschumi's *folies*: bright red constructions which function as burger bars, workshops and even a jazz club.

There are ten themed gardens, which include the **Jardin des Miroirs** (Garden of Mirrors) and the **Jardin des Frayeurs Enfantins** (Garden of Childhood Fears).

Parc de la Villette

The park will not appeal to all tastes, as the futuristic design is a world apart from a picturesque English-style garden or the French formal gardens more familiar in Paris. Its trees are too young to have made much difference so far, and the watery element is the dead-straight **Canal de l'Ourcq**. The quirky visual elements such as the *folies*, however, make it worth seeing.

Parc des Buttes Chaumont

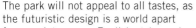

Parc de Belleville

The **Parc des Buttes Chaumont** is a popular oasis in a residential area of high-rise blocks. It was created in 1863 as part of Napoleon III's plans to make Paris a healthier place.

The park features steep hills and plunging paths, all carefully landscaped by Haussmann to give the impression of natural countryside.

There is a lake, several waterfalls, man-made cliffs, a classical temple and plenty of areas of thick woodland. The park is popular with the youth of the area who flock here on warm evenings with drums and guitars.

Further south is the smaller **Parc de Belleville**. This modern park is built on the side of a hill and covers 11 acres (4.5 hectares), and offers an unusual and unexpected view of Paris from the top.

Parc des Belleville

The hill was formerly a vineyard, and a staircase wends its way up through vines, artificial grottos, pools and waterfalls.

. . . Open Spaces . . .

The **Cimetière du Père Lachaise** is the biggest cemetery in Paris and is famous throughout the world for its notable residents.

Pere Lachaise

In the 17th century the land had belonged to Père La Chaise, Louis XIV's confessor, and the cemetery was created under Napoleon's decree in 1804. Prefect Frochot, who was in charge of its creation, purchased the remains of Abélard and Héloïse, Molière and La Fontaine to start the ball rolling, and such eminent residents had the desired effect.

More famous corpses joined them and the cemetery became the most desirable resting place in Paris. With its tree-lined paths and rich and poor areas, it is a veritable 'city of the dead'.

In order to be buried here you have to have Parisian connections. Alongside French celebrities such as Marcel Proust, Honoré de Balzac, Victor Noir and Georges Bizet, Oscar Wilde secured his plot by dying in a Paris hotel with the immortal quip: 'Either that wallpaper goes, or I do'. His tomb was sculpted by Jacob Epstein.

Balzac

Jim Morrison

Jim Morrison, the lead singer of the Doors, also died in Paris and has the most visited grave in the cemetery. Fans keep a constant vigil, and the surrounding graves have to be scrubbed clean of Jim-related graffiti every so often.

The **Columbarium** contains the ashes of cremated notables, including Isadora Duncan, and the **Mur des Fédérés** marks the spot where the last of the Communard rebels were executed in 1871.

. . . Open Spaces

The **Parc de Bercy**, in a industrial part of the 12th *arrondissement*, is a modern park which has been designed to reflect the history of its location. The area was formerly the unloading point for wine and foodstuffs coming along the Seine from outside Paris.

Parc de Bercy

Warehouses once stood on this site, which now comprises geometric planning, French garden-style terraces and broad paths. Four areas represent the seasons, and the lawns are broken up by trees and paths.

The **Bois de Vincennes**, together with the Bois de Boulogne, was once a huge area of woodland surrounding the early settlement which was to become Paris.

In the 12th century the land became a hunting ground,

Château de Vincennes

and the keep of the **Château de Vincennes** was constructed in the 15th century, with other buildings being added in the 16th and 17th centuries.

The château was originally a royal castle, but Louis XIV favoured Versailles for his country seat and the château was used as a prison.

Parc de Bercy

Today you can visit the keep, the exhibitions of sculpture, the replica of Ste-Chapelle and the bedroom where England's Henry V died of dysentery in 1422. (☎ *01 43 28 15 48. Mon-Sun: 10am-5pm.*)

The Bois de Vincennes was almost cleared to become a military training site in the 19th century, but was spared following the public success of the Bois de Boulogne. It was then landscaped in a similar style with lakes, waterfalls and slopes.

Bois de Vincennes

Attractions in the park include the **Vincennes Zoo**, the **Floral Park** with children's amusements, a racetrack, the **Buddhist Temple**, a theatre and a baseball field.

Eating and Drinking

The majority of restaurants in this area are centred around the main squares such as **Place de la Nation** and **Place de la République**, and along the boulevards that extend from them.

Menilmontant

After relaxing in the **Parc des Buttes Chaumont**, try the nearby **L'Olympe** (page 158) for Middle Eastern cuisine, or **Chinatown** (page 159) where every evening karaoke draws crowds of Parisians and visitors alike. A multilingual song list ensures that anyone can take the spotlight.

Late-night restaurants and cafés create a vibrant atmosphere in **Menilmontant**. The main thoroughfare is the **rue Oberkampf**.

L'Olympe *for less*

North African / Oriental

62 rue Botzaris, 19th
☎ 01 42 01 01 36

Average meal: 150-200F
for less discount: 20%
AM/VS

HOURS

Tue-Sun: 12noon-3pm, 7.30pm-10pm. Mon: closed

L'Olympe is located opposite the Parc des Buttes Chaumont. It serves specialities such as *couscous* and *tajines.* Also available are traditional pastries and mint tea.

Le Savoyard *for less*

French

3 avenue du Trône, 11th
☎ 01 43 73 06 13

Average meal: 150-200F
for less discount: 20%
AM/VS/MC/DC

HOURS

Mon-Sat: 12noon-2pm, 7.30pm-10.30pm. Sun: closed

Le Savoyard serves traditional French dishes. The speciality here is cuisine from the Savoy region in the east of France. Particularly recommended is the *fondue savoyarde* and the *tartiflette.*

Le Navarin

French

**3 avenue
Philippe Auguste, 11th
☎ 01 43 67 17 49**

Average meal: 100-150F
for less discount: 20%
VS/MC

HOURS

Mon-Fri: 12noon-2pm,
7pm-10pm.
Sat: 7pm-10pm.
Sun: 12noon-2pm.

Le Navarin is located close to Place de la Nation. It serves traditional French dishes such as *foie gras* and lamb specialities. The décor in the restaurant is charming and old-fashioned.

 # Chinatown

Chinese / Karaoke

**27-29 rue du
Buisson St-Louis, 10th
☎ 01 42 38 19 28**

Average meal: 100-150F
for less discount: 20%
AM/VS/MC

HOURS

Mon-Sun: 12noon-3pm,
7pm-2am.
Karaoke: 9pm-2am.

Chinatown specializes in traditional Chinese cuisine, and Thai and Vietnamese dishes are also served. The informal, friendly restaurant doubles as a venue for karaoke evenings.

 # Sin an Kiang

Chinese / Thai

**8 avenue de la
République, 11th
☎ 01 47 00 43 05**

Average meal: 100-150F
for less discount: 20%
AM/VS/MC/DC

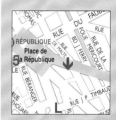

HOURS

Mon-Sun: 12noon-
2.30pm, 7pm-11pm

Sin an Kiang has been serving fine food for nearly 30 years. The restaurant has an authentic Chinese feel, and the oriental specialities include *canard Pékinois,* or Peking Duck.

HOURS

Mon-Sat: 12noon-2.30pm,
7pm-10.30pm.
Sun: closed

Da Pippo

Italian

**47 avenue de
St-Mandé, 12th
☎ 01 43 44 91 25**

Average meal: 100-150F
for less discount: 20%
AM/VS/MC

Da Pippo has an informal, friendly atmosphere. House specialities include delicious fresh pasta dishes. Try the *scampi fritti* or one of their special Gorgonzola sauce dishes.

HOURS

Mon-Fri: 12noon-
12midnight.
Sat: 7pm-1am.
Sun: closed

Les Fleurs du Berry

French

**197 avenue Daumesnil, 12th
☎ 01 43 43 24 61**

Average meal: 100-150F
for less discount: 20%
AM/VS/MC/DC

This restaurant is close to the Place Félix Éboué. It takes its name from the Berry area in the centre of the country, and the delicious regional specialities include *escargots en noisette*.

HOURS

Mon-Sun: 11.30am-
3.30pm, 6.30pm-
10.30pm.

La Sardana

Spanish

**4 rue de Chaligny, 12th
☎ 01 43 43 02 84**

Average meal: 100-150F
for less discount: 20%
AM/VS/MC/DC

Le Sardana specializes in classic dishes from the Catalan area. Enjoy your meal in friendly and cosy surroundings. Try the Serano ham or the delicious tortillas.

Au Bon Coin

French

10 rue Pixiérécourt, 20th
☎ 01 46 36 67 71

Average meal: 50-100F
for less discount: 20%
AM/VS/MC

HOURS

Mon-Sat: 6am-6pm
Sun: closed

Au Bon Coin has a mouth-watering French menu which changes every day. The décor is charming and traditional to reflect the food, and this characterful restaurant has been a location for several films.

La Nouvelle Epoque

French

15 bis rue de Chaligny, 12th
☎ 01 43 43 33 29

Average meal: 50-100F
for less discount: 20%
AM/VS/MC

HOURS

Mon-Sat: 12noon-2pm,
7pm-10.30pm. Sun:
closed

La Nouvelle Epoque serves traditional French food. The décor in the restaurant is old-fashioned and elegant, and classic dishes such as *foie gras* and *escargots* are on the menu.

La Saporita

Italian

156 blvd Voltaire, 11h
☎ 01 43 79 52 66

Average meal: 50-100F
for less discount: 20%
AM/VS

HOURS

Mon-Sat: 12noon-2.30pm,
7pm-11.30pm.
Sun: closed

La Saporita offers traditional Italian fare. Authentic Sicilian dishes are a particular speciality here. The delicious food is complemented by the charming, relaxed atmosphere.

Shopping

The ethnic diversity of the **Belleville** area is reflected in its shops, most of which are small and independently

owned. Despite the trendy eateries springing up here and in nearby **Menilmontant**, this is as far from touristy Paris as one can get and the prices of goods here are lower than in central Paris.

This is also the place to sample cuisine from around the globe. Many *traiteurs* sell snacks and samplings of their cuisine on the street where a passerby can pick up a Turkish dessert or a treat from North Africa without spoiling dinner. If possible, visit on a Tuesday or Friday when the **boulevard de Belleville** is transformed into a street market.

Shopping in Belleville

Richard

Hairdressing

182 avenue Daumesnil, 12th
☎ **01 43 07 97 82**

for less discount: 20%
AM/VS/MC

HOURS

Tue-Fri: 9.30am-7pm. Sat: 9am-6pm.
Sun-Mon: closed

Richard's salon is known and recommended throughout Paris. The speciality here is haute-coiffure for men. Richard's prides itself on cutting hair to its clients' specifications.

British Shoes

Shoes

8 rue de Prague, 12th
☎ **01 43 41 98 18**

for less discount: 20%
VS/MC

HOURS

Mon-Fri: 12noon-7pm.
Sat: 10am-7pm.
Sun: closed

British Shoes stocks excellent brands in quality materials. There are city and country styles for men and women. Famous names include Timberland, Alden and Paraboot.

Place d'Italie and Paris South

Introduction . . .

This area, which is made up almost entirely of the 13th *arrondissement*, is largely residential and commercial. Until recently it was somewhat neglected and

Place d'Italie

desolate. Until quite recently **Place d'Italie**'s only claim to fame was being the location of the first horse-butcher in France.

All this began to change when President Mitterrand chose this outer part of the Left Bank as the site of the new **Bibliothèque Nationale** (page 167). As the last of the *grands projets* intended to spruce up the more neglected parts of Paris, like La Villette and La Défense, it seemed that the most southerly *arrondissement* was about to receive a long-overdue facelift.

REFLECTIONS

'I enjoyed seeing Paris again; I looked at the boulevards, the rue de Rivoli, the sidewalks, as though I were back among them after being away a hundred years; and I don't know why, but I felt happy in the midst of all that noise and all that human flood' - *The Letters of Gustave Flaubert*

The additional plans involved its transformation into a modern residential and commercial neighbourhood, with improved links to the centre of town. The development seems to have slowed, however, perhaps due to the

Bibliothèque Nationale

public disappointment with the 8 billion franc library, which is said to have worryingly leaky foundations due to its proximity to the Seine.

The area does, however, have some points of historical interest. As the home of the **Manufacture Nationale des Gobelins**, it has played an important part in the history of the city.

Chinatown

The famous tapestry factory was founded in the early 17th century and functions both as a production centre and as a residential school for the hand-picked, carefully trained apprentices (artist-weavers) who carry on the traditional trade of exquisite tapestry-making.

. . . Introduction

The area is also home to Paris's **Chinatown**, located in the largely high-rise, south-eastern corner from **rue Tolbiac** to the **boulevard périphérique**. The residents here are immigrants from China, Vietnam, Laos, Cambodia, Thailand and various other Asian countries, and have given this area a delightful community feel.

It is at its liveliest at Chinese New Year, when the streets fill with colourful parades, music and dancing.

The area south of the rue Tolbiac is a gastronome's delight, with restaurants, shops and supermarkets selling an enviable choice of Far Eastern dishes and ingredients.

Buddhist Temple, Chinatown

The other 'village' in this otherwise soulless area is **Butte-aux-Cailles**, largely ignored by tourists and Parisians alike. Its several points of interest, good cafés and restaurants, and community atmosphere make it a valuable find.

The rue de la Butte-aux-Cailles is a winding, cobbled street which was the site of the landing of the first manned balloon flight, and the neighbouring, almost

rural streets share its unspoilt feel.

The area's ambience is a combination of the fashionable social

Cité Universitaire

scene and a traditional working community, with workers' co-operative retaurants sitting side-by-side with trendy bistros.

South-west of the Butte-aux-Cailles is the lovely **Parc Montsouris** (page 169), neighbour to the extensive, multicultural campus of the **Cité Universitaire** (page 168). This was founded in 1920 and still provides accommodation for thousands of foreign University of Paris students every year.

Manufacture des Gobelins

The Gobelin family established themselves as dyers and tanners in the early part of the 16th century, and were set apart from their competitors in this part of the city as a result of their discovery of a new scarlet dye.

Their factory, the **Manufacture des Gobelins**, began to produce tapestries in the 17th century under the decree of Louis XIV, who assembled the most talented craftsmen in the country in a quest to build an unrivalled tapestry industry for France.

As they perfected their technique, the weavers became the official suppliers to royalty. The Palace of Versailles was decorated with many of their tapestries, and the intricate style became well-known throughout the world.

ADDRESS

42 avenue des Gobelins,
13th *arrondissement*
☎ 01 44 61 21 69

GETTING THERE

Métro: Gobelins

HOURS

Guided tours:
Tue-Thu: 2pm

PRICES

Adult 45F
Child 35F
(under 7 free)
Senior 35F
Student 35F

During the 1848 revolution the area south of the Manufacture des Gobelins, around the Place d'Italie, was the scene of a temporary victory for the radicals (many of them Gobelins weavers and workers), when they forced a government general to sign a treaty promising to give aid to the needy in Paris.

However, this was not honoured, and the radicals

Manufacture des Gobelins

paid greatly for their daring. Post-revolution governments suppressed the production of original tapestries and instead had the weavers churn out tapestry copies of oil paintings. This was rectified after the Commune of 1871 and the weaving became decorative and original again.

Until 1910 the area was home to the river Bièvre, which ran beside the factory. However, it was covered over after it became a health-hazard, having been polluted by the Gobelins dyes.

Despite all these set-backs, tapestries are still made today using the old methods; it is misleading to think of the Manufacture des Gobelins as a factory, as the technique involves painstakingly slow handiwork.

It is open for guided tours, during which visitors can watch the process and visit the adjoining 18th-century chapel.

Other Attractions . . .

The last of Mitterand's *grand projets* of development, the new **Bibliothèque Nationale**, towers by the Seine at the edge of the 13th *arrondissement*.

A competition was launched to determine the design of the building, and was won by Dominique Perrault, hitherto unknown.

Bibliothèque Nationale

Bibliothèque Nationale

Four towers, supposed to look like open books, flank a concrete square and sunken gardens. It all looked good on paper, but unfortunately the real thing is far from attractive, the glass walls having had to be modified with screens that are more conducive to the protection of printed material.

The Parisian response to the new building has not been positive. Although the need for more space for the ever-growing collection is appreciated, they lament the fact that it is moving from the stately building in the 2nd *arrondissement* (see page 59) to this edge-of-town eyesore, known derisively as the TGB (Très Grande Bibliothèque).

Saltpêtriere hospital

Nevertheless, more than 10 million books have been moved here from the old Bibliothèque Nationale to join the CD-Rom resources and expansive sound and picture archives. *(Quai François-Mauriac, 13th, ☎ 01 53 79 59 59. Tue-Sat: 10am-7pm. Sun: 12noon-6pm. Mon: closed.)*

Close by is the gigantic **Saltpêtrière** hospital, once the largest hospital in the world. Under Louis XIV it functioned as an orphanage, a workhouse for the poor and a prison for prostitutes and female offenders.

It later became a research centre into mental illness, and, in the 1880s, was briefly the workplace of Sigmund Freud.

Saltpêtrière hospital

South of rue Tolbiac, towards **Chinatown**, there are some attractive 19th-century buildings, a few interesting modern structures and a Salvation Army building designed by Le Corbusier at 12 rue Cantagrel.

. . . Other Attractions . . .

The Chinese atmosphere is prevalent here, and in Avenue d'Ivry there is a lantern-bedecked **Buddhist temple**.

Château de Reine Blanche

The **Cité Universitaire**, on the edge of the 14th *arrondissement*, is the part of the University of Paris set aside for its 5,000 foreign

Buddhist temple

students. Its buildings are built in the typical architectural styles of different countries. You can walk around the lively, landscaped campus and admire the buildings, some of which are the designs of famous architects such as Le Corbusier. *(19-21 boulevard Jourdan, 14th, ☎ 01 44 16 64 00.)*

Well hidden among workshops is a piece of Gobelins heritage: the fairy-tale **Château de Reine Blanche** (4 rue Gustave-Geffroy). This was built by the Gobelin family in the 16th century on the site

Cité Universitaire

of a previous castle built for Queen Blanche. The remains are not open to the public, but you can look at the delicate architecture of the exterior.

The **Paris Observatoire**, commissioned by Louis XIV in 1667, is recognizable for its white dome. The Paris meridian, which runs through it, was initially the line of longitude which provided the base measure for the world. Greenwich took over this honour in 1884, although France kept to its own meridian until 1911.

Observatoire

Observatoire

The observatory has been the centre of important astronomical discoveries and progress, such as the mapping of the moon and the discovery of Neptune. *(61 avenue de l'Observatoire, 14th, ☎ 01 40 51 22 21. Tours only on the first Saturday of the month: write in advance to book.)*

. . . Other Attractions

Paris's grisliest attraction is located underground here. The **Catacombes** were originally quarries, dug out in Roman times to provide stone. In 1785 it was decided that the corpses should be removed from Paris's overcrowded cemeteries and stored here instead.

The removals took more than a year, with decomposing bodies being wheeled through the streets of the city after dark.

Catacombes

Catacombes

Visitors can walk the mile (1½ km) of underground tunnels, neatly lined with the skeletons of pre-1785 Parisians. The inscription above the doorway welcomes you to the "Empire of the Dead", where famous remains include those of Mirabeau and Madame de Pompadour. *(1 place Denfert-Rochereau, 14ᵗʰ, ☎ 01 43 22 47 63. Tue-Fri: 2pm-4pm. Sat-Sun: 9am-11am, 2pm-4pm. Adult 27F, child 19F, senior 19F, student 19F.)*

Open Spaces

The **Parc Montsouris**, beside the Cité Universitaire, is one of the most delightful parks in Paris and well worth the *RER* trip to reach it.

It was landscaped under the auspices of Haussmann in 1865 as part of his campaign to make the city a greener place.

Parc Montsouris

Landscape gardener Alphand, who designed the Parc des Buttes-Chaumont (page 155) repeated his successful formula of valleys, thickets, lakes and grottos.

Today the park is popular with the neighbouring students but big enough to guarantee finding an isolated spot to picnic or sunbathe. Huge pines line the hillsides,

Parc Montsouris

wooden bridges span the clear streams and there are many colourful flowerbeds.

Look carefully around the banks of the large lake and you may see turtles basking in the sun.

Eating and Drinking

Paris's **Chinatown**, like its namesakes in London and New York, is an ideal place to come for a cheap and

filling meal. It has a multitude of bustling Oriental restaurants which offer delicious, authentic food from the many nearby food stores.

Regional Chinese, Japanese, Thai and even Vietnamese cuisine may be found in abundance here, lovingly prepared by those truly in the know.

Chinatown

One of the best places is **La Chine Masséna** (*13 place de Vénétie, 13th,* ☎ *01 45 83 98 88*). It seats 400 people and has a menu with 300 dishes. It is a cheap and lively place to try regional Chinese specialities, and there is Asian dancing at weekends.

The **Bangkok-Thailand** (*35 boulevard Auguste-Blanqui,* ☎ *01 45 80 76 59*) offers pure Thai food, unsullied by Chinese or other influences, in bright, kitsch surroundings with Buddhas of all shapes and sizes wherever you look.

La Chine Massena

Just as reasonable but rather more upmarket is **Dao Vien** (*82 rue Baudricourt, 13th,* ☎ *01 45 85 20 70*), a Vietnamese restaurant offering friendly service and Saigon specialities.

The **Butte-aux-Cailles** area specializes in hip bars, bistros and restaurants for a youngish crowd, reflecting the bohemian atmosphere of the area.

Chez Paul (*22 rue de la Butte-aux-Cailles, 13th,* ☎ *01 45 89 22 11*) is a chic, lively bistro which offers traditional French dishes. For Basque food and décor and a party atmosphere, try **Chez Gladine** (*30 rue des Cinq Diamants, 13th,* ☎ *01 45 80 70 10*).

Pavillion Montsouris

La Folie en Tete (*33 rue de la Butte-aux-Cailles*) is perfect for a laid-back, friendly meal and occasional musical entertainment. Its sister bistro at no. 11, **Le Merle Moqueur**, has been popular for many years and still offers good food and live bands.

One of Paris's most romantic restaurants, **Pavillion Montsouris**, is located beside the Parc Montsouris at 20 rue Gazan (☎ *01 45 88 38 52*). Mata Hari and Lenin are among those who have enjoyed the shady terrace and excellent, traditional French cuisine.

Pause Gourmande

French

**27 rue Campagne-
Première, 14th**
☎ 01 43 27 74 51

Average meal: 50-100F
for less discount: 20%
VS

HOURS

Mon-Fri: 8.30am-7pm.
Sat-Sun: closed

Pause Gourmande specializes in provençale cuisine,
serving a good range of delicious salads and savoury
tarts. For dessert, try the *gateau au chocolat avec crème
anglaise.*

Le Pascal

North African

**14 rue des
Cinq Diamants, 13th**
☎ 01 45 80 97 20

Average meal: 50-100F
for less discount: 20%
VS/MC

HOURS

Tue-Sun: 12noon-3pm,
7pm-12midnight.
Mon: closed

Le Pascal is located close to the Place d' Italie. It has
been serving Moroccan and Algerian cuisine for 25
years, and its speciality is the large selection of different
couscous dishes.

L'Art Home

Café

44 boulevard Arago, 13th
☎ 01 43 31 32 33

Average meal: 50-100F
for less discount: 20%
VS/MC

HOURS

Tue-Sat: 9.30am-8pm.
Sun: 10am-6pm.
Mon: closed.

L'Art Home café holds exhibitions of the work of young
artists. In the summer you can sit outside under the trees.
Specialities include delicious cakes and old-fashioned
hot chocolate.

Shopping

Chinatown offers some unusual shopping opportunities in this area, as does the under-rated **Butte-aux-Cailles** neighbourhood. While Chinatown shops tend to concentrate on produce and cooking ingredients, Butte-aux-Cailles is cashing in on its slowly increasing tourist trade.

Butte-aux-Cailles

For an unusual gift, visit Paris's best honey shop, **Les Abeilles** *(21 rue Butte-aux-Cailles, 13ᵗʰ)*. It stocks honey from all over France and other parts of Europe.

The area's good open air food market takes place on Tuesdays, Fridays and Sunday mornings at **boulevard Auguste-Blanqui** near the Place d'Italie.

L'Atelier Bleu

Home Furnishings / Gifts

3 rue de la Butte aux Cailles, 13ᵗʰ
☎ 01 45 80 58 33

for less discount: 20%
No credit cards

HOURS

Tue-Sat: 11am-1pm,
3pm-7.30pm.
Sun-Mon: closed

L'Atelier Bleu sells hand-painted furniture and items for the home. Choose a creatively decorated frame or candlestick for a great gift. The artist makes sketches from your photos and adds a personalized border.

Laquaris

Jewellery / Gifts

7 blvd de Port Royal, 13ᵗʰ
☎ 01 47 07 10 91

for less discount: 20%
AM/VS/MC/DC

HOURS

Tue-Sat: 10am-7pm.
Sun-Mon: closed

All the items in this unique shop have a maritime connection. There is a great selection of jewellery made of pearls and seashells. Among the original gift ideas are starfish, coral, minerals and rocks.

Montparnasse

Introduction. . .

Montparnasse began life as the haunt of students, an all-night venue for drunken revelry and poetry readings. Its name is a derivation of Mount Parnassus, the holy mountain of Apollo, god of poetry and art.

During the Middle Ages the area became the chief supplier of flour for the Left Bank bakeries, and its windmills remained until the end of the 18th-century. The main thoroughfare, boulevard Montparnasse, was completed in 1761.

Gare Montparnasse

REFLECTIONS

'Paris was the place that suited those of us that were to create the twentieth-century art and literature, naturally enough' - Gertrude Stein

It became an elegant promenade, but the area only began to develop its own identity at the beginning of the 19th century, when a flurry of dancehalls and cabarets opened up.

It became residential after the opening of the **Montparnasse railway station**, serving Brittany, and a strongly Breton community developed here.

Montparnasse station was the site of a spectacular accident in 1895 when a steam engine, failing to stop, shot out of the front of the building and landed in the square. No-one on the train was hurt, although a woman in the street was killed. The old station was replaced by a new glass-fronted one in 1974.

Montparnasse, like Montmartre, is famous as the home of writers, philosophers and artists.

In the late 19th century Verlaine and Baudelaire lived here. They were followed by Modigliani at the turn of the century, who left Montmartre in protest at the rising rents. At the beginning of this century the area became the centre of development of Cubism when Picasso moved to the neighbourhood.

La Coupole, a favourite café of Hemingway's

The eastern part of the 15th *arrondissement* also has an artistic heritage. **La Ruche**, a polygonal design of Gustave Eiffel's, was built as the wine pavilion for the

. . . Introduction

1900 World Fair and re-erected off the rue de Dantzig as studios for struggling artists who included Chagall and Fernand Léger.

Gertrude and Leo Stein established themselves here before the First World War. At this time, too, the area was popular with Russian revolutionaries, Lenin and Trotsky among them.

La Ruche

However, the real heyday of Montparnasse was between the wars, and it is more famous for its American residents than the native French. Nightclubs began to spring up after the First World War, as did the first all-night bar in Paris.

Many Americans, including Hemingway, Miller and Scott Fitzgerald came, partly to escape prohibition, and spent much of their time in the cafés around Montparnasse, many of which still remain (page 179).

An added bonus for the exiles was the good exchange rate: Americans moving to Paris between the wars were instantly rich, which allowed them to pursue a hedonistic lifestyle.

The Second World War signalled the end of

Institut Pasteur

Montparnasse's hedonism. The artists, many of whom were Jewish, fled to safer locations, and the Germans took over the boulevard Montparnasse cafés.

By the time the war was over, St-Germain-des-Prés had taken over as the centre of Parisian nightlife, although it was never to capture the carefree atmosphere of the 1920s and 30s. Today, parts of the area have been spoilt by new buildings such as the ugly **Tour Montparnasse**, but other parts, including the Boulevard Montparnasse, still boast lively nightlife and attractive architecture.

REFLECTIONS

'How 'ya gonna keep 'em down on the farm (after they've seen Paree)? - Sam M. Lewis and Joe Young, American songwriters

Tour Montparnasse

Montparnasse Attractions . . .

The **Tour Montparnasse** is the tallest office building in France. It is said to have the best view in Paris because it is the only place in the city from which it cannot be seen.

You can ride up to the open terrace for spectacular 25 mile (40km) views, or go to the bar on the 56th storey

Tour Montparnasse

(three floors from the top) for enclosed surveillance. *(33 avenue du Maine, 15th, ☎ 01 45 38 52 56. Mon-Sun: 9.30am-10.30pm. Adult 42F, child 26F, senior 36F, student 33F.)*

The area is home to a remarkable church, **Notre Dame du Travail** (Our Lady of Work) *(59 rue Vercingetorix, 14th)*. The ironwork building was designed at the turn of the century and displays an unusual Art Nouveau interior.

The **Musée Antoine Bourdelle** is a frequently overlooked delight, hidden down a side street of newish blocks near to the Tour Montparnasse.

Musée Bourdelle

This collection of Bourdelle's sculpted works is displayed in his former studios and apartments. The ivy-covered courtyard garden dotted with some of his stunning bronzes is perhaps the highlight of the museum.

The workshops and apartments are reached from the gardens: closed doors do not mean you are not permitted to enter the little rooms. A second, narrow garden is lined with busts and statues and evokes a silent, almost eerie atmosphere.

The great hall exhibits larger sculptures and Bourdelle's sparse apartments are the setting for some of his private possessions. A new extension displays his tools, photographs of him at work and the works of other sculptors in temporary exhibitions. *(18 rue Antoine Bourdelle, 15th, ☎ 01 49 54 73 73. Tue-Sun: 10am-5.40pm. Adult 27F, chid 19F, senior 19F, student 19F.)*

Musée de la Poste

Just around the corner, the **Musée de la Poste** is undergoing renovations until 1999 but is open for several temporary exhibitions, covering such themes as football-related stamp art and 18th-century

. . . Montparnasse Attractions

postcards. *(34 boulevard de Vaugirard, 15th, ☎ 01 42 79 23 45. Mon-Sat: 10am-6pm. Adult 25F, child 15F (under 8 free), senior 15F, student 25F. Call for dates of temporary exhibitions.)*

for less The **Musée Pasteur** comprises the living quarters of Louis Pasteur, the famous microbiologist. They are part of the Institut Pasteur, which is still a working research centre.

Institut Pasteur

The rooms have been fully restored to the way they

would have been in Pasteur's day. The portraits, paintings, ornaments and trinkets give the visitor an insight into the home life of the great man.

There are portraits of his family, and a special collection of the instruments that Pasteur used in his research, including lenses, test tubes and flasks. Visitors can also see his tomb, which lies in a specially built, ornate funeral chapel. *(25 rue de Docteur Roux, 15th, ☎ 01 45 68 82 83. Mon-Fri: 2pm-5.30pm. Sat-Sun: closed. Closed in August. Adult 15F, Child 8F, Senior 15F, Student 8F. 2 for the price of 1 with voucher on page 275.)*

Institut Pasteur

Aquaboulevard

for less **Aquaboulevard** is located just outside the city boundaries. This Water Park is known as the 'beach of Paris', and comprises pools, slides, watersports and games. It is a great place to spend a day whatever the weather, as the indoor attractions are maintained at a constant temperature of 29°C (85°F).

In addition to indoor and outdoor swimming pools, water slides and beaches, there are waterways for boating and water-tobogganing. There is plenty to do for visitors of all ages and swimming abilities.

In the summer there is an outdoor beach area, so that you can soak up the sun without travelling to the real coast.

The complex also caters for more sedentary pursuits with bars, restaurants and a games room. *(4 rue Louis Armand, 15th, ☎ 01 40 60 10 00. Mon-Thu: 9am-11pm. Fri: 9am-12midnight. Sat: 8am-12pm. Sun: 8am-11pm. Weekends: Adult 77F, Child 56F. Week: Adult 69F, Child 50F. 2 for the price of 1 with voucher on page 275.)*

Aquaboulevard

Open Spaces

Montparnasse cemetery, founded in 1824, is the resting place for many of the famous people who made this area their home. The 44 acre (18 hectare) plot is the second-largest cemetery in Paris.

Montparnasse cemetery

Napoleon commissioned the cemetery to replace the many cramped burial grounds in the centre of the city, which were becoming a health hazard.

Like the Cimetière du Père Lachaise (page 156), it is criss-crossed with tree-lined paths which divide it into areas.

Among the notable figures buried here are Jean-Paul Sartre, who lived on boulevard Raspail, Andre Citröen, Guy de Maupassant and César Frank.

Parc Georges-Brassens

A Cenotaph in memory of Baudelaire, sculpted by José de Charmoy, stands near the middle of the cemetery, and the centrepiece is a bronze angel, 'Eternal Sleep', by Daillion.

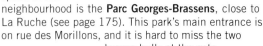

A bronze bull outside the Parc Georges-Brassens

The only other open space in the neighbourhood is the **Parc Georges-Brassens**, close to La Ruche (see page 175). This park's main entrance is on rue des Morillons, and it is hard to miss the two bronze bulls at the gate.

Parc Georges-Brassens

The park, a sea of trees in the midst of some quite ugly apartment buildings, is on the site of the Vaugirard cattlemarket and abattoir. The clocktower from the original building is still standing, inscribed 'Vente à la criée' (Sale by Auction).

There is a pond, a scented garden for the blind, rocks, streams and even a vineyard. Every weekend the neighbouring rue Briançon hosts a market of old books just outside the gates.

Eating and Drinking

Boulevard de Montparnasse is lively with legendary cafés, many of which were frequented by the American expatriates at the beginning of this century. **La Rotonde**, at 105 boulevard du Montparnasse, was the favourite of the Russian revolutionaries and was often

visited by Edna St. Vincent Millay, the American poet, during her 1922 sojourn in Paris. Picasso and Modigliani also enjoyed many evenings here.

La Rotonde

La Rotonde

The **Café du Dôme**, opposite La Rotonde, was one of the favourites of Ernest Hemingway and his circle. Nowadays it is the most touristy of them all.

La Coupole, at no. 102, has retained most of its Art Deco features and remains one of the trendiest places to be seen in Paris. The pillars supporting the ceiling of the huge dining room were decorated by the artists who frequented it, applying their decorative skills in return for a meal. Léger and Chagall were among them.

Le Select, at no. 99, was another of Hemingway's haunts. It was the rowdiest of the cafés, the location of many a fight in the 1920s. One of them involved the dancer Isadora Duncan, who was arguing the case for a pair of convicted anarchists.

Le Select

Bergamote

French

1 rue Niepce, 14th
☎ **01 43 22 79 47**

Average meal: 100-150F
for less discount: 20%
AM/VS/MC

HOURS

Tue-Sat: 12noon-2.30pm, 7.30pm-10.30pm. Sun-Mon: closed. Aug: closed. Fri-Sat night by reservation.

This restaurant has a range of delicious provençale dishes. Try a traditional speciality such as the *daube provençale aux côtes du Rhône*. There are mouthwatering desserts and a good wine list.

Palais du Agra

Indian

142 avenue du Maine, 14th
☎ 01 43 21 00 21

Average meal: 100-150F
for less discount: 20%
VS/MC

Mon-Sun: 12noon-
2.30pm, 7pm-11.30pm.

Enjoy an Indian meal in these exuberant surroundings. The specialities include chicken or lamb *kofta agra*. Try *anarkali* (red) or *chabari* (white) Indian wine with your meal.

L'Amanguier

French

46 blvd du
Montparnasse, 15th
☎ 01 45 48 49 16

Average meal: 100-150F
for less discount: 20%
with voucher on page 281
AM/VS/DC

Mon-Sun: 12noon-3pm,
8pm-12midnight

Dining at L'Amanguier is in a relaxed, garden atmosphere. The imaginative dishes are made from the freshest ingredients, and there are delicious meals and snacks to suit any appetite.

Le Sawa

Cameroonian

196 avenue du Maine, 14th
☎ 01 45 43 12 88

Average meal: 100-150F
for less discount: 20%
VS/MC

Mon-Sat: 12noon-2.30pm,
7pm-12midnight.
Sun: closed

Cameroonian cuisine is rich with spices and flavours. Try the *ndomba*, lamb cooked in banana leaves with coconut milk. The African masks and plants give the restaurant an authentic feel.

Shopping

There is a branch of **Galeries Lafayette** at the Montparnasse shopping mall which is barely comparable to the grand original in the 9th *arrondissement* (page 64). The mall itself has little atmosphere but is handy for bargain hunting or holiday essentials.

The **rue d'Alesia**, which runs through the middle of the 14th *arrondissement* towards Chinatown, is the setting for an attractive open-air food market on Thursdays and Sundays. The street is also known for its good *dépot-ventes* and other inexpensive clothes stores. Look out for the **Salle des Ventes**, more an indoor market than a shop, with old jewellery, china and other French trinkets to inspire gift-buying. *(123 rue d'Alésia, ☎ 01 45 45 54 54.)*

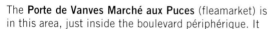

Fleamarket at Vanves

The **Porte de Vanves Marché aux Puces** (fleamarket) is in this area, just inside the boulevard périphérique. It dates back many centuries, and is a great place to rummage through bric-a-brac in search of a real treasure. Serious collectors and dealers can often be seen here, and it is best to arrive early in the morning before the bargains disappear.

Books, postcards, china, furniture and linens dominate the charming stalls, which line avenues Marc Sangnier and Georges Lafenestre up to the Porte de Vanves *métro* stop. There is a market here every weekend, and on Sundays it is joined by a food market.

Rue d'Alésia

 ## Caillou

Jewellery

71 rue Lecourbe, 15th
☎ 01 43 06 53 19

for less discount: 20%
AM/VS/MC

HOURS

Mon-Sat: 9.30am-7.30pm.
Sun: closed

Caillou sells a wide range of jewellery for all occasions. There are items made with pearls, rubies, emeralds and cubic zirconias. You will find a good range of engagement and wedding rings here.

Women's Clothing

111 rue d'Alésia, 14th
☎ **01 45 42 19 09**

for less discount: 20%
AM/VS/MC/DC

HOURS

Mon-Sun: 10.30am-
7.30pm. Sun: closed

Womens' ready-to-wear designer labels are the speciality at Perlyne. There is a wide selection of items by George's Rech, and other designs represented include those by La Perla and Rochas.

Melbury

Shoes

139 rue d'Alésia, 14th
☎ **01 45 42 96 38**

for less discount: 20%
AM/VS/MC

HOURS

Tue-Sat: 10am-7pm. Mon:
1pm-7pm.
Sun: closed

Melbury has sold shoes at this location for more than 30 years. There are English-made shoes of the highest quality for men, and for women, the best designer names are stocked.

Le Comptoir de la Mode

Women's Clothing

118 rue d'Alésia, 14th
☎ **01 40 44 78 97**

for less discount: 20%
AM/VS/MC/DC

HOURS

Mon-Sat: 10.30am-
7.30pm.
Sun: closed

This shop sells great brands at reasonable prices, with women's garments of every style in stock. You will find items here by Valentino, Givenchy, Nina Ricci and Escada.

Paris West

Introduction. . .

Paris West is one of the most select areas in which to live. It is made up of the expensive 16th *arrondissement*, the west side of the 15th to the Seine,

and is bordered by the Bois de Boulogne. It has tree-lined, broad avenues, attractive houses and apartments, and has a similar ambiance to London's Mayfair or New York's Park Avenue.

Smart houses in the 16th

The area started life as two villages, **Passy** and **Auteuil**, which merged to make a separate *quartier* in 1860. The former villages have managed to retain their distinctive architecture and styles.

Passy has *belle époque* apartment blocks and a provincial air. In the 18th century its thermal springs attracted Parisians, and the royal court resided in the Château de la Muette for a time.

Castel Béranger

All that remains of the Muette estate today is the **Jardin du Ranelagh** (page 190) on the west. The opulence has remained, however, with expensive apartments dominating the surrounding streets.

REFLECTIONS

'This great city appears to be in many respects the most ineligible and inconvenient for the residence of a person of small fortune that I have seen; and vastly inferior to London' - Arthur Young

Honoré de Balzac, author of *Le Père Goriot*, lived in the area from 1840 to 1847 (see page 187). Other famous visitors and residents are buried in the little Passy cemetery, including Debussy and Manet.

Auteuil, an ecclesiastical settlement, was famous for its vines until the Revolution. It was annexed to the village of Boulogne, now a suburb of Paris, until the 14th century. Like Passy, it had thermal springs renowned for their supposed health-giving qualities, and Molière and Racine were among those who sampled them.

Maison de Balzac

It was later the home of **Proust**, who lived on the rue La Fontaine. After a period of neglect in the 19th

. . . Introduction

century, when it became a largely industrial area, it was refurbished with the architectural masterpieces of Hector Guimard. He was the designer of the Art Nouveau *métro* entrances and the carved advertising boards inside many of the stations.

Buildings by Le Corbusier

Guimard's buildings incorporate features such as wrought-ironwork and tiling. He designed his houses in meticulous detail, even specifying the kind of furniture. His most famous construction is Castel Béranger at 14 rue La Fontaine. Built in 1895 as an apartment building, it was dubbed 'Castle Dérangé' (Crazy Castle) by Guimard's critics, but won a prize for its distinctive façade.

Art Nouveau métro entrance by Guimard

The area is also a showcase for the buildings of Le Corbusier, the Swiss modernist architect (page 189).

The **Bois de Boulogne**, bordering the west of the 16th *arrondissement*, is the Hyde Park or Central Park of Paris, with twice as much history and mythology surrounding it. Until the reign of Louis XI, who made it a hunting reserve, it was a thick forest, home to Parisian Robin Hoods and gangs of bandits.

Napoleon III, having seen Hyde Park in London,

Bois de Boulogne

wanted something like it for Paris and so commissioned Haussmann to emulate it and opened the Bois de Boulogne to the public.

Nowadays, it is criss-crossed with paths and roads and is a pleasant, organized arrangement of gardens, grassy areas, lakes and woods. By day it is a pleasant place to walk, but it has always had something of a reputation at night, ever since being used as an illicit rendezvous for lovers in the 17th century.

ADDRESS

17 place du Trocadéro, 16th *arrondissement*

GETTING THERE

Métro: Trocadéro

HOURS / PRICES

Cinémathèque Française
(☎ 01 45 53 21 86):
Wed & Sun: 7pm & 9pm
Tickets 28F

Musée des Monuments
(☎ 01 44 05 39 10):
Wed-Mon: 10am-6pm
Adult 36F
Others 24F

Musée de la Marine
(☎ 01 45 53 31 70):
Wed-Mon: 10am-6pm
Adult 38F
Others 25F

Musée du Cinéma Henri
Langlois
(☎ 01 45 53 21 86):
Guided tours every hour
Wed-Sun: 10am-5pm
Adult 30F
Others 20F

Musée de l'Homme
(☎ 01 44 05 72 72):
Wed-Mon: 10am-5pm
Adult 30F
Child 20F

Palais de Chaillot

The **Palais de Chaillot** was built for the 1937 Paris Exhibition in the neo-classical style. The square between its two pavilions is a gathering-place for jugglers, skateboarders and rollerbladers, and the two colonnaded wings house four museums and a cinema (see page 205).

Palais de Chaillot

The **Musée du Cinéma Henri Langlois** comprises thousands of examples of film memorabilia, including props, costumes, scripts, stills, even preserved film sets.

The **Musée des Monuments Français** is in the same wing. It opened in 1880 and displays models and reproductions of architecture in France. At the time of writing this wing and both the museums are closed indefinitely for refurbishment.

The **Musée de l'Homme** is devoted to anthropology, ethnography and archaeology, with exhibits to illustrate the cultural and artistic heritage of many different parts of the world.

Gilt statues decorate the Palais

Items on display include shrunken heads, musical instruments, tribal uniforms, fetishes and mummies, frescoes and statues.

The neigbouring **Musée de la Marine** is a fascinating history of all things nautical. The exhibits follow maritime developments from the earliest boats to today's advanced submarines and navigation systems.

The museum's curved halls house Napoleon's own barge, scale models, seafaring paintings, displays of navigational instruments, huge ropes, lighthouse lamps and audiovisual exhibits.

Following the display chronologically is a little difficult owing to the layout of the museum, but all periods of French maritime history are covered, and there are even earlier exhibits from other parts of the world.

Other Attractions . . .

for less The **Musée du Vin** is housed within the beautifully preserved 14th-century cellars of the old Passy Abbey.

It was home to the Minim monks, who grew their vines on nearby Chaillot Hill until the closure of the Abbey during the French Revolution.

Musée du Vin

Musée du Vin

The museum charts the history of wine making and examines the traditional and modern techniques of the wine-producing regions of the country. In addition, there are displays of artefacts such as bottles, corkscrews and other tools of the trade. It doubles as a wine bar and restaurant, and your visit finishes with a complimentary tasting. *(Rue des Eaux / 5 sq. Charles Dickens, 16th, ☎ 01 45 25 63 26. Tue-Sun: 10am-6pm. Mon: closed. Adult 35F, Child 29F, Senior 30F, Student 29F. 50% discount with your for less card.)*

La Maison de Balzac, also located in the old village of Passy, was Honoré de Balzac's home for seven years. His personal quarters, including the study where he wrote *The Human Comedy* and *Cousine Bette* are beautifully preserved.

Maison de Balzac

Balzac's letters, books, his cane and even his ever-full coffee pot are on display, alongside portraits of the famous writer by, among others, Rodin and Falguière. Visitors can also see the peaceful garden where Balzac spent many hours. *(47 rue Raynouard, 16th, ☎ 01 42 24 56 38. Tue-Sun: 10am-5.40pm. Mon: closed. Adult 17.50F, child free, senior 9F, student 9F.)*

Maison de Balzac

Radio-France

The **Musée de Radio-France** is housed in the distinctive 1963 headquarters of France's national radio and charts the history of communication to the present day. Exhibits include the first 18th-century telegraph and the latest state-of-the-art television sets. Visitors also gain an insight into how television and radio programmes are actually produced. *(116 av. du Président*

Radio France

. . . Other Attractions . . .

Musée Kwok-On

Kennedy, 16th, ☎ 01 42 30 15 16. Tours Mon-Sat: 10.30am-11.30am, 2.30pm-4.30pm. Sun: closed. Adult 18F, child 18F, senior 12F, student 12F.)

The stretch of the Seine alongside Radio-France is the location of the **Ile des Cygnes**, said to have been formed from the bones of horses. At the Pont de

Ile des Cynges

Grenelle end stands a miniature **Statue of Liberty.**

The **Musée Kwok On** specialises in folk culture from Asia, in particular the myths and legends which form part of the heritage of Asian communities.

The 10,000-item collection, which includes props from the Peking opera, Chinese festival dragons, Japanese puppets, lucky charms, masks, costumes and engravings, provides a visual history of the oral literature of many Asian countries. *(57 rue du Théâtre, 15th, ☎ 01 45 75 85 75. Mon-Fri: 10am-5pm. Sat-Sun: closed. Adult 15F, child 10F, senior 10F, student 10F.)*

Musée Dapper

Thai tapestry at the Musée Kwok-On

The **Musée Dapper** is approached through a lovely bamboo garden and hosts temporary exhibitions of African interest.

Musée Dapper

Particular subjects, such as hunting, or specific tribes or countries provide the themes for the displays. The attractive setting, a townhouse on the posh avenue Victor Hugo, has been adapted to display the precious artefacts with low-level lighting and an atmospheric soundtrack of Afrrican music. *(50 av. Victor Hugo, 16th, ☎ 01 45 00 01 50. Mon-Sun: 11am-7pm. Adult 20F, child 10F, senior 10F, student 10F.)*

. . . Other Attractions

The **Musée Marmottan** focuses on Impressionist paintings, especially those of Monet following his son's 1971 bequest of more than 150 paintings. Other artists represented here are Sisley, Pissarro and Renoir.

The museum also contains a selection of medieval manuscripts and the collection of First Empire furniture belonging to 19th- century historian Paul Marmottan. *(2 rue Louis-Boilly, 16th, ☎ 01 42 24 07 02. Tue-Sun: 10.30am-5.30pm. Mon: closed. Adult 40F, child 25F (under 8 free), senior 25F, student 25F.)*

Musée Marmottan

The **Fondation Le Corbusier**, housed in two of Le Corbusier's innovative Cubist buildings, contains the architect's letters, documents, art collections and furniture. The setting itself and the lectures about his inimitable style offer the biggest insight into his life and work. *(8-10 sq. du Docteur Blanche, 16th, ☎ 01 42 88 41 53. Mon-Fri: 10am-12.30pm, 1.30pm-6pm (5pm on Fri). Adult 15F, child 15F, senior 15F, student 10F.)*

Musée de la Contrefaçon

The unusual **Musée de la Contrefaçon** was set up by the French manufacturer's union to exhibit all types of fake luxury items, such as perfume, brandy and watches, illustrating the problems caused by counterfeiters over the years.

Musée Marmottan

To dissuade anyone from turning their hand to this lucrative business, the museum is careful to emphasize the fate awaiting those who are caught. *(16 rue de la Faisanderie, 16th, ☎ 01 45 01 51 11. Mon-Thu: 2pm-5pm. Fri: 9.30am-12noon. Sun: 2pm-6pm. Sat: closed. Adult 15F, child 15F, senior 15F, student 15F.)*

The **Musée d'Ennery** is a collection of Far Eastern artefacts dating from the 17th century onwards. Assembled by Adolphe d'Ennery in the late 19th century, the collection resides in a luxurious Napoleon III townhouse. *(59 av. Foch, 16th, ☎ 01 43 53. Thu & Sun: 2pm-5.45pm. Admission free.)*

Musée d' Ennery

Open Spaces

 The **Jardin de Ranelagh** is dwarfed by the nearby Bois de Boulogne but is popular with children for its open-air *guignol*

theatre. The **Marionnettes de Ranelagh** perform their traditional Punch and Judy-style shows on summer afternoons. *(Avenue Ingres, 16th, ☎ 01 45 83 51 75. Wed and Sat-Sun: 3.15 and 4.15pm (closed Dec-Feb). Tickets 13F. 2 for the price of 1 with your **for less** card.)*

Marionnettes de Ranelagh

Marionnettes de Ranelagh

The huge **Bois de Boulogne** borders almost all of the 16th a*rrondissement* and covers more than 2,100 acres (850 hectares). It is all that remains of the western part of the massive forest which surrounded the early settlement of Paris.

Becoming a royal park in the 13th century, it was named after a pilgrimage to Boulogne made by Philippe IV. Napoleon III renovated it and the Bois became the popular destination of weekending Parisians that it remains today.

Nowadays, the Bois comprises landscaped gardens, woodland, lakes and paths. The **Jardin de Bagatelle** surrounds one of several small *châteaux*, and the **Jardin d'Acclimatation** is an amusement park. There are even two racecourses, **Longchamp** (see page 256) and **Auteuil**.

Musée en Herbe

Jardin de Bagatelle

Musee en herbe

 For less cardholders can take advantage of the discount offered by the **Musée en Herbe**. This museum, located in the Jardin d'Acclimatation, is dedicated to introducing children to art. Permanent displays uncover the techniques of the great artists, and themed activities include prehistoric cave painting. *(☎ 01 40 67 97 66. Mon-Sun: 10am-6pm. Exhibitions 16F, workshops 25F. 2 for the price of 1 with your **for less** card.)*

Eating and Drinking

Reflecting the area's elegance, even the brasseries and cafés tend to be expensive in Paris West, despite the fact that it is not central.

Dining at **Le Pré Catalan** in the Bois de Boulogne is a delightful experience. The restaurant is one of the city's best, so it is advisable to book well ahead. The cuisine is French with Asian influences. *(Route de Suresnes, ☎ 01 45 24 55 58.)*

Le Pré Catalan

Guy Savoy has a bistro, **La Butte Chaillot**, in the 16th. Stylish Parisians dine here on food which is instantly recognizable as the creation of the best chef in Paris. *(110 bis avenue Kléber, ☎ 01 47 27 88 88.)*

 # Nikita

Russian

6 rue Faustin-Helié, 16th
☎ **01 45 04 04 33**

Average meal: 200-250F
for less discount: 20%
AM/VS/MC

HOURS

Mon-Sat: 8.30pm-2am.
Sun: closed

Nikita is sumptuously decorated in the Belle Epoque style. The Russian fare is complemented by a traditional bar. Impromptu violin concerts entertain you while you dine.

 # La Petite Tour

French

11 rue de la Tour, 16th
☎ **01 45 20 09 31**

Average meal: 200-250F
for less discount: 20%
AM/VS/MC/DC

HOURS

Mon-Sat: 12noon-2.30pm,
7.30pm-10.30pm.
Sun: closed

The chef at La Petite Tour uses traditional methods. Specialities include *escargot* casserole with aromatic spices, and the delicious desserts include home-made iced nougat.

Mon-Sun: 11.45am-
2.30pm, 7.45pm-
11.30pm.

Lal Qila

Indian

88 avenue Emile Zola, 15th
☎ 01 45 75 68 40

Average meal: 100-150F
for less discount: 20%
AM/VS/MC/DC

Lal Qila specializes in traditional tandoori dishes. The décor represents the grandeur of 16th- and 17th-century India, and Indian music adds to the authentic atmosphere.

Mon-Fri: 12noon-2.30pm,
7.30pm-11.30pm.
Sat: 7.30pm-11.30pm.
Sun: 12noon-4pm

Durand Dupont

Italian / Provençale

14 rue Cauchy, 15th
☎ 01 45 54 43 43

Average meal: 100-150F
for less discount: 20%
AM/VS/MC

Durand Dupont has an authentic Mediterranean ambiance. The table are adorned with Italian urns and bottles of olive oil. The dishes are made with fresh, aromatic ingredients.

Mon-Sun:
9am-11pm

Au Regal

Russian

4 rue Nicolo, 16th
☎ 01 42 88 49 15

Average meal: 100-150F
for less discount: 20%
VS

Au Regal has been serving fine Russian food since 1934. All the favourites are on the menu, including *bortsch* and *tarama*. Live music provides entertainment on weekend evenings.

Rajas

Indian

129 rue de la Tour, 16th
☎ 01 45 03 38 48

Average meal: 100-150F
for less discount: 20%
VS

HOURS

Mon-Sat: 12noon-2pm,
7pm-11pm. Sun: closed

Rajas is the perfect place for a relaxing meal. The specialities are dishes from the Indian subcontinent, and there is a huge range of curries and accompaniments to suit all palates.

La Villa des Anges

Italian

45 avenue Emile Zola, 15th
☎ 01 45 79 98 52

Average meal: 100-150F
for less discount: 20%
AM/VS/MC

HOURS

Mon-Sun: 12noon-3pm,
7pm-11pm

La Villa des Anges serves a great selection of the finest Italian cuisine. The owner recommends the delicious *veal saltimbocca*. The relaxing restaurant is decorated like a veranda.

L'Infini

French

15 rue Mesnil, 16th
☎ 01 47 55 96 44

Average meal: 50-100F
for less discount: 20%
VS/MC

HOURS

Mon-Fri: 11am-3pm.
Group reservations only in
the evening

The delicious French cuisine at L'Infini includes *gigot d'agneau*. The fresh dishes are based around traditional market produce, and the décor is reminiscent of the country, with dried flowers and sunny colours.

Shopping

The proximity of the *haute couture* fashion houses in the neighbouring 8th *arrondissement* and the sheer wealth of the residential area combine to make shopping in the 16th a luxurious but expensive experience.

Shops in the 16th

The largest, most famous *dêpot-vente* in Paris, **Réciproque**, is located at 92,103 and 124 rue de la Pompe (☎ *01 47 04 30 28*). Here you may be lucky enough to find last season's reasonably priced Chanel and even Lacroix items.

Les Caprices de Sophie *for less*

Second-hand Designer Labels

24 avenue Mozart, 16th
☎ **01 45 25 63 02**

for less discount: 20%
AM/VS

HOURS

Tue-Sat: 10.30am-6.30pm.
Mon: 2pm-6.45pm.
Sun: closed

This bright, airy shop specializes in cut-price Chanel and Hermès items. There are suits, bags, shoes, belts and various accessories. You will also find items by other designers such as Louis Vuitton.

Richard Gampel *for less*

Accessories

13 rue du Passy, 16th
☎ **01 42 15 24 25**

for less discount: 20%
AM/VS

HOURS

Mon: 1pm-7.30pm. Tue-Sat: 10.30am-2pm, 2.30pm-7.30pm.
Sun: closed

Richard Gampel has a range of accessories for men and women. It sells belts, wallets and bags made from high-quality leather. The more unusual items make great presents.

La Défense

Introduction. . .

La Défense is officially outside Paris, being beyond the *boulevard périphérique*, but its status as one of the top tourist attractions merits its inclusion in any guidebook, and it has been unofficially honoured with

Place de la Defense

the title of 21st *arrondissement*. It is, however, like no other part of Paris and were it not for the distant glimpses of the Arc de Triomphe, you might feel you had left the city altogether.

The area was once part of a huge royal hunting ground and park. After the Revolution a statue commemorating the defence of Paris was built there, and it is after this monument that the complex is named.

For much of the 18th and early 19th centuries the area was a grim, industrial wasteland. In the mid-1950s the first plans were laid to transform it into a modern business complex. Paris itself had little to do with the decision: it was the brainchild of the national government.

Building began in 1958, and the glass skyscrapers which quickly appeared were like nothing Paris had seen before. The area soon

Taki's fountain

became a futuristic, corporate ghetto and hundreds of businesses relocated there.

In 1960 the complex covered just 3 miles^2 (4.8km^2)

but was home to 700 factories and businesses and more than 25,000 workers.

However, the development almost halted in the 1970s due to lack of finance, and it was only after a cash injection from the national government that the building could recommence.

Sculpture by Miro

The government persuaded a dozen or so leading French businesses to move in, and as a result the area became a prestigious corporate address.

The developers had further plans for La Défense. As

. . . Introduction

well as establishing a modern, American-style business complex, they wanted to use the site as a showcase for modern art, architecture and achievement.

This led to plans being made for the building of the most adventurous structure of all, the **Grande Arche de la Défense**. Designed by a Danish architect, von Sprechelsen, the Arche was opened in 1989, the bicentenary of the Revolution.

CNIT Building

Like the Eiffel Tower, it met with a mixed reception. The 367 foot (112 metre) near-perfect cube of white marble is thought by some to be a beautiful and fitting memorial to the 20th century, while others have declared it an eyesore, with the hollow design wasting precious space.

Some of the other outlandish plans have yet to be realized; Jean Nouvel's Tour Sans Fin (Tower without End) has been put on hold following the recession. It is intended to be the tallest building in the world, the pin-point tip of which will be lost in the clouds.

Perhaps the most surprising thing about La Défense is the fact that 35,000 people actually live here, in the huge, hideous blocks of flats to the south of the Place de la Défense. Working here is one thing, but it seems amazing that people would choose to reside here when Paris is on the doorstep.

INSIDER'S TIP

At weekends there are often stalls set up on the Place de la Défense selling an array of clothing and gifts.

Ile de la Grande Jatte

The area is almost always busy, either with office workers during the week or with sightseers and shoppers at weekends, but there is something rather soulless about it even on a busy day. The restaurants and shops around the Place de la Défense give it some colour, but turn a corner and you may well find yourself alone among the unfriendly glass and concrete façades.

Critics of the complex have to remember that its proximity to Paris has allowed for the growth of modern business while saving the city centre from development.

Grande Arche de La Défense

With the unveiling of von Sprechelsen's innovative **Grande Arche** in 1989, La Défense's most ambitious project to date was realized. It also made the area the focal point of that year's French Revolution bicentenary celebrations.

The previously unknown Danish architect was selected by President Mitterand himself, but unfortunately he died before his project was completed. Construction took six years, with a desperate hurry at the end to complete it in time for the 1989 celebrations.

Grande Arche de la Défense

It is made of Carrara marble and weighs 300,000 tonnes, the space in the middle wide enough and high enough to contain the Champs-Elysées or Notre Dame. To the naked eye it is an almost perfect cube, with a few feet extra in height than in width.

From outside it is hard to believe that the faceless marble walls contain office space, but both the Ministry of Transport and the Foundation for the Rights of Man have their headquarters inside.

Twice as high as the Arc de Triomphe, the Grande Arche offers a tremendous view all way along the *vie triomphale* to the Louvre. The external lifts rise past the surreal 'cloud' canopy suspended in the void, and the rooftop viewing area is 360 feet (110 metres) above the ground.

The 'cloud' canopy

It is not quite aligned with the rest of the *vie triomphale*: from a distance the slight tilt is very noticeable.

The monument also contains galleries, a restaurant, a bar and shops.

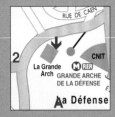

ADDRESS

La Défense
☎ 01 49 07 27 57

GETTING THERE

Métro: Grande Arche de la Défense

HOURS

Apr-Oct: Mon-Sun: 9am-8pm.
Nov-Mar: Mon-Sat: 10am-6m. Sun: 9am-7pm

PRICES

Adult 40F
Child 30F
Senior 30F
Student 30F

Other Attractions . . .

for less Following the success of the Petit Train de Montmartre, the Petit Train de La Défense began service in 1995.

This miniature train runs from the Grande Arche de la Défense past all the major sites, taking in the dazzling new high-rise towers and examples of modern sculpture along the way.

The tour, with music and a commentary, enables visitors to discover the

Petit Train de la Défense

history of the complex and see how the future has taken shape here.

Tours run every day from Easter to late October and the trip lasts about thirty minutes. To join a tour, buy your ticket as you board in front of the Grande Arche. (*☎ 01 42 62 24 00. Apr-Oct: Mon-Sun: 10am-6.30pm. Tours run every thirty minutes. Adult 25F, child 15F, senior 25F, student 25F. 50% discount with voucher on page 275.*)

Petit Train de la Défense

Miro's figures

The office buildings at La Défense are attractions in themselves, despite their humdrum purpose. There are four generations of towerblocks: the first set, built from 1963 onwards, are 328 feet (100 metres) high. The next generation, built from 1974, are 656 feet (200 metres) high, and so on to 1312 feet (400 metres).

CNIT building

The **CNIT** building, the first to be constructed in the complex, has a concrete covering like a seashell. The **Elf**, **PFA** and other high-rise towers have been constructed using glass for amazing mirror and dazzle effects.

Office buildings

All in all, the complex deserves its nickname 'the Parisian Manhattan', although there is something rather anonymous and eerie about the towers from the outside. The blank glass façades make it hard to believe that they are occupied by human beings.

. . . Other Attractions

During the week, however, the area is full of office workers, a reminder that the futuristic complex really is a working sector of Paris.

Esplanade

The esplanade leading from the Grande Arche is a showcase of sculpture. Artists represented are Miro, whose colourful, abstract figures can be seen in the **Place de La Défense**, Calder, sculptor of the huge red iron **Stabile**, and Takis. The latter's **fountain**, at the Paris end of the esplanade, is computer-controlled and lit with coloured lights which can be seen at night from the Arc de Triomphe.

There is a multitude of shops, restaurants, brasseries and bars. Europe's biggest shopping complex, the **Quatre Temps**, is also here.

Dôme IMAX

Musée de l'Automobile

The **Musée d'Automobile** is the only museum in the complex. With the help of more than 100 cars from several eras, the museum traces the history of motoring from its origins to the present day.

Models on display include the earliest prototype cars from before 1900, the pioneering designs from the turn of the century which heralded the true dawn of the age of the motorcar, and vintage examples of Rolls Royces, Fords and Bugattis. *(1 place du Dôme, ☎ 01 46 92 46 00. Mon-Sun: 12.15pm-7.30pm. adult 45F, child 35F, senior 45F, student 45F.)*

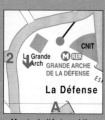

Musée de l'Automobile

Dome IMAX

The **Dôme IMAX**, near to the Grande Arche, offers a futuristic cinematic experience. The hemispherical screen almost makes you feel you are part of the film. *(Colline de la Défense, 1 place du Dôme, ☎ 01 46 92 45 50. Cinema tickets 55F (75F on Sat) or 45F for concessions.)*

Paris by Night

Introduction

Whatever your taste in evening entertainment, Paris has something for you. A typically Parisian way of spending an evening is to watch cabaret, but the city also has a rich theatrical heritage.

The new developments such as La Villette and La Défense have contributed important new venues to the city.

REFLECTIONS

'Why did Paris still draw us to its fascination, why did it draw those who felt themselves creative - talent or no talent? ... Why did art, literature, and sex, and the feeding and drinking seem more genuine there?' - *We All Went to Paris*, Stephen Longstreet

Perhaps the most typical, and certainly the cheapest, way of spending an evening is sitting outside one of Paris's countless cafés and watching the world go by. Street life is as enthralling as a stage production, and you will never be hurried along.

If you prefer more organized drama, there are dozens of theatres dotted around the city, staging both national productions and fringe shows, or playing host to touring companies.

A typically French phenomenon is the *café-théâtre*, where new talent airs itself on stage in front of a relaxed audience. To enjoy the shows, which are often comedies, a good grasp of French is needed.

Classical music, opera or ballet lovers can head for one of the large venues, such as the Opéra Bastille or the sumptuous Opéra Garnier. Dozens of smaller venues cater for almost every other taste, with jazz clubs especially abundant.

Take time to sample the café culture

Those used to London's stringent drinking laws will be happy to discover that most bars in Paris stay open until 1am or 2am, and there are plenty of late-night bars and nightclubs.

Paris has more than 200 cinemas, and its taste has always been eclectic. As well as catching the latest Hollywood blockbusters, you can be sure of sampling the work of little known, talented international directors.

Listings magazines such as *Pariscope*, which contains a section in English, are produced every week and are widely available. See pages 208-212 for details about the ***for less*** discounts available at various night spots around the city.

Theatres and Cabaret

The **Comédie Française** (*2 rue de Richelieu, 1ˢᵗ, ☎ 01 40 15 00 15*) is the home of France's national theatre company, the oldest in the world, which was founded in 1680.

Today, as in the past, it is devoted to presenting classical theatre while encouraging the talent of recognized new playwrights. Classical masters Molière and Racine still dominate the repertoire, with well-established contemporaries taking second place.

Comedie Française

The **Odéon Théâtre de l'Europe** (*1 place de l'Odéon, 6ᵗʰ, ☎ 01 44 41 36 36*) presents a more varied repertoire, staging international plays alongside French ones and offering a venue to famous visiting companies.

Independent theatres include the old, tiny **Théâtre Montparnasse** (*31 rue de la Gaîté, 14ᵗʰ, ☎ 01 43 22 77 74*), and the Bouffes-du-Nord (*37 bis blvd de la Chapelle, 10ᵗʰ, ☎ 01 46 07 34 50*), where British playwright Peter Brooks produces and directs.

National theatres close in August, but several of the independent ones stay open. The **Shakespeare Garden** in the Bois de Boulogne, Paris's most unusual 'theatre', stages open-air productions all summer long.

The most famous cabaret venue in Paris is the **Moulin Rouge** (*82 blvd de Clichy, 18ᵗʰ, ☎ 01 46 06 00 19*), still sporting its famous windmill. The images of bohemian pleasure-seeking immortalized by Toulouse-Lautrec are hard to find these days, as the cabaret scene has lost its music-hall charm and is frequented largely by groups of businessmen.

Moulin Rouge

Moulin Rouge

Other notable venues where you can see a show are the **Lido** (*116 bis av des Champs-Elysées, 8ᵗʰ, ☎ 01 47 23 68 75*), which is still home to the Bluebell girls, and the FoliesBergères. This, the oldest music hall in Paris, was refurbished in 1993 and offers a show somewhat tamer than its first in 1886. (*32 rue de Richer, 9ᵗʰ, ☎ 01 44 79 98 98.*)

Opera, Ballet and Classical Concerts

Opera has been moved from the stately Opéra Garnier (page 54) to the modern **Opéra Bastille**, forfeiting aesthetics and acoustics for a better view.

Performances vary from the classical to the avant-garde, with the great works of Verdi, Mozart and Puccini sometimes being subjected to postmodern interpretations. *(120 rue de Lyon, 12th,* ☎ *01 44 73 13 00)*

Opéra Bastille

The **Opéra Comique** or *salle Favart* premièred many famous operas in its time and now specializes in international operettas. It offers a discount to ***for less*** holders (page 208).

Théâtre de la Ville

The **Opéra Garnier** is now the home of Paris's ballet company, one of the best in the world. As well as classical ballet favourites, it stages other dance performances and the occasional opera.

For modern dance productions, head for the **Théâtre de la Ville** *(2 place du Châtelet, 1st,* ☎ *01 42 74 22 77)*, which was once owned by the great actress Sarah Bernhardt.

The classical music scene in Paris is now better than ever. The city has three symphony orchestras and plays host to touring orchestras from all over the world.

Opéra Garnier

The major venue for classical concerts is the **Salle Pleyel** *(252 rue du Faubourg-St-Honoré, 8th,* ☎ *01 45 61 53 00)*, home of the Orchestre de Paris. It can hold an audience of over 2,000, and stages an average of two concerts a week.

Of growing importance is the **Théâtre du Châtelet**, closed until the end of the century for a major overhaul which will make it a principal classical music venue. *(2 rue Edouard-Colonne, 1st,* ☎ *01 40 28 28 40.)*

The **Cité de la Musique** at La Villette (page 153) stages free concerts by the students of the *conservatoire* and has an impressive concert hall. The repertoire since its inauguration just a few years ago has included diverse performances of both contemporary and early music.

Cinema

Paris, being the birthplace of New Wave cinema in the 1950s, has an international reputation as a showcase for weird and wonderful cinematic achievement.

Hollywood movies are predominant in many venues, but others are almost totally devoted to New Wave, experimental, independent and international films.

Grand Rex

There are lots of cinemas along the Champs-Elysées, most of which charge the earth to present subtitled Hollywood hits.

Paris also has its fair share of multi-screen cinema complexes, which tend to rob the smaller, older and more characterful cinemas of customers.

Paris cinema

To sample a real Parisian cinema experience, go to one of the surviving 'picture palaces'. The Baroque **Grand Rex** *(1 boulevard Poissonnière, 2ⁿᵈ, ☎ 01 42 36 83 93)*, built in 1932, even runs 'backstage' tours of the projection room and behind the screen.

The **Cinémathèque Française** is the repertory cinema of the New Wave, with one screen at the Palais de Chaillot and two at the Palais de Tokyo. Film fans in search of an obscure classic can search its film archives.

A film poster

There are 200 other general and speciality cinemas dotted all over the city, and tickets cost around 50F, except on Wednesday, Paris's half-price cinema day. The code "v.o." means a film is in its original language with French subtitles. The dreaded "v.f" means that it has been dubbed into French.

Futuristic cinematic experiences can be had at both La Villette, where the Géode (page 153) offers the largest cinema screen in the world, and at La Défense, where the Dôme IMAX (page 200) engulfs you with its wrap-around screen.

Géode

For constantly updated cinema information (in French) for the whole of Paris, call the information service on ☎ 01 47 47 74 85.

Nightclubs and Bars

Paris's nightclub scene may not be as cool and trendy as London's or New York's, but its abundance of well-established clubs and late-night music bars caters for every taste.

Le Palace

The most famous nightclub in the city is **Le Palace** *(8 rue du Faubourg Montmartre, 9th, ☎ 01 42 46 10 87)*, closely followed by **Les Bains** *(7 rue du Bourg-L'Abbé, 3rd, ☎ 01 48 87 01 80)*, popular with the fashion and showbusiness crowd, and **Le Bataclan** *(50 boulevard Voltaire, 11th, ☎ 01 47 00 30 12)*.

Le Balajo, formerly a music hall frequented by Piaf, is situated on the lively rue de Lappe

'Queen' nightclub in Paris

and has an atmospheric 1930s interior *(9 rue de Lappe, 11th, ☎ 01 47 00 07 87)*. For an unusual setting, try **Le Colonial**, a yacht moored on the Seine. *(port Debilly, quai de New York, 16th, ☎ 01 53 23 98 98.)*

Le Balajo

These clubs, as well as the many smaller ones scattered around the city, feature theme nights and different DJs, mostly inspired by the scene in Britain or America. The dominant sound is currently house music and its spin-offs.

The dress code in Paris nightclubs is quite strict, with no jeans and trainers allowed, but you can rarely go wrong if you wear black. Entrance prices are sometimes very high, although admission often includes the first drink.

There are several bars in Paris which offer live music and late hours. Irish and Cuban sounds are especially well represented. Live bands are usually listed on a board outside the venue. **Le Café Noir** *(65 rue Montmartre, 2nd, ☎ 01 40 39 07 36)* has a more French 'feel' than some of the others and features nightly blues and other music.

Le Lapin Agile, a famous Montmartre nightspot

For a quieter night and to sample the famous Montparnasse atmosphere of the 1940s, visit **La Closerie des Lilas** *(171 boulevard du Montparnasse, 6th, ☎ 01 43 26 70 50)*. A pianist provides the music, and the bar, which was one of Hemingway's favourites, is famous for its cocktails.

Jazz Clubs

There are dozens of jazz venues in the city, with big American names appearing frequently. There is even an annual jazz festival held in July at the Grande Halle de la Villette (page 153). Paris can certainly be said to be the jazz capital of Europe.

La Villette is also home to the newest venue, **Hot Brass** (*211 avenue Jean-Jaurés, 19th, ☎ 01 42 00 14 14*). Salsa and funk also feature here.

New Morning (*7-9 rue des Petites-Écuries, 10th, ☎ 01 45 23 51 41*) is the most popular jazz club in town, where some of the most famous musicians often play. R&B is also staged here.

Socializing Parisians

Magazines such as *Pariscope* list jazz clubs and their nightly-changing repertoire, and you can usually expect to see an important gig somewhere in the city. Two of the best jazz clubs offer discounts to **for less** cardholders (see page 211).

Café-Théâtre and Comedy

Café-Théâtres stage monologues, sketches or mini-plays performed in front of a drinking and sometimes eating audience, a form of entertainment endlessly popular with Parisians. The performances are often comic or satirical, so a very good knowledge of the French language and current affairs is essential.

Café-Théâtres are the closest thing Paris has to comedy venues, staging a mixture of good and bad stand-up, musical performances and small-scale cabaret. Touring comedians such as Eddie Izzard have performed in these venues.

Café de la Gare

Café-Théâtre

Café de la Gare (*41 rue du Temple, 4th, ☎ 01 42 78 52 51*) is housed in a former stables and launched Depardieu into the limelight.

Point Virgule (page 209), another of the most important venues, offers a discount to **for less** cardholders.

Opéra-Comique

Place Boïeldieu, 2nd
☎ 01 42 44 45 46

*(Box office open Mon-Sat:
11am-7pm. AM/VS/MC/DC.
Tickets 50-610F.)*

DISCOUNT

20% discount on day of
performance only with *for
less* card, subject to
availability.

The Opéra-Comique performs from September to July in
the magnificent *salle Favart*. It has always played a major
musical rôle in Paris, presenting a spectacular repertoire
of operas ranging from the Baroque to the modern.

Théâtre de la Bastille

76 rue de la Roquette, 11th
☎ 01 43 57 42 14

*(Tue-Sat: shows begin 7.30pm
and 9pm (call for details). Sun:
begins 5pm. Mon: closed.
Adult 120F, others 80F.)*

DISCOUNT

40F off adult ticket (120F)
with *for less* card, subject
to availability.

This theatre stages experimental dance and drama
productions. The dance performances range from ballet
to contemporary choreography, and the theatre has a
reputation for staging controversial drama.

Théâtre de la Cité International

21 boulevard Jourdan, 14th
☎ 01 43 13 50 50

*(Call for times and to make
reservations. Tickets 110F (80F
on Mon) and 55F for those
under 26. No credit cards.)*

DISCOUNT

2 for the price of 1 with *for
less* card, subject to
availability.

The Théâtre de la Cité International is a popular venue
for dance, comedy and drama, with a special commitment
to contemporary and unusual theatre. Performances
range from cabaret to opera and comedy to tragedy.

Théâtre de Nesle

8 rue de Nesle, 6th
☎ 01 46 34 61 04

(Call the Box Office for performance times and to purchase tickets. Tickets 60-90F.)

The Théâtre de Nesle stages innovative new French works. It is one of the few theatres in Paris which holds English language productions. The work of American writers is well represented here.

DISCOUNT

2 for the price of 1 with *for less* card, subject to availability.

La Balle au Bond

Opposite 3
quai Malaquais, 6th
☎ 01 40 51 87 06

(Mon-Sun: 8.30pm-1.30am (drama 8.30pm, bar and concert 10pm. AM/VS/MC. Tickets 50-100F.)

This dinner show is held on a boat moored in the heart of Paris. Performances include drama, jazz and comedy productions. From October to April it is moored opposite 55 quai de la Tournelle, 5th.

DISCOUNT

50% discount with voucher on page 273, subject to availability.

Point Virgule

7 rue Ste-Croix
de la Bretonnerie, 4th
☎ 01 42 78 67 03

(Mon-Sun: shows at 8pm, 9pm and 10.30pm. 1 show 80F, 2 shows 130F, 3 shows 150F.)

This *café-théâtre* is very popular with the locals. There are three performances of drama, comedy or recital every night, and a good grasp of French is necessary to appreciate the evening.

DISCOUNT

2 for the price of 1 with voucher on page 273, subject to availability.

DISCOUNT

20% discount with voucher on page 273, subject to availability.

DISCOUNT

20% discount with *for less* card, subject to availability.

DISCOUNT

20% discount with voucher on page 275, subject to availability.

A L'Abbé Constantin

6 rue Fontaine, 9th
☎ 01 40 16 13 07

(Call for performance information and to book. VS/MC. 340F / 480F menus inc. food and wine.)

A L'Abbé Constantin provides an evening of true Parisian cabaret. The show includes comedy, song and magic. There is a choice of two menus of the highest quality French cuisine.

Cabaret la Bohème

3 rue des Déchargeurs, 1st
☎ 01 42 36 10 29

(Shows at 7pm, 8.30pm and 10pm. Call to make reservations. 80F / 100F.)

This cabaret venue is located in the lively Les Halles area. An evening here evokes the golden era of traditional French entertainment. It is a great place for music and dancing.

Le Canotier

62 blvd Rochechouart, 18th
☎ 01 46 06 02 86

(Call for performance times - reservations required. VS/MC. Ticket price (210F) includes free drink.)

At Le Canotier you can experience an evening of pure Parisian cabaret. The show involves jugglers, singers, comics, dancers and musicians, with wonderful costumes from past and present.

Au Duc des Lombards

42 rue des Lombards, 1st
☎ 01 42 33 22 88

(Tue-Sat: performances start at 10pm. Sun-Mon: call for times. Ticket prices vary. VS.)

DISCOUNT

2 for the price of 1 with voucher on page 273, subject to availability.

This jazz club has a relaxed and intimate atmosphere. Famous international stars often play here, with names such as Kirk Lightsey and Steve Grossman appearing regularly.

Caveau de la Huchette

5 rue de la Huchette, 6th
☎ 01 43 26 65 05

(Sun-Thu: 9.30pm-2.30am. Fri-Sat: 9.30pm-4am. Mon-Thu & Sun: 60F (students 55F) Fri-Sat: 70F.)

DISCOUNT

2 for the price of 1 with *for less* card, subject to availability.

This jazz- and nightclub is housed within atmospheric medieval cellars. Trumpeter Harry 'Sweets' Edison is a regular act at this venue of rock, swing, blues and folk music.

Le Rive Gauche

1 rue du Sabot, 6th
☎ 01 42 22 51 70

(Thu-Sat: 11pm-6am. Sun-Wed: closed. Thu free, Fri 80F, Sat 100F. VS/MC.)

DISCOUNT

Free admission with *for less* card, subject to availability.

This club is located in the heart of the lively St-Germain-des Près area. It is a great place to meet for a drink or dancing, with late opening hours and a youthful atmosphere.

DISCOUNT

Free admission with *for less* card, subject to availability.

DISCOUNT

Free admission with *for less* card, subject to availability.

DISCOUNT

20% discount with voucher on page 275, subject to availability.

Le Saint

7 rue St-Séverin, 5th
☎ 01 43 25 50 04

(Tue-Sat: 11pm-6am. Sun-Mon: closed. VS/MC/DC. 60F during the week, 80-90F at weekends.)

The atmospheric cellars housing this club date from the 13th century. A range of musical tastes are catered for, and the venue is popular with students. The entrance price during the week includes one drink.

Slow Club

130 rue de Rivoli, 1st
☎ 01 42 33 84 30

(Tue-Sat: 10pm-3am. 60F Tue-Thu, 75F Fri & Sat. V/MC.)

The Slow Club jazz venue is located in the Châtelet area, and used to be a fruit store for the market. Like its sister club Caveau de la Huchette (page 211), the music here is varied and caters for a young crowd.

Maxwell Café

17 blvd Vital-Bouhot, Neuilly
☎ 01 46 24 22 00

(Thu-Sat: from 10.45pm. 80F Thu, 100F Fri-Sat.)

Maxwell Café, Quai du Blues, is on the Ile de la Grande Jatte in the Seine. The live music here is mostly blues, R&B, soul and gospel, and plays from 10.45pm until early in the morning.

Tours

TOURS

for less Walking Tours

From the traditional gardens of the Bois de Vincennes to more unique open spaces such as the Père Lachaise cemetery, these walking tours offer an interesting perspective on the city of Paris.

Created in 1984, **Paris Côte Jardin** currently offers more than 100 different tours each year. Although each tour is unique, they share a common theme: nature within the urban landscape.

Led by knowledgeable guides, the walks include Paris's most famous green spaces such as the Luxembourg Gardens and the Tuileries. They may also focus on a particular architectural or historic element, such as the development of a Parisian neighborhood or a visit to the Roman ruins of Arènes.

Jardin de Luxembourg

NOTE: All tours are given in French, though some guides may also speak English. Please call the number above for more information about particular tours.

INFORMATION

Call ☎ 01 40 30 47 15 for information about tour dates, prices and times

DISCOUNT

20% discount with **for less** card

for less River Trips

Cruise the river Seine and the Canal Saint Martin while taking in Paris' most famous sights. During the 3-hour **Paris Canal** cruise, an English commentary is provided as you glide past monuments and landmarks such as the Louvre, Notre Dame and the Ile-St-Louis before arriving at the entrance to the Canal Saint Martin.

Discover the eerie subterranean waterways that run below the Paris streets. You pass directly under the Place de la Bastille before emerging near the Place de la République. The journey continues along the tree-lined canal past ancient locks and swing bridges before arriving at La Villette.

Notre Dame from the Seine

Morning tours originate at the quai Anatole France, by the Musée d'Orsay, while the afternoon tours begin at the centre of the Parc de la Villette. *(Daily departures (with additional cruises during peak seasons) from mid-March-mid-November: Musee d'Orsay: 9.30am-12.30pm (arrives at Parc de la Villette). Parc de la Villette: 2.30pm-5.15pm (arrives at Musee d'Orsay).)*

PRICES

Adult 95F
Child (under 12) 55F
Senior 70F
Student (12-25) 70F

DISCOUNT

20% discount with **for less** card.
Reservations necessary – call ☎ 01 42 40 96 97. Tickets are purchased on the boat immediately prior to departure.

![for less] Open Top Bus Tours

One of the best ways to get an overview of Paris is to take a tour on a hop-on, hop-off open-top double-decker bus.

L'Opentour bus

L'Opentour is a unique open-top bus service new to Paris in 1998 which offers a 20% discount on its city tours to *for less* cardholders.

Tours run every day of the year and pass the most famous and notable buildings in the city, so it is a great way to make sure you see everything.

Tickets are valid for one day, and you can get on and off as often as you like at the places you wish to see in more detail. The buses run every 25 minutes at the moment, and the frequency will be increased next year as more buses join the circular route. There are 21 stops, so you never need wait long to reboard.

Eiffel Tower

There is a commentary in English pointing out all the major sites on the tour route, which include the Opéra Garnier, the Louvre, Bastille, St-Germain, the Latin Quarter, the Musée d'Orsay, Les Invalides, the Champs-Elysées, the Eiffel Tower and the Place de la Concorde.

In addition, your ticket entitles you to ride the complimentary shuttle bus link between Madeleine and the funicular train which runs up to the Sacre Coeur in Montmartre.

Notre Dame and the Square Rene Viviani

L'Opentour bus stops are clearly marked with a yellow sign, and the frequent departure times are listed at each stop.

Luxembourg bus stop

Petit Pont bus stop

Cityrama Coach Tours

Cityrama, Paris's premier tour operator, runs a large number of coach, boat and walking tours both within and outside the city. Many of these tours offer a 20% discount to **for less** cardholders.

Cityrama's unique coaches are comfortable, air-conditioned and allow panoramic views. Tours often include entrance prices and sometimes lunch, and you do not waste time queuing, parking or waiting for public transport.

Cityrama tour bus

CITYRAMA OFFICE

4 place des Pyramides, 1st *arrondissement*
☎ 01 44 55 60 00
For more information, view the website at www.cityrama.com

Whatever your interests, Cityrama has a tour to suit you. There are orientation tours of Paris, night-time trips which introduce the city in all its illuminated glory and incorporate a cabaret (pages 218-219). Some tours involve a romantic cruise along the Seine (page 218). Cityrama also offers a walking tour of the Louvre museum (page 218), and for those who wish to venture further afield, there are trips to Versailles (page 219), Château Country (page 220), Normandy (page 222) and even Bruges in Belgium (page 222).

To reserve places on a tour, call ☎ 01 44 55 60 00. There is no need to mention *Paris for less* until you pay for your tour at the departure point at 4 place des Pyramids, 1st, at which point you must present your *for less* card.

Cityrama office

Cityrama request that you arrive at the departure point at least 15 minutes before the tour is scheduled to begin. *(No reservations required for tours C (below) and I (page 218). Passport required for tour BR1 (page 222).)*

Tour C: Cityrama Tour

Apr-Oct: Mon-Sun: every hour from 9.30am-4.30pm (Nov-Mar: last tour 2.30pm)	Adult 150F, child under 12 free *for less* discount: 20% (present card at 4 place des Pyramides)

The 2-hour Cityrama tour of Paris, which runs every day of the year, is the perfect introduction to the city. Most of the important sights are on the itinerary.

The tour begins at Place des Pyramids and takes in the Iles, Le Marais and Bastille before continuing through the Latin Quarter to the Left Bank.

HIGHLIGHTS

Guided coach tour through Paris

Les Invalides, the Eiffel Tower, the Arc de Triomphe and the Champs-Elysées are next on the list, and the tour ends in the heart of the city.

Tour PA: Paris Artistic

Adult 295F, child 147.50F **Mon, Wed, Fri, Sat**
for less discount: 20% **(+ Thu Apr-Oct): 9.45am**
(present card at 4 place des Pyramides)

Paris's historic and artistic heritage is the central theme of this tour. It begins with a drive through the old areas of Le Marais and the Latin Quarter.

This is followed by a guided visit to the ancient Cathédral de Notre Dame on the Ile de la Cité, the oldest part of the city.

The 3½-hour tour ends with a guided tour of Paris's greatest museum, the Louvre, during which the most famous items in its vast collection are highlighted.

HIGHLIGHTS

Le Marais &
Latin Quarter coach tour
Notre Dame
Louvre

Tour PS: Paris Seinorama

Adult 280F, child 140F **Mon-Sun:**
for less discount: 20% **2.15pm (2pm Nov-Mar)**
(present card at 4 place des Pyramides)

The Seinorama tour incorporates some of Paris's best-loved buildings and monuments, starting with the stately Place de la Concorde.

After a visit to the Champs-Elysées, the tour continues into the prestigious 16th *arrondissement*, home of the wealthiest Parisians.

Following an hour-long cruise along the Seine, you are taken on a guided tour to the 2nd floor of the Eiffel Tower for a view of the city (1st floor in winter).

HIGHLIGHTS

Champs-Elysées
Seine Cruise
Eiffel Tower

Tour PJ: Paris Full Day

Adult 510F, child 255F **Mon, Wed, Fri and Sat**
for less discount: 20% **(+ Thu Apr-Oct) 9.45am**
(present card at 4 place des Pyramides)

The full day Paris tour combines both the Paris Artistic and the Paris Seinorama tours, providing an in-depth introduction to almost all of the city's highlights.

You have the choice of taking one tour in the morning, breaking for 1½ hours for lunch, and continuing with the second tour in the afternoon.

Alternatively, you may split the tours over two consecutive days, giving yourself more time to spend at the Louvre or the Eiffel Tower.

HIGHLIGHTS

Combination of Paris
Artistic and Paris
Seinorama tours

Tour GL: Grand Louvre

Fri (+ Mon Apr-Oct):   Adult 190F, child 95F
2.30pm   *for less* discount: 20%
(present card at 4 place des Pyramides)

HIGHLIGHTS

Guided walking tour
through the Louvre

You are taken on a guided tour of the biggest museum
in the world, beginning with a stroll around the
commercial area of the Louvre.

The expert guide ensures that none of the highlights of
the museum are overlooked in this three-hour walk,
which takes in all the best-known and important works.

Almost all of the seven types of collection are visited,
from the Egyptian antiquities to the Italian paintings
and the famous Mona Lisa.

Tour MP: Montmartre and the Fleamarket

Sun (+ Mon   Adult 245F, child 122.50F
Apr-Oct): 2pm   *for less* discount: 20%
(present card at 4 place des Pyramides)

HIGHLIGHTS

Sacré-Coeur
Place du Tertre
St-Ouen fleamarket

Montmartre is one of the most picturesque parts of
Paris, with a strong artistic heritage. This tour begins
with a visit to the Basilique de Sacré Coeur.

It proceeds through the hilly streets to the Place du
Tertre, where portrait painters and other artists can be
seen at work.

The tour continues to the famous and ancient
fleamarket of St-Ouen, where you can spend some
time rummaging for bargains.

Tour I: Illuminations of Paris

Mon-Sun: Adult 150F, child under 12 free
10pm (7pm Nov-Mar)   *for less* discount: 20%
(present card at 4 place des Pyramides)

HIGHLIGHTS

Night-time coach tour
through Paris

All of Paris's monuments are spectacularly floodlit at
night, making an evening tour an unforgettable
experience.

This 1½ hour tour passes all the major sights,
including the Eiffel Tower, Notre Dame, the Louvre and
the Champs-Elysées.

The drive is accompanied by a headphone commentary
in a choice of 12 languages, and you do not need to
reserve seats in advance.

Tour CR: Cruise and Illuminations

Adult 185F, child 92.50F
for less discount: 20%
(present card at 4 place des Pyramides)

Mon-Sun:
7.30pm (7pm Nov-Mar)

This tour begins with an romantic evening cruise along the river, past the Eiffel Tower, the Louvre, the Musée d'Orsay and the Iles of the Seine.

Once darkness has fallen, the trip continues with a guided coach tour of the illuminated monuments of the city.

Commentary on the coach tour, which takes in the Champs-Elysées and most of the most important buildings, is available in 12 languages.

HIGHLIGHTS

Seine cruise
Paris illuminations

 # Tour IL: Illuminations and Lido Show

Adult 595F (winter 590F)
for less discount: 20%
(present card at 4 place des Pyramides)

Mon-Sun:
10pm (8.30pm Nov-Mar)

This tour begins with a drive past the illuminated monuments of the city, including the Eiffel Tower, the Arc de Triomphe and Notre Dame.

Afterwards you are taken to the prestigious Lido on the Champs-Elysées for a spectacular evening of Parisian entertainment.

Take your seats for 'C'est Magique', the celebrated cabaret. The tour price includes one glass of champagne per person.

HIGHLIGHTS

Paris illuminations
Lido show (not recom-
mended for children)

 # Tour CRM: Cruise and Moulin Rouge Show

Adult 495F
for less discount: 20%
(present card at 4 place des Pyramides)

Mon-Sun:
8.30pm (Apr-Oct only)

Discover the floodlit beauty of Paris's greatest monuments and bridges during a relaxing cruise along the Seine.

In complete contrast, the tour followed by a visit to the Moulin Rouge, the most famous cabaret venue in the world.

The prestigious show, 'Formidable', includes the famous French can-can. Your ticket includes a glass of champagne.

HIGHLIGHTS

Seine cruise
Moulin Rouge Show (not
recommended for children)

HIGHLIGHTS

Versailles State Apartments
Gardens

Tour VO: Versailles Orientation

Tue-Sun: Adult 200F, child 100F
9.30am & 2.30pm (9.30am &   *for less* discount: 20%
1.45pm Nov-Mar)   (present card at 4 place des Pyramides)

The outward journey incorporates a recorded
commentary about the Palace of Versailles, its history
and what to see when you get there.

On arrival, you are free to explore Louis XIV's
spectacular creation at your leisure, concentrating on
the parts which interest you most.

Your entrance fee is included in the price of the tour,
and allows admission to the glorious State Apartments
and the stunning gardens.

HIGHLIGHTS

Beauce countryside
Chartres cathedral

Tour CH: Chartres

Tue, Sat (+ Thu   Adult 275F, child 137.50F
Apr-Oct): 1.45pm   *for less* discount: 20%
                      (present card at 4 place des Pyramides)

This trip to Chartres cathdral begins with a drive
through the open farmland of the Beauce region of
France.

Arrival in Chartres is followed by a guided tour of the
cathedral, recognized as a World Heritage Site by
UNESCO.

Afterwards there is some free time left for a leisurely
stroll around the cathedral to admire the famous
stained glass and 13th-century architecture.

HIGHLIGHTS

Château de Fontainebleau
Fôret de Fontainebleau
Barbizon

Tour F: Fontainebleau and Barbizon

Nov-Mar: Wed & Sun: 1.45pm   Adult 330F, child 165F
Oct-Apr: Mon,Wed & Sat: *for less* discount: 20%
1.45pm   (present card at 4 place des Pyramides)

This trip begins with a guided tour of the Château de
Fontainebleau, the Renaissance palace of kings and
emperors.

The tour continues with a drive through the ancient
hunting ground of François I, the 96 miles^2 (250km^2)
Fôret de Fontainebleau.

Before returning to Paris there is a short stop at
Barbizon, the picturesque village made famous by
artists Rousseau and Millet.

Tour G: Giverny

Adult 345F, child 172.50F   Apr-Oct only:
for less discount: 20%   Tue-Sat:
(present card at 4 place des Pyramides)   2pm

Monet settled in Giverny in 1883, entranced by the beauty and peace of the surrounding countryside. Many of his most famous works were completed here.

This tour begins with a guided tour of the wonderful flower gardens which inspired his *'Waterlilies'* paintings.

This is followed by free time to explore the artist's former home and studio, and the afternoon finishes with shopping or a visit to the American Museum.

HIGHLIGHTS

Monet's house and garden
American Museum

Tour CL1: Châteaux Country

Adult 760F, child 684F   Daily except Wed: 7.15am
for less discount: 20%   (Nov-Mar: Tue, Thu & Sun
(present card at 4 place des Pyramides)   only)

The Loire Valley is famous the world over for its stunning Renaissance castles. This tour takes in some of the highlights.

It begins with a guided tour of the Château at Blois for a potted history of the region. After lunch there is a tour of Chenonceau castle.

The tour passes Cherverny castle before stopping again at the Château at Chambord for another guided tour.

HIGHLIGHTS

Blois
Chenonceau
Cherverny
Chambord

Tour MS1: Mont-St-Michel

Adult 980F, child 882F (2 meals included)   Mon, Wed & Fri
for less discount: 20%   (Nov-Mar: Sat & Wed):
(present card at 4 place des Pyramides)   7.15am

A drive through picturesque Normandy includes a stop for regional brunch (drinks included) at Le Dauphin restaurant in L'Aigle.

This is followed by a guided tour of the Abbey of Mont-St-Michel, an important centre of pilgrimage since the Middle Ages.

There is some free time to explore the village in the afternoon, and on the return journey there is a stop for dinner at the village of Pont l'Evênque.

HIGHLIGHTS

Normandy
Mont-St-Michel Abbey
and Village
Lunch and dinner

HIGHLIGHTS

Basilique de St-Remi
Tour of Reims
Champagne cellars

Tour RC: Reims Champagne

Tue & Fri (Mar-Oct only):	Adult 470F, child 235F
8am	*for less* discount: 20%
	(present card at 4 place des Pyramides)

This tour begins in Reims, the capital of the Champagne region, and includes a visit to the Basilique de Saint-Remi.

From the Gothic Reims cathedral an orientation tour of Reims allows you to choose somewhere for a leisurely lunch.

The afternoon comprises a visit to the cellars of Mercier or Moët et Chandon, which also includes champagne tasting.

Tour NP1: Landing Beaches of Normandy

HIGHLIGHTS

Memorial at Caen
American cemetery
Landing beaches
Lunch

Sat (Mar-Oct):	Adult 855F, child 769.50F
7.15am (from Jun: Tue also)	*for less* discount: 20%
	(present card at 4 place des Pyramides)

This tour concentrates on the area where the Allies fought for freedom. It begins with a visit to the Memorial Peace Museum in Caen.

A stop at Point du Hoc allows for an hour's visit to the American cemetery at Sainte Laurent, followed by Longues-sur-Mer.

The tour continues through Arromanches to the landing beaches of Gold Juno and Sword, arriving back in Paris at about 9pm.

Tour BR1: Bruges

HIGHLIGHTS

Walking tour of Bruges
Shopping
Canal cruise

Wed & Sun:	Adult 720F, child 648F
7.15am	*for less* discount: 20%
	(present card at 4 place des Pyramides)

Bruges, one of the best preserved medieval towns in Europe, is famous for Belgian chocolate, lace and the canals which earned it the name 'Venice of the North'.

The day begins with a walking tour of the town, passing the Beguine Convert, the Grand Place, Les Halles and the gothic-style Town Hall.

After lunch, time is allowed for shopping, exploring or a visit to the museum of Flemish art. The afternoon finishes with a cruise along the canals.

Outside Paris

Versailles

The huge and sumptuous **Château of Versailles** is one of the world's most treasured monuments, with a rich and chequered history going back to the 17th century.

The village of Versailles was tiny when, in 1623, Louis XIII built the original château which was little more than a hunting lodge. It was extended by Louis XIV, the Sun King, who moved here in 1682.

The Revolution saw the abandonment of the château until 1837, when Louis-Philippe opened it as a history museum. After a brief period as headquarters for the Prussians in the Franco-Prussian war, the building was fully restored and opened to the public.

Palace of Versailles

The château is comprised of the **Grands Appartements**, or the ceremonial quarters, and the **Petites Appartements**, the private quarters of the monarchy.

The ceremonial quarters, including the magnificent **Hall of Mirrors**, are open to visitors, and there are guided tours of the private chambers.

The two smaller palaces in the grounds of the château can also be visited. The **Grand Trianon** was Louis XIV's personal refuge, and was refurnished by Napoleon who also spent time there.

The **Petit Trianon** was the favourite of Marie-Antoinette and has an English-style garden. It offers an insight into life at the end of the Ancien Régime. Other buildings comprising the royal court include the beautiful **stables**, the **chapel**, and the **Jeu de Paume** tennis court.

The **Parc de Versailles** covers more than 1,970 acres (800 hectares). The area adjacent to the château, the **Petit Parc**, is a series of typically French formal gardens, laid out by Le Nôtre at the end of the 17th century. Features here include small lakes, parterres, statues and fountains.

The **Grand Parc**, beyond it, is a large wood bisected by the **Grand Canal**. The canal, covering 60 acres (24 hectares) held a fleet of 9 ships in the château's heyday.

ADDRESS

78000 Versailles
☎ 01 30 84 76 18

GETTING THERE

Versailles is 14 miles (23km) south-west of Paris

RER: line C to Versailles-Rive Gauche

HOURS

Château: Tue-Sun: May-Sep: 9am-6pm. Oct-Apr: 9am-5pm.
Gardens: 7am-sunset

PRICES

Adult: 45F (35F on Sun)
Child: free
Senior: 45F (35F on Sun)
Student: 35F

REFLECTIONS

'Versailles must be ranked very highly. It must be defended against all comers. We are on Versailles's side; what am I saying? We are a part of it' - Henri de Montherlant

Disneyland Paris

Disneyland Paris, based on the successful Disney theme park in California, opened in 1992 and has welcomed more than 60 million visitors (or 'guests', as they are called) since then.

Disneyland Parade

A stay here plunges the whole family into a 24-hour Disney extravaganza. There are several 2- to 4-star hotels in the complex, all with an American theme: choose from the brownstone **Hotel New York** for a taste of the Big Apple; the **Sequoia Lodge** to evoke a sojourn in a Rockies log cabin; or even the **Hotel Cheyenne** for a Wild West experience. There is so much to do that a visit of at least two days is recommended.

The rides and shows are divided into five themed areas, in which every detail contributes to the authenticity. As well as 42 permanent attractions, there are parades and shows at frequent points during the day.

The different 'worlds' are **Frontierland**, **Main Street USA**, **Discoveryland**, **Adventureland** and **Fantasyland**.

Château de la Belle au Bois Dormant (Sleeping Beauty's Castle)

Each has corresponding themed restaurants, shops and rides. The famous pink-turreted **Sleeping Beauty's Castle** is in Fantasyland, the kingdom of fairy-tales.

Discoveryland is based on science fiction, space travel and the future, with attractions inspired by the imaginations of Jules Verne and George Lucas of *Star Wars* fame, and Main Street USA is based on a turn-of-the-century small American town not unlike the one in which Walt Disney himself grew up.

In addition to these 'lands', the **Disney Village** at the entrance to the park has a downtown American feel, and stages several shows of music and dancing every day, as well as a **Buffalo Bill Dinner Show**, a multiplex **Gaumont cinema** and several all-American restaurants and shops. Outside the complex there is a 27-hole golf course.

VISITOR INFORMATION

For information and reservations call
☎ 01 60 30 60 30 or contact a travel agent

GETTING THERE

Disneyland is 19 miles (32km) east of Paris

RER: line A to Marne-la-Valley-Chessy

HOURS

Park open Mar-Oct. Summer: Mon-Sun: 9am-11pm. Reduced opening hours during Mar, Apr,Sep and Oct.

PRICES

One day 'passport': Mar-Jul: Adult 200F, child (up to 11) 155F. Jul-Oct: Adult 210F, child 165F.

Two days: Adult 385F, child 300F.

Three days: Adult 545F, child 420F.

Annual passports also available.

Fontainebleau

The elegant, royal town of Fontainebleau, surrounded by forest, is famous for its huge Renaissance château. It incorporates the medieval keep of the original castle built here at the beginning of the 12th century.

Château de Fontainebleau

François I commissioned the construction of today's building, which combined French and Italian styles, in the 16th century. At the beginning of its life the *Mona Lisa* hung here.

Catherine de Médicis, Louis XIV, Napoleon and Louis-Philippe all had a hand in the expansion of the château and its grounds, which were designed by landscape gardener *extraordinaire* Le Nôtre.

It survived the Revolution unscathed, unlike many other French châteaux, and was taken over by the Germans in the Second World War. After the war it was opened to the public.

GETTING THERE

Fontainebleau is 40 miles (65km) south-east of Paris

Train: 50-minute journey from Gare de Lyon to Fontainebleau-Avon, with a bus connection to the château

The rambling building, surrounding five courtyards, is beautifully furnished with items dating from as far back as the Renaissance. It is a showcase of carving, tapestry, panelling and paintings. The ***Grands Appartements*** (state rooms) contain some wonderful 16th-century frescoes and Renaissance ornamentation.

VISITOR Information

Office de Tourisme de Fontainebleau-Avon 4 rue Royale 77300 Fontainebleau ☎ 01 60 74 99 99

The château incorporates a **Chinese museum** and the **Musée Napoleonien**, displaying many of the Emperor's personal possessions and clothes.

Forêt de Fontainebleau

The **gardens** comprise a formal French area, a **Jardin Anglais**, a carp lake and the **Grand Canal**, and is home to dozens of peacocks. *(☎ 01 60 71 50 70. Château: Wed-Mon: Summer: 9.30am-6pm. Winter: 9.30am-12.30pm, 2pm-5pm. Gardens only: dawn until dusk everyday. Adult 32F, child free, senior 32F, student 20F. Free admission to gardens only.)*

The huge **Forêt de Fontainebleau** covers more than 96 miles^2 (250km^2) and was François I's hunting ground. It now attracts joggers, walkers, horse riders, cyclists and even mountain climbers with its miles of tracks and deep gorges.

Chartres

Chartres is a beautifully preserved old town lining the banks of the river Eure and boasting the most complete medieval monument in Europe.

The cathedral, which replaced a Romanesque one largely destroyed by fire in 1194, has two steeples, one dating from the 12th century and the other a Gothic spire built in 1513 to replace the previous wooden one. The copper roof is bright green with verdigris.

The three entrances all boast superb ornamentation but the **Royal Portal**, facing west, is the only one which still has most of the original statues and carvings which date from 1150.

The nave, the choir and the transept are 13th-century, and the cathedral contains some magnificent stained glass which dates from this period. Three windows predate the 12th-century fire and incorporate glass of the famous "Chartres blue". (*☎ 02 37 21 75 02. Mon-Sat: 7.30am-7.15pm. Sun: 8.30am-7.15pm. Admission free.*)

Chartres cathedral

The stained glass theme continues at the **Centre International de Vitrail**, devoted to the study of this art form. The exhibitions concentrate on technique, history, iconography and renovation, and there is an adjoining research centre which holds lectures and workshops. (*5 rue du Cardinal Pie, ☎ 02 37 21 65 72. Exhibitions: Mon-Sun: 9.30am-12.30pm, 1.30pm-6pm.*)

The **Conservatoire de l'Agriculture**, housed in a 19th-century steam engine shed, is France's only museum dedicated to agriculture. It has a unique and huge collection of tractors, threshers, ploughs and harvesters. Interactive exhibits illustrate the social and technical history of farming. (*Pont de Mainvilliers, 28000 Chartres, ☎ 02 37 30 99 38. Tue-Fri: 10am-12.30pm, 1.30pm-6pm. Sat-Sun: open until 7pm. Adult 25F, child 10F, senior 20F, student 20F.*)

The **Musée des Beaux Arts**, in the former Bishop's palace, has an important collection of paintings, sculpture, documents relating to the history of Chartres and a unique collection of François I enamels. (*29 cloître Notre-Dame, ☎ 02 37 36 41 39. Mon & Wed-Fri: 10am-12noon, 2pm-6pm (until 5pm Nov-Apr). Sun: 2pm-6pm (until 5pm Nov-Apr). Adult 10F, child 5F, senior 5F, student 5F).*

VISITOR INFORMATION

L'Office de Tourisme
Place de la Cathédrale
28005 Chartres
☎ 02 37 21 50 00

GETTING THERE

Chartres is 56 miles (90km) south-west of Paris

Train : a hour-long journey from Gare Montparnasse

REFLECTIONS

'All the steam in the world could not, like the Virgin, build Chartres' - *The Education of Henry Adams*, Henry Adams

Chantilly

The château at **Chantilly** (☎ *01 44 57 08 00)*, an imposing but graceful building surrounded by a moat, has an important collection of paintings from the 15th to the 19th centuries. Many people visit it simply to see its stunning gardens.

Château at Chantilly

The castle consists of the **Petit Château**, built in 1570 for Anne de Montmorency, who served as a diplomat at the beginning of the 16th century . It contains the **Prince's Apartments** and a library of precious medieval manuscripts.

The adjoining **Grand Château** was rebuilt in the late 19th century in the Renaissance style after being destroyed during the Revolution. This part of the building contains the museum of art which includes works by, among others, Raphael, Lippi and Fouquet. The latter was the creator of an exquisite 15th-century Book of Hours, an intricately illuminated calendar. It also displays furniture and sculpture.

The **Grands Écuries** (stables) date from 1740 and are big enough to house 2,240 horses. Today, the stables are home to the **Musée Vivant du Cheval** (☎ *01 44 57 13 13)* and have just 30 horses in residence. The museum stages daily equestrian demonstrations and incorporates displays of equipment and horse paintings.

Part of the **gardens** of the château were laid out in the formal style by Le Nôtre, who also designed the garden of Versailles (page 224). The **Jardin Anglais** and **Jardin Anglo-Chinois** are wilder, and the park as a whole is bisected by the **Canal** and its subsidiaries.

The stately **town** of Chantilly is a significant centre of horseracing, and hosts several important events every year.

The 24 mile^2 (63 km^2) **Forêt de Chantilly** is southeast of the town and the château, and is home

The gardens

to deer. It is popular with walkers and riders who follow the long-distance paths through the trees. Guided hikes are also available (☎ *01 44 57 03 88)*.

VISITOR INFORMATION

Office de Tourisme de Chantilly
60 av du Maréchal Joffre
Boite Postale 60233
60631 Chantilly CEDEX
☎ 03 44 57 08 58

GETTING THERE

Chantilly is 25 miles (40km) north of Paris

Train: from the Gare du Nord

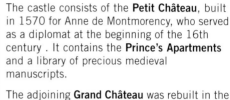

Auvers-sur-Oise

Auvers-sur-Oise has been made famous by the many 19th-century landscape painters who chose to make it their subject.

The village's location, sandwiched between the river Oise and the Vexin plateau, attracted the artists with its wide pastures, quaint stone buildings and, most of all, the superb and rare quality of light.

Cézanne lived here for 18 months until 1874. He, Pissarro, Sisley, and Renoir were often entertained by the great eccentric and painter Doctor Gachet, many of whose own paintings now hang in the Musée d'Orsay.

Van Gogh was Auvers' most famous visitor. He came in 1890 and was to spend just seventy days in the village before shooting himself. During his time here he

executed many of his best works, including the famous *Church at Auvers* and *Self-portrait*.

Church at Auvers

Museums at Auvers include the **Musée Daubigny** *(Manoir des Colombières, rue de la Sansonne,* ☎ *01 30 36 80 20)*, which exhibits 19th-century and naïve art, and the **Musée de l'Absinthe** *(44 rue Callé,* ☎ *01 30 36 83 26)*, devoted to the mythical drink which was a favourite among the 19th century painters.

The picturesque village offers riverside walks, good restaurants and interesting architecture.

![for less] Château d'Auvers-sur-Oise

Auvers-sur-Oise
☎ **01 34 48 48 50**

(Apr-Sep: Tue-Sun: 10.30am-6pm. Oct-Mar: Tue-Sun: 10.30am-4.30pm. Mon: Jun-Aug: 10.30am-4.30pm. Adult 60F, Child 40F, Senior 50F, Student 40F.)

The Château d'Auvers-sur-Oise is a recently renovated 17th-century castle. The beautiful building is devoted to the Impressionist movement, and a multimedia exhibition introduces visitors of all ages to the world of art.

GETTING THERE

Auvers-sur-Oise is 18 miles (30km) north of Paris

Train: from the Gare du Nord or Gare St-Lazare, changing at Persan-Beaumont or Pontiose

RER: line A to Cergy-Préfecture, then take the bus in the direction of Butry

REFLECTIONS

'I am entirely absorbed by these plains of wheat on a vast expanse of hills like a ocean of tender yellow, pale green, and soft mauve, with a piece of worked land dotted with clusters of potato vines in bloom, and all this under a blue sky tinted with shades of white, pink and violet' - Vincent van Gogh, 1890

DISCOUNT

2 for the price of 1 with voucher on page 277

France Miniature

25 route du Mesnil,
Elancourt
☎ 01 30 62 40 79

*(Mon-Sun: Mar 15th-Nov 15th:
10am-7pm (last admission 6pm).
Adult 75F, Child 50F, Senior
75F, Student 65F.)*

In this 12 acre (5 hectare) garden you can see the famous monuments, palaces and castles of France, all in miniature. The reconstruction celebrates more than a thousand years of French architecture.

DISCOUNT

50% discount with
voucher on page 277

Château Vaux-le-Vicomte

77950 Maincy
☎ 01 64 14 41 90

*(Apr-Oct: Mon-Sun: 10am-6pm.
Nov-Mar: closed. Adult 56F,
Child 46F, Senior 46F, Student
46F.)*

The Baroque-style château of Vaux-le-Vicomte was built in the 17th century for Nicolas Fouquet, Louis XIV's finance minister, and was the inspiration for the château at Versailles. It is full of charm despite its grand scale.

DISCOUNT

2 for the price of 1 with
voucher on page 277

Château de Thoiry

Thoiry
☎ 04 34 87 52 25

*(Summer: Mon-Fri: 10am-6pm,
Sat-Sun: 10am-6.30pm. Winter:
Mon-Sun: 10am-5pm. Adult
98F, Child 78F, Senior 98F,
Student 98F.)*

Thoiry, an impressive 16th-century Renaissance château, has stunningly preserved interiors. It is surrounded by 300 acres (120 hectares) of magnificent landscaped gardens, including a game reserve.

DISCOUNT

2 combined tickets
(castle, gardens and
reserve) for the price of 1
with voucher on page 277

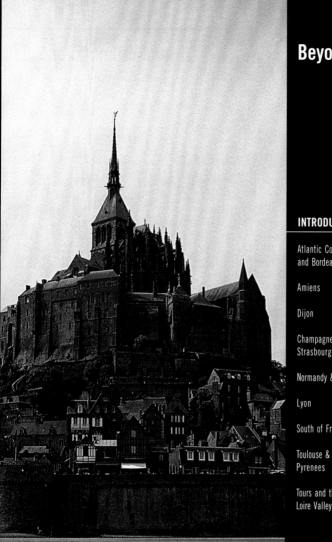

Beyond Paris

Introduction

France, the largest country in Western Europe, is physically and climatically diverse, with many regions having their own particular styles of architecture and dialects.

France is hemmed in on the south and south-east sides by two of Europe's mountain ranges, the Alps and the

Fort St-Jean Vieux, Marseille

Pyrenees. The hillwalking and skiing country here is a world apart from the flat northern land of Champagne and Lorraine. In the middle of the country is France's own mountain range, the Massif Central, which covers roughly a sixth of the country.

A vineyard

Many of France's regions are famous for their contributions to the country's gastronomic or artistic or output, or simply for their natural beauty or architectural features. The Loire Valley is renowned for its many châteaux, legacies of the kings and dukes who settled here between the Middle Ages and the Renaissance. Champagne and Burgundy are famous for their wines, and Normandy for its cider and cheese.

Some regions are so un-French they seem to be individual countries or parts of neighbouring Italy, Germany or Spain. In Alsace the language is Alsatian, more German than French though with no official written form. Basque people speak a language related to no other, which is also found in

A Loire château

the neighbouring parts of Spain. Catalan, a Spanish dialect, is spoken in the far south-east of France.

Atlantic Coast and Bordeaux

The flat, green region bordering the Atlantic is famous for wine, cognac and seafood. The wines vary in quality, with the best coming from **Médoc** in the northwest. Much of the wine produced here is red and is what the English call claret.

The little town of **Cognac** has been making the eponymous brandy since the 1700s. Surprisingly, many of the chief producers, including Hennessey and Martell, have been English. This is still reflected in the labelling of cognac: the letters VSOP stand for 'very special old pale'.

The region has other English links, having been ruled by that country for more than 300 years following the marriage of Henry II to Eleanor of Aquitaine in 1152.

The capital of the Aquitaine region is **Bordeaux**, the fifth-largest French city and capital of France on three separate occasions in its history. The most recent time was at the beginning of the Second World War before the Vichy government was proclaimed.

The heart of the city is **Place Gambetta**, a peaceful oasis in amongst the lively shops and attractions. During the Revolution it was the site of a guillotine and 300 noblemen were executed here. An 18th-century city gate, the Porte Dijeaux, stands at the south-east corner of the square.

The **Cathédrale St-André**, south of Place Gambetta, has an exquisitely sculpted 13th-century west portal and a separate 15th-century belfry. (Place Pey-Berland, ☎ 05 56 52 68 10. Mon-Sun: 8am-11am-2pm-6pm.)

The Bordeaux region is famous for its wines

The most beautiful building in the city is the 18th-century **Grand Théâtre** (Place de la Comédie, ☎ 05 56 48 58 54), whose Classical façade features a huge colonnade decorated with Muses and Graces. Operas and ballets are put on here, but you can take a guided tour of the sumptuous interior without seeing a performance.

The river Garonne flanks the east of the city and is spanned by one of France's loveliest bridges, the **Pont de Pierre**. This Napoleonic construction has no less than 17 arches.

Of the city's many museums, the **Musée d'Aquitaine** is the most outstanding, giving a concise history of the region from prehistoric times to the present century. (20 cours Pasteur, ☎ 05 56 01 51 00. Tue-Sun: 10am-6pm.Adult 20F, child 10F, senior 10F, student 10F.)

GETTING THERE

Trains run from the Gare Montparnasse

VISITOR INFORMATION

Office de Tourisme (Bordeaux)
12 cours du 30 Juillet
33000 Bordeaux
☎ 05 56 00 66 00

REFLECTIONS

'Bordeaux is dedicated to the worship of Bacchus in the most discreet form' - *A Little Tour of France*, Henry James (1882)

Amiens

Amiens is famous for its cathedral and as the home of the great 19th-century writer Jules Verne, author of *Around the World in Eighty Days*. Although the town was badly damaged in the First and Second World Wars, the cathedral and the medieval quarter remained unscathed, and the town retains much of its original charm.

Hortillonages, Amiens

The **cathedral** is the largest Gothic building in France, and was constructed in just 60 years, thus avoiding the influence of any later architectural styles. Its stunning and monumental sculpted façade hides a cavernous nave, 138 feet (42 metres) high, its chapels wonderfully embellished with statues and gilt. The choirstalls, which date from 1522, display beautiful oak carvings. *(Mon-Sun: Easter-Sep: 8.30am-7pm. Oct-Easter: 8.30am-12noon, 2pm-5pm. Free admission.)*

The medieval quarter, **Saint-Leu**, calls itself the 'little Venice of the North'. Its carefully renovated buildings are clustered on the banks of several canals, and it is a lovely part of town to wander around, with plenty of restaurants and shops.

Old quarter, Amiens

To learn more about the Picardie region, visit the **Musée de Picardie** *(48 rue de la République, 80000 Amiens, ☎ 03 22 97 14 00)*. Housed in a 19th-century mansion, this collection comprises archaeological artifacts, sculptures, *objets d'art*, statuary and paintings.

Another fascinating museum is the **Maison Jules Verne**, former home of the famous author and adventurer. He moved to Amiens after marrying a local woman and stayed here for 20 years. The museum charts his life and travels with artefacts, models and documents. *(2 rue Charles Dubois, 80000 Amiens, ☎ 03 22 45 09 12. Mon-Fri: 9am-12noon, 2pm-6pm. Admission free.)*

Set among the waterways just outside the town are the *hortillonages*, or market gardens, which have supplied the town with flowers and produce since the Middle Ages. You can walk around the gardens or join a boat trip along the rivers *(☎ 03 22 92 12 18)*.

GETTING THERE

Trains run north from the Gare du Nord

VISITOR INFORMATION

Office de Tourisme Amiens
6 bis rue Dusevel
80010 Amiens
☎ 03 22 71 60 50

Dijon

Dijon, one of the most attractive cities in France, reflects the wealth of the Burgundy region in its buildings. Its name, however, is most commonly linked with its worldwide gastronomic contribution, mustard. The condiment has been produced here since the Middle Ages, and Dijon has a museum devoted solely to it. *(Le Musée Amora, 48 quai Nicolas Rolin, 21000 Dijon, ☎ 03 80 44 11 41. Open by appointment only; contact the Tourist Office.)*

Rue de la Liberté, Dijon

Under the dukes of Burgundy Dijon was the capital of the region, and their legacy remains in the form of the **Palais des Ducs et des États de Bourgogne** (place de la Libération). This Classical building, remodelled in the 17th and 18th-century, was the seat of the dukes and later became the Burgundian parliament's headquarters. Parts of the palace now act as the town hall.

The only part of the original building is the **Tour de Bar**, which dates from the mid-1300s and now houses part of the **Musée des Beaux-Arts**, one of the best of such museums in France. *(☎ 03 80 74 52 70. Wed-Mon: 10am-6pm. Tue: closed. Adult 18F, child free, senior 9F, student free.)*

The **Église Notre Dame**, behind the palace, was built in the early 1300s in the Burgundian Gothic style. Its tiers of gargoyles, however, date from the 19th-century.

The city has several important museums, some of them located in beautiful and historic buildings. The **Musée Rude**, dedicated to the Dijon-born sculptor François Rude, is inside a former church. *(Rue Vaillant, ☎ 03 80 66 87 95. Jun-Oct: Wed-Sun: 10am-12noon, 2pm-5.45pm. Admission free.)* The **Musée Magnin** comprises more than 2,000 works of art, showcased in a magnificent 17th-century hôtel which was the ancestral home of the Magnin family. *(4 rue des Bons Enfants, ☎ 03 80 67 11 10. Tue-Sun: 10am-6pm. Adult 15F, child 10F, senior 10F, student 10F.)*

South of Dijon lies the **Côte d'Or**, the famous wine region where Burgundy's best vintages are produced. Many of its villages offer wine-tasting opportunities and tours of their cellars and vineyards.

GETTING THERE

Trains run to Dijon and Lyon from the Gare de Lyon

VISITOR INFORMATION

Office de Tourisme de Dijon
34 rue des Forges
/ Place Darcy
21022 Dijon
☎ 03 80 44 11 44

Palais des Ducs

Champagne, Reims & Strasbourg

Only wine made in the Champagne region can be labelled with the sought-after name. 'Bubbly' has been produced here since the late 17th-century, when wine-producer Dom Pérignon perfected the technique for making sparkling wine.

Today, in order to preserve the exclusivity of champagne, only about 200 million bottles per year are produced, using just three particular types of grape. Britain is now the largest consumer of champagne in the world, even over France itself.

GETTING THERE

Trains from the Gare de l'Est go to Champagne and Alsace

Reims, the capital of Champagne, is named after Saint-Rémi, the bishop who converted Frankish king Clovis to Christianity in the Dark Ages. Its **basilica** is the largest Romanesque church in Northern France. It also has a splendid Gothic **cathedral** which was immortalized in a series of paintings by Monet. The cathedral was begun in 1211 and was the site of French coronations for many centuries, in memory of the baptism of Clovis in 498. Much of the exterior and interior features have been restored with donations from local champagne houses. Look out for the famous Smiling Angel statue which stands above the west portal. *(Mon-Sun: 7.30am-7.30pm.)*

VISITOR INFORMATION

L'Office de Tourisme de Reims
2 rue Guilaume de Machault
F-51100 Reims
☎ 03 26 77 45 25

The **Musée-Abbaye Saint-Rémi** exhibits historical and archaeological artefacts related to Reims and there is a large military history section. The building itself is the former quarters of the Benedictine monks of Saint-Denis. *(52 rue Simon, ☎ 03 26 85 23 36. Mon-Fri: 2pm-6.30pm. Sat-Sun: 2pm-7pm. Adult 10F, child 10F, senior 10F, student 10F.)*

The nearby **Palais du Tau**, built in 1690, was formerly an archbishop's palace and now houses the museum of the cathedral. The collection includes tapestries, sculptures and artefacts from the coronations of several French kings. The impressive **Salle du Tau** was the banqueting hall used for post-coronation feasts. *(☎ 03 26 47 81 79. Mon-Sun: 9.30am-12.30pm, 2pm-6pm (until 5pm in winter). Adult 28F, child 15F, senior 28F, student 18F.)*

Reims cathedral

Another of Reims's claims to fame is that it was the location of the signing of the German surrender on May 7th 1945 which brought hostilities in Europe to an end. Visitors can see the map room of Eisenhower's quarters, housed in the **Musée de la Reddition**. *(12, rue*

Champagne, Reims & Strasbourg

*Franklin Roosevelt, ☎ 03 26 47 84 19. Apr-Nov: Wed-Mon:
10am-12noon, 2pm-6pm. Adult 10F, child free, senior 10F,
student free.)*

Other attractions in the city include the **Musée des
Beaux-Arts** *(☎ 03 26 47 28 44)* and the **Musée-Hôtel Le
Vergeur** *(☎ 03 26 47 20 75)*, which is housed in one of
the most beautiful buildings in Reims. You can also

have guided tours
of many of the
champagne
cellars.

Alsace and
Lorraine border
Champagne and
are two separate
regions even
though they are
frequently spoken
of as if they were
linked. In fact, the
language and food

Musée-Hôtel le Vergeur

of Alsace are more
reminiscent of Germany than France, whereas
Lorraine, the birthplace of Joan of Arc and quiche
lorraine, is very French.

The capital of Alsace is Strasbourg. Most of the city,
which is just 2.5 miles (4km) from Germany, is on an
island sandwiched between two tributaries of the river
Ill.

The pink sandstone **cathedral** is visible from any part
of town. It was completed in 1439, and boasted the
tallest spire of the time. *(☎ 03 88 32 75 78. Mon-Sun:
7am-11.45am, 12.45pm-7pm.)*

Strasbourg's most important museum,
the **Musée de l'Oeuvre Notre-Dame**,
contains a priceless collection of wood
and stone sculpture, including pieces
taken from the nearby cathedral for
preservation. It also exhibits the oldest
stained glass in France. *(3 place de
Château, ☎ 03 88 52 50 00. Tue-Sun: 10am-
12noon, 1.30pm-6pm (5pm on Sunday).
Adult 15F, child free, senior free, student 8F.)*

Strasbourg

The prettiest part of town is the second,
tiny island to the south-west of the centre, known as
La Petite France. It is connected to the main island by
bridges and its 16th- and 17th-century houses, which
line winding streets, are decorated with flowers.

REFLECTIONS

'Champagne certainly
gives one werry gentle-
manly ideas, but for a
continuance, I don't know
but I should prefer mild
hale' - *Jorrock's Jaunts and
Jollities*, R.S. Surtees
(1838)

VISITOR INFORMATION

Office de Tourisme
de Strasbourg
17 place de la Cathédrale
F 67082 Strasbourg
☎ 03 88 52 28 28

Normandy and Rouen

Normandy, a region of patchwork fields often compared to the English countryside, is renowned for its agricultural produce. The particular specialities are its rich dairy products: Camembert originated here, and the area produces about half of the dairy requirements of the whole country. Its long coastline means that seafood dishes are abundant, too, as are apples and cider from the many orchards.

GETTING THERE

Trains for Normandy leave from the Gare St-Lazare

Rouen, the loveliest city in the region, has almost 1,000 half-timbered medieval houses and one of France's most famous Gothic cathedrals.

The **cathédrale Notre Dame de Rouen** was one of Monet's favourite subjects by virtue of its magnificent sculpture on the west façade. It is a perfect example of French Gothic dating from the 13th- to the 16th- centuries, although the crypt dates from an earlier,

Gros Horloge

VISITOR INFORMATION

Office de Tourisme Rouen
25 place de la Cathédrale
76008 Rouen
☎ 02 32 08 32 40

Romanesque cathedral destroyed by fire. *(Mon-Sat: 8am-7pm. Sun: 8am-6pm. Free admission.)*

The old city, thoughtfully restored after the Second World War, surrounds the cathedral. **Place de Vieux Marché** was where Joan of Arc was executed in 1431, and the pedestrian **rue du Gros Horloge** boasts, among other splendid buildings, a 16th-century gatehouse and a medieval clocktower.

Rue Damiette

Another striking building is the **Palais du Justice** *(rue aux Juifs)*, extensively restored after war damage. It is an example of ornate 16th-century Gothic, with gargoyles and statuary.

Rouen has plenty of memorials to Joan of Arc, including the **Tour Jeanne d'Arc** *(rue du Donjon, ☎ 02 35 16 21)* where she spent her last days.

Another famous name connected with the city is that of Gustave Flaubert. The author of *Madame Bovary* was born here, and the museum about his life and work also contains exhibits charting the history of medicine, since Flaubert's father was the chief surgeon of Rouen. *(Hôtel-Dieu, 51 rue de Lecat, ☎ 02 35 15 59 95. Tue-Sat: 10am-12noon, 2pm-6pm. Admission free.)*

Lyon

Lyon lies just south of Burgundy in the Rhône Valley. The city of just under 450,000 people is divided into nine *arrondissements*, and the centre of town occupies the strip of land between two rivers, the Rhône and the Sâone. During the Second World War 26 of the 28 bridges connecting the centre to the rest of Lyon were destroyed.

Place Bellecour, Lyon

The old town (**Vieux Lyon**) is on the left bank of the Sâone and is overlooked by the **basilica**, high on Fourvière Hill. It was built for the same reasons as Paris's Sacré Coeur (page 140) and to similarly flamboyant specifications. It does, however, afford a spectacular view of the town. The **Credit Lyonnais** building, looking like a cylindrical version of London's Canary Wharf, towers above everything else.

Lyon's traditional industry, the silk trade, has left its legacy in the **Croix-Rousse** area, north of the centre. Some old looms can still be seen in action at **La Maison des Canuts** (*10-12 rue Ivry, ☎ 04 78 39 88 89*), a museum devoted to the history of Lyonnais silk.

The Croix-Rousse quarter is also famous for its *traboules*, pedestrian passageways linking streets through apartment buildings. These came into being to provide easy and sheltered access for silk workers carrying their wares through the town.

VISITOR INFORMATION

Office de Tourisme (Lyon)
Place Bellecour
69002 Lyon
☎ 04 78 42 25 75

Lyon

Lyon has dozens of other museums, including the unusual **Musée de la Miniature** (*☎ 04 72 00 24 77*), which features tiny dolls-house items and miniature handmade objects. Another interesting museum is the **Musée Gallo-Romain** (*☎ 04 72 38 81 90*), an important collection of local remains and artefacts dating from the Roman Occupation.

The **Musée des Beaux-Arts** (*☎ 04 72 10 17 40*) is one of the largest in France and is a must for fans of European painting from the Middle Ages onwards.

South of France

The south-east coast between Marseille and the Italian border is made up of Provence, the Côte d'Azur and, though not strictly France, the tiny Principality of Monaco. Part of this coast is also known as the French Riviera, the playground of the rich and famous.

GETTING THERE

The South of France is 8 hours away from Paris by regular train and 4½ hours away by high-speed TGV.

VISITOR INFORMATION

Office de Tourisme Marseille
4 la Canebière
13001 Marseille
☎ 04 91 13 89 00

VISITOR INFORMATION

Office de Tourisme Toulon
Place Riaux
83000 Toulon
☎ 04 94 18 53 00

Château d'If, Marseille

Marseille's position as a gateway to the Mediterranean led to its historical importance as a centre of maritime activity, and to this day it is the setting for important boat shows and regattas. Hemmed in between mountains and the sea, it is renowned for its climate, natural beauty and glorious views.

The old port, blessed with an average of 2,600 hours of sunshine per year, is surrounded by an archipelago known as the Frioul Islands. The **Château d'If**, former prison of Mirabeau, the Man in the Iron Mask and the Count of Monte Christo, guards the bay.

This part of the coastline is made up of creeks or *calanques* which make it a popular destination for swimmers, walkers, canoeists and even climbers, all of whom benefit from the miles of sandy beaches and picturesque cliffs surrounding them.

The city itself stands in terraces overlooking the sea, topped by **Notre Dame de la Garde**. This Romanesque-Byzantine basilica was built between 1853 and 1864 and is 505 feet (154 metres) above sea-level.

The city is a mixture of architectural styles, from the 14th-century abbey of **Saint-Victor** to the 19th-century edifices of **Palais Longchamp**. Culturally Marseille is France's second city, with a plethora of theatres and 22 museums, including the **Musée d'Archeologie Mediterranéene**. This has one of the finest Egyptian collections in France.

Nice

Moving eastwards along the coast brings you to **Toulon**, the base of France's Mediterranean Naval fleet. It is built around a sheltered bay, with the liveliest and oldest part of town looking out to sea. The most interesting museum in the town is the **Musée de la Marine**, housed in the arsenal building. *(Place Monsenergue, ☎ 04 94 02 02 01. Wed-Mon: 9.30am-12noon, 2pm-6pm. Adult 29F, child 19F, senior 29F, student 19F.)*

South of France

Nice, with its 8,175 yards (7,500 metres) of beaches and 18 museums and galleries, is well-established as the capital of the Riviera. Its wonderful climate has attracted a fashionable crowd for many years, although these days the reality is rather less glamorous than it used to be.

The charming town is France's second most important tourist region. It has its own language, Nissart, which is related to Italian, and its gastronomic tradition is influenced by the proximity of Italy and of the sea.

Marketplace, Nice

The **Promenade des Anglais** epitomises the Nice of the brochures. The walkway, lined with palm trees, skirts the Bay of Angels for 3 miles (5km).

In addition to sun, sea and sand, Nice has a rich cultural heritage. It was home to Chagall, Dufy and Matisse, and today has museums devoted to each one. The old town has recently undergone a process of gentrification and has examples of Classical, Renaissance and Baroque architecture.

VISITOR INFORMATION

Office de Tourisme (Nice)
5 Promenade des Anglais
06000 Nice
☎ 04 92 14 48 00

Monaco, despite being the size of London's Hyde Park, is an individual Principality whose royals appear in the world's tabloids almost as much as the members of the British monarchy. The official language is French, but the culture and lifestyle displays a substantial Italian influence.

Monaco is divided into five separate areas. **Monaco-Ville** is the old capital, luxurious **Monte Carlo** is famous for its casinos, **Larvotto** is the beach area, **La Condamine** is the old port and **Fontvielle** is a new suburb.

VISITOR INFORMATION

Office Nationale de
Tourisme (Monaco)
2a blvd des Moulins
9800 Monaco
☎ 04 92 16 61 66

It is cheaper to stay in nearby Nice and take day trips to the principality, as hotel prices there are sky-high. Although gambling at the renowned Monte Carlo casinos is the main attraction, Monaco also offers a carefully engineered charm and several museums and points of interest, including the world famous **Musée Océanographique de Monaco** aquarium *(Ave Saint-*

Yachts at Monte Carlo

Martin, Monaco-Ville, ☎ 04 93 15 36 00. Mon-Sun: 9am-7pm (8pm in summer). Adult 60F, child 30F, senior 60F, student 30F.)

Toulouse, Pyrenées

The south-west of France borders Spain and incorporates the Toulouse area, the Pyrenees and the French Basque country.

Toulouse is the capital of a small region, the **Pays Toulousain**, which was once part of the neighbouring Languedoc area. It became a separate entity in the 1960s when French regional boundaries were redrawn.

GETTING THERE

This area of the country is served by the Gare Montparnasse

Toulouse

The capital is primarily a university town, nicknamed *la ville rose* because of the abundance of red-brick buildings. There are more students here than in any other city outside Paris, and the student life gives the town its vibrancy and youthful ambience.

The leading industry in Toulouse since the Second World War has been aeronautics, but even before then Antoine de Saint-Exupéry, aviator and author of *The Little Prince*, used its airfields as the starting point for his pioneering flights to Africa and across the

Salle des Illustres

Atlantic in the 1920s. Today, Ariane rockets and Concorde are produced here.

The city, which lies on the right bank of the wide **Garonne** river and the left bank of the **Canal du Midi**, boasts an untouched 18th-century *Vieux Quartier* (old quarter). To the north is the impressive 1750s **city hall**. The interior, including the beautiful *Salle des Illustres,* can be visited on weekdays. (*Place de Capitol.* ☎ *05 61 22 29 22*).

Canal du Midi

Toulouse's cathedral, **St-Etienne**, is a hotchpotch of

Toulouse, Pyrenées

architectural styles. It was begun in the 12th century and the last portal was added as late as 1929. Its layout is unusual, too, as the nave is out of line with

the choir. *(Rue de Metz. Mon-Sun: 7.30am-7pm.)*

Pont Neuf

Other important monuments include the more uniform **Basilique Saint-Sernin** *(Place St-Sernin, Mon-Sun: 8am-12noon, 2pm-6pm)*, built in the 11th and 12th centuries, and the classical-style **Hôtel d'Assézat**, home to the Fondation Bemberg art collection. *(Place d'Assézat, ☎ 05 61 12 06 89.)*

The most visited museum in Toulouse is the **Galerie Municipale du Château d'Eau**. This early 19th-century pumping station overlooking the 16th-century **Pont Neuf** is the setting for important exhibitions of contemporary international photography. *(Place Laganne, ☎ 05 61 77 09 40. Wed-Sun: 1pm-7pm. Adult 15F, child under 12 free, senior 15F, student 10F.)*

Carcassonne

While in the area, pay a visit to **Carcassonne**, strictly part of neighbouring Languedoc-Roussillon but only a 50 minute train journey from Toulouse. The fortress city is the stuff of medieval knights and damsels, and the old turrets are stunningly floodlit at night. It was the location for Kevin Costner's 1991 Hollywood film *Robin Hood, Prince of Thieves.*

The **Pays Basque** begins just north of the Pyrenées. The area includes part of the north of Spain, and its customs and folklore are influenced by both countries. However, the unofficial language spoken here is a linguist's dream, being entirely unrelated to any other in Europe.

The **Pyrenees** are endlessly popular with walkers. Some stalwarts walk all the way from the Atlantic to the Mediterranean, but the central **Parc National des Pyrénées**, which covers about 62 miles (100km) in the middle, has the most beautiful scenery and the highest peaks.

VISITOR INFORMATION

Office de
Tourisme de Toulouse
Donjon du Capitole
31080 Toulouse
☎ 05 61 11 02 22

VISITOR INFORMATION

Office de
Tourisme (Carcassonne)
Porte Narbonnaise
11000 Carcassonne
☎ 04 68 25 07 04

Tours and the Loire Valley

The **Loire**'s surfeit of châteaux stems from the 15th-century, when kings and dukes began to adopt the area as the perfect spot for a country retreat. Some of the region's older castle were once fortresses, but the majority of the 15th- to 18th-century examples were built with aesthetics in mind.

GETTING THERE

Tours is served by the Gare d'Austerlitz.

Tours is the liveliest town in the Loire Valley by virtue of its important university. It is thought to be where the purest French is spoken, and has a bourgeois, well-bred ambience.

Tours

The old quarter of town boasts examples of 12th- to 15th-century timbered houses, but the most impressive structure is the Renaissance **Hôtel Gouin**, home of the **Musée de la Société Archéologique de Touraine**. Here, works of art dating from prehistory and Gallo-Roman times up to the Renaissance can be viewed. *(25 rue du Commerce, ☎ 02 47 66 22 32. Mon-Sun: 10am-12.30pm, 2pm-6.30pm. Adult 18F, child 12F, senior 15F, student 12F.)*

The **Musée des Beaux Arts**, whose lovely French-style garden has a 200-year-old cedar, is home to works by Rembrandt, Rubens, Degas and Delacroix, to name a few. The building itself is the former archbishop's palace, and the rooms evoke 18th-century life. *(18 place François-Sicard, ☎ 02 47 05 68 73. Wed-Mon: 9am-12.45pm, 2pm-6pm. Adult 30F, child 15F, senior 15F, student 15F.)*

VISITOR INFORMATION

Office de Tourisme
78 rue Bernard Palissy
37000 Tours
☎ 02 47 70 37 37

Contact this Office for information about guided tours to the outlying *châteaux*

Just two towers of the medieval **Château de Tours** remain and are annexed to the **Aquarium Tropical**. Marine creatures from five continents are on display here in more than 34,000 litres of water. *(25 quai d'Orleans, ☎ 02 47 64 29 52. Mon-Sun: 2pm-5.30pm. Adult 30F, child 18F, senior 22F, student 22F.)*

The **Historial de Touraine** wax museum, which uses 165 figures as well as soundtracks and music to illustrate the history of the area, is in the same building. *(Mon-Sun: 9am-12noon, 2pm-6pm.)*

Other museums include one devoted to the wines of the region, the **Musée des Vins de Touraine** *(16 rue Nationale, ☎ 02 47 61 07 93)*, and a unique collection of trade guild crafts comprising items by joiners, cartwrights and even clogmakers at the **Musée du Compagnonnage**. *(8 rue Nationale, ☎ 02 47 61 07 93.)*

Visitor Information

Calendar of Events . . .

January

La Grande Parade de Montmartre, a parade to celebrate the New Year. *(Jan 1. Place Pigalle to place Jules-Joffrin.)*

Festival Mondial du Cirque de Demain, international circus event. *(5 days at the end of Jan. Cirque d'Hiver Bouglione, ☎ 01 44 61 06 00.)*

February

Foire à la Feraille de Paris, antiques fair / fleamarket. *(Parc Floral, Bois de Vincennes, ☎ 01 40 62 95 95.)*

Salon de l'Agriculture, agricultural show. *(End Feb-beginning Mar. Parc des Expositions, ☎ 01 49 09 60 00.)*

March

Salon de Mars, antiques and art fair. *(By the Eiffel Tower, ☎ 01 44 94 86 80.)*

Festival d'Art Sacré de la Ville de Paris, church music recitals and concerts all over Paris. *(End Mar-beginning Apr. ☎ 01 45 61 54 99.)*

Foire de Trône, 12th *arrondissement* funfair. *(End Mar-end May. Pelouse de Reuilly / Bois de Vincennes, ☎ 01 46 27 52 29.)*

April

Marathon International de Paris, 42km race from the Place de la Concorde to the Hippodrome de Vincennes. *(Sun, mid-late Apr. ☎ 01 53 17 03 10.)*

Foire de Paris, gastronomic fair. *(End Apr-beginning May. Parc des Expositions, ☎ 01 49 09 60 00.)*

May

Mai 1er, May day celebratory marches. *(May 1, Place de la Bastille.)*

Vintage Car Rally. *(Sun closest to May 15. Montmartre, ☎ 01 46 06 79 56.)*

International de France de Tennis, French Open tennis championships. *(Last week of May, first week of Jun. Stade Roland Garres, ☎ 01 47 43 48 00.)*

June

Fête de la Musique, free concerts and bands at several venues. *(Jun 21. ☎ 01 40 03 94 70.)*

Festival Chopin à Paris, candlelit piano concerts. *(Mid-Jun-mid Jul. Orangerie de Bagatelle, Bois de Boulogne. ☎ 01 45 00 22 19.)*

Feux de la Saint-Jean, fireworks for St-Jean's Day. *(3rd week in Jun. Parc de la Villette / quai St-Bernard.)*

Gay Pride, march. *(☎ 01 43 57 21 47.)*

Course des Garçons de Café, waiters race through the streets carrying trays of drinks. *(Late Jun / early Jul. Hôtel de Ville, ☎ 01 46 33 89 89.)*

Halle that Jazz, jazz festival. *(End Jun-beginning July.*

. . . Calendar of Events

Grande Halle de la Villette, ☎ 01 40 03 75 75.)

Foire St-Germain, antique fair, concerts and exhibitions. *(Jun-Jul. St-Germain-des-Prés, ☎ 01 40 46 75 12.)*

La Goutte d'Or en Fête, international music festival. *(1st week of Jul. ☎ 01 42 62 11 13.)*

Bastille Day, fireworks and dancing. *(July 14. Place de la Bastille.)*

Arrivée du Tour de France Cyclistes, participants cross the finishing line in the Champs-Elysées. *(3rd or 4th Sun in Jul.)*

Festival du Cinéma en Plein Air, open-air cinema. *(Jul 15-Aug 15. Parc de la Villette. ☎ 01 40 03 75 00.)*

Fête de l'Assomption, procession. *(Aug 15. Ile de la Cité, ☎ 01 42 34 56 10.)*

Fête de l'Humanité, music, food, fireworks and exhibitions sponsored by the Communist Party. *(2nd weekend in Sep. La Courneuve, ☎ 01 49 22 72 72.)*

Journées Portes Ouvertes, government buildings are opened to the public. *(Weekend closest to Sep 15. Throughout Paris and France, ☎ 01 44 61 20 00.)*

Nouveau Festival International de Danse de Paris, dance festival. *(End Sep-beginning Oct. Théâtre du Châtelet, ☎ 01 40 28 28 40.)*

Fête des Vendanges, grape harvest. *(1st or 2nd Sat in Oct. Montmartre vineyard, ☎ 01 42 62 21 21.)*

FIAC, contemporary international art show. *(Early Oct. By the Eiffel Tower, ☎ 01 49 53 27 00.)*

Prix de l'Arc de Triomphe, horse race. *(First weekend in Oct. Longchamp, ☎ 01 49 10 20 30.)*

Salon de Champignon, mushroom-fanciers fair. *(Mid-late Oct. Jardin des Plantes, ☎ 01 40 79 36 00.)*

Marjolaine, ecological food and gift fair. *(First 10 days in Nov. Parc Floral de Paris, Bois de Vincennes. ☎ 01 43 43 92 95.)*

Mois de la Photo, photographic exhibitions at several venues. *(All Nov. ☎ 01 43 59 41 78.)*

Fête du Beaujolais Nouveau, the arrival of the new vintage. *(3rd Thu in Nov. All France.)*

Lancement des Illuminations des Champs-Elysées, switching-on ceremony of the Christmas lights. *(End Nov. Avenue des Champs-Elysées.)*

Children's Paris . . .

Attractions - many of the attractions and museums offering discounts to **for less** cardholders are of interest to children. These include France Miniature (page 230), Musée Grevin (page 52), Musée en Herbe (page 190), the Centre de la Mer et des Eaux (page 98), and the Marionettes de Champ-de-Mars (page 117). Paristoric (page 57) is a good introduction to the city for any age.

Mammoth at the Muséum National d'Histoire Naturelle

Other museums guaranteed to keep children occupied include the Cité des Sciences (page 152), with its hands-on exhibits, the Museum Nationale d'Histoire Naturelle (page 99), the Musée de la Curiosité (page 78), the aquarium at the Musée d'Arts Africains et Océanographiques (page 154) and Musée de la Poupée (page 76).

Childrens' taste for the unusual or gruesome can be satisfied by a visit to Les Egouts (page 115) or the Paris Catacombes (page 169).

Toddlers are often allowed into museums free. The childrens' reduced admission rate, found at most museums, usually applies to those up to the age of 12, 16 or even 18.

Muséum National d'Histoire Naturelle

Tours - children enjoy the trips on miniature trains offered at Montmartre and La Défense (see pages 141 and 199), and the boat trips along the Seine.

Sightseeing - there is multitude of places in Paris to enjoy a bird's-eye view, always popular with children. The Eiffel Tower, of course, is a hit, especially when Paris is lit up at night. The exterior glass escalators at the Centre Pompidou (page 72) make an exciting change, and a visit to the Sacré Coeur (page 140) is made more child-friendly by the carousel at the bottom of the hill.

Bois de Boulogne

Parks - many of Paris's parks have children's playground areas. There are lots of amusements and

. . . Children's Paris

activities for children in the Bois de Boulogne (page 185) and the Bois de Vincennes (page 151), including boating lakes and cycle trails. The Jardin d'Acclimatation in the Bois de Boulogne comprises a zoo, a funfair and a children's theatre.

La Villette (pages 149 to 162), with its themed gardens, is a good bet for keeping children amused for hours.

The Jardin des Halles offers crèche facilities so that you can lose the kids for a hour or two.

Bois de Vincennes

Restaurants, bars and hotels - children are well catered for in most restaurants in Paris, and even the bars are quite welcoming. Some of the chain restaurants have a special children's menu.

Fussy eaters need not be a problem, as there are plenty of hamburger chains to fall back on. The superb quality and choice of supermarket, delicatessen and bakery food makes a picnic an ideal alternative in good weather.

Several of the hotels listed in this book offer baby-sitting facilities. See the separate listings for details.

Sport - Aquaboulevard (page 177), which offers a *for less* discount, is a great place for children to swim and play water games in a safe and temperature-controlled environment.

Outside Paris - Disneyland Paris (page 225) is hugely

popular with adults and children alike. The Disneyland complex comprises hotels, a campsite, restaurants and shops, as well as the terrific rides, shows and atmosphere made famous by its American counterpart.

Disneyland Paris

Shopping - you can deck your children out in chic Parisian fashion from

Bonpoint *(67 rue de l'Universitaire, 7th, ☎ 01 45 55 63 70).* There are plenty of toy and book shops, some, such as **Chantelivre** *(13 rue des Sèvres, 6th, ☎ 01 45 48 87 90)* with children's books in English.

Bonpoint

. . . Visitor Information . . .

British Embassy

INSIDER'S TIP

You will find additional visitor information that will be helpful before you go to Paris, when you arrive, and when planning your itinerary on pages 16-22.

US Embassy

CLIMATE

Although Paris has less rainfall than the rest of the north of France, showers occur quite often. The temperature seldom drops far below 0°C (32°F) in winter, and in the height of summer can reach 30°C (86°F).

CUSTOMS

Import restrictions on tax/duty free goods from EU countries are: **Tobacco**: 300 cigarettes; **Alcohol**: 5 litres of wine plus 2.5 litres of spirits or 3 litres of drinks under 22°; **Perfumes**: 75g.

The restrictions for non-EU visitors are: **Tobacco**: 200 cigarettes; **Alcohol**: 2 litres of wine plus 1 litre of spirits or 2 litres of drinks under 22°; **Perfumes**: 50g.

ELECTRIC CURRENT

Electricity in France runs on 220V, so British appliances simply need a two-prong convertor, which is widely available at airports and in shops. American 110V appliances need a transformer.

EMBASSIES

Australia *(4 rue Jean-Rey, 15ᵗʰ, ☎ 01 40 59 33 00)*, Britain *(35 rue du Fbg-St-Honoré, 8ᵗʰ, ☎ 01 44 51 31 00)*, Canada *(35 avenue Montaigne, 8ᵗʰ, ☎ 01 44 43 29 00)*, Ireland *(4 rue Rude, 16ᵗʰ, ☎ 01 44 17 67 00)*, New Zealand *(7ter rue Léonard-de-Vinci, 16ᵗʰ, ☎ 01 45 00 24 11)*, South Africa *(59 quai d'Orsay, 7ᵗʰ, ☎ 01 45 55 92 37)*, United States *(2 av Gabriel, 8ᵗʰ, ☎ 01 43 12 22 22)*.

EMERGENCIES

Dial ☎ 17 for the Police, ☎ 18 for the Fire Service and ☎ 15 for an ambulance. These are all 24-hour services.

French ambulance service

All hospitals in Paris have a 24-hour emergency ward. For a complete list of hospitals in and around the city, call the *Hôpital Assistance Publique (☎ 01 40 27 30 00)*.

ETIQUETTE

Parisians use courtesies such as *Monsieur* and *Madame* in almost every situation. Most Parisians are only too pleased to give directions and help tourists around the city.

. . . Visitor Information . . .

Smoking in restaurants and other public places is more widely tolerated in France than in countries such

as Britain. The obligatory non-smoking areas of some restaurants are very small. Smoking is not allowed in most theatres and cinemas. It is also banned everywhere on the *métro*, but a surprising number of Parisians ignore this rule.

Few grassy areas in Paris are meant to be sat on. 'Pelouse interdite' means 'keep off the grass' and these signs are rife in the Tuileries and the Jardin du

Smoking is a popular pursuit

Luxembourg, with patrolling *gendarmes* making sure the law is kept. Go to one of the outlying parks to feel the grass beneath your feet.

HEALTH AND SAFETY

EU nationals are entitled to treatment from the French health service provided they have form E111. Non-EU nationals should take out comprehensive travel insurance which includes medical coverage.

There are plenty of grassy spaces in the Bois de Boulogne

Paris is generally quite safe, but as in any large city, watch out for pickpockets. The tramps that hang around the *métro* are harmless enough, though often drunk and smelly.

Report thefts to the police for insurance purposes and call the following 24-hour helplines to cancel lost or stolen cards (all have English speaking staff):
American Express (☎ *01 47 77 72 00*), Diner's Club (☎ *01 47 62 75 75*), MasterCard (☎ *01 45 67 84 84*), Visa (☎ *01 42 77 11 90*).

LANGUAGE

Although English is often spoken in tourist offices, most hotels, museums and large shops, you may need a little French in smaller shops and restaurants. In any case it is useful to know some basic phrases, and the French are usually helpful towards people attempting to speak their language.

Hello / Goodbye	*Bonjour / Au revoir*
Yes / No	*Oui / Non*
Please / Thank you	*S'il vous plaît / Merci*
What's your name?	*Comment vous appelez-vous?*

INSIDER'S TIP

Forget what your teachers told you. Summoning a waiter with 'Garçon!' is likely to cause offence these days.

. . . Visitor Information . . .

Do you speak English?	*Parlez-vous anglais?*
I am English	*Je suis anglais/e*
How do you say it in French?	*Comment ça se dit en français?*
Sorry / Excuse me	*Pardon / Excusez-moi*
I don't understand	*Je ne comprends pas*
Please speak more slowly	*S'il vous plaît, parlez moins vite*
OK	*D'accord*
It doesn't matter	*De rien*
Where is...	*Où est...*
How much is it?	*C'est combien?*
How are you?	*Ça va?*
I would like...	*Je voudrais...*
Exit	*Sortie*
Open	*Ouvert*
No Vacancies	*Complet*
Out of Order	*En panne*
Prohibited	*Interdit*
Information	*Renseignements*

Bureau des Objects Trouvés

INSIDER'S TIP

When buying fruit and vegetables from markets or grocers, do not touch the produce yourself. Let the stallholder select it for you.

LOST PROPERTY

Contact the *Bureau des Objects Trouvés* in person at 36 rue des Morillons, 15th *(8.30am-5pm Mon-Fri, until 8pm Tue & Thu)*. You must take some form of identification and be specific about where and when you lost your item. There is a charge for returned items.

MAIL / POST

Post offices are open from 8am to 7pm Monday to Friday, and 9am until noon on Saturday. Most have automatic weighing machines which print out a stamp for your letter or parcel.

Poste Restante - You can collect Poste Restante letters (make sure the sender puts your surname in capitals) from the post office at 52 rue du Louvre, 75001 Paris.

MARKETS

Fruit and vegetable market

As well as the famous book stalls along the banks of the Seine (see page 103) and the flower market on the Ile de la Cité, Paris has three big *Marchés aux Puces*, or flea markets, selling just about anything and everything.

... Visitor Information ...

Montmartre and NW Paris - Marché aux Puces St-Ouen, 18th, *métro* Porte de Clignancourt. Open Sat-Mon: 5am-6pm.

Paris East - Marché aux Puces de Montreuil, 20th, *métro* Porte de Montreuil. Open Sat-Mon: 7.30am-7pm.

Montparnasse - Marché aux Puces de Vanves, 14th, *métro* Porte de Vanves. Open Sat-Sun: 7.30am-7pm.

There are several street markets in the city offering a choice of produce. Market streets include rue Montorgueil (1st), rue Mouffetard (5th) and rue de Buci (6th).

Rue Mouffetard

MEDIA

Newspapers: British and American papers and

magazines, along with many other foreign language papers, can be found at larger outlets. Of the French daily papers, *Le Monde* is the most respected.

Listings: Listings magazines such as *Pariscope*, which contains an English-language supplement, are published weekly and include everything you will need to know about current cinema and theatre offerings, temporary exhibitions and

Newspaper stand

more.

Radio: Tune into Chante France to submerge yourself in totally French music. Since 1996 radio policy has been to devote 40% of musical airtime to chanson française, although on some of the other channels this may not be apparent.

France Musique is a classical music station, and for international news in French the state-run France Inter is good. France Info offers 24-hour news headlines and bulletins. The BBC World Service is accessible for news in the English language.

Television: There are six channels in France: TF1 and the state-run FR2 and FR3 are aimed at the mass-market; Canal +, a private subscribers' channel, concentrates on sport and films; Arte is co-run with Germany for quality cultural programmes; and M6 is popular with 20- and 30-somethings.

. . . Visitor Information . . .

MONEY

One French franc is made up of 100 centimes. Francs come in 500, 200, 100, 50 and 20F notes and 20, 10, 5, 2 and 1F coins. At the time of printing, 10F is worth just under £1 or about $1.60.

French francs

French prices are written with a comma where the British or American decimal point would be. For example, 12,50F is 12 francs and 50 centimes.

Money changing - You can change money at banks or at bureaux de change. Although bureaux de change keep longer hours, they sometimes charge high commissions (transaction fees).

With the **for less** vouchers, you pay no transaction fee at Travelex outlets in the US or UK (see left).

Credit cards - Major credit cards are accepted just about everywhere in Paris.

NATIONAL HOLIDAYS

On national holidays many businesses and shops close, but most restaurants and museums stay open.

Le Jour de L'An	1 Jan 1998 /1 Jan 1999
Lundi de Paques	13 Apr 1998/5 Apr 1999
Fête du Travail	1 May 1998/1 May 1999
Fin de la Guerre	8 May 1998/8 May 1999
L'Ascension	21 May 1998/13 May 1999
Pentecoste	1 Jun 1998/24 May 1999
Le 14 Juillet	14 Jul 1998/14 Jul 1999
Assomption	15 Aug 1998/15 Aug 1999
La Toussant	1 Nov 1998/1 Nov 1999
L'Armistice	11 Nov 1998/11 Nov 1999
Le Jour de Noël	25 Dec 1998/25 Dec 1999

OPENING HOURS

Banks - Standard opening hours are 9am to 4.30pm Monday to Friday, and 9am-12noon on Saturdays.

. . . Visitor Information . . .

Some banks close at lunchtime, and all are closed on national holidays (see page 254), sometimes from noon the previous day.

Bars / Restaurants - Most restaurants close for a few hours between lunch and dinner. As a rule, the latest you can order a meal is about 10pm.

Brasseries / Cafés - these are generally more flexible with their serving times. Bar opening times vary greatly, with some closing well after midnight.

A Parisian bank

Shops - Business hours are normally from 8am or 9am to 7pm or 8pm, though some shops close for an hour or two at lunchtime. Some are also closed during August, when Parisians typically tkae a whole month's holiday.

ORIENTATION

Paris is divided into 20 *arrondissements* or areas which begin in the centre and spiral outwards. In this book the *arrondissement* number (1st, 2nd) is given after the address.

RELIGIOUS SERVICES

Paris has several English-speaking churches, including the American Church in Paris *(65 quai d'Orsay, 7th, ☎ 01 40 62 05 00)* and St George's Church *(7 rue Auguste-Vacquerie, 16th, ☎ 01 47 20 22 51)*.

SPECIAL TRAVELLERS

Disabled: *Tourisme pour Tout le Monde*, available at 60F from tourist offices, gives information and advice about disabled access in Paris. Most major attractions and museums have easy access, but the transport service is not wheelchair-user-friendly.

Elderly: Concessions are usually available for senior citizens but may not always be advertised, so be sure to ask. Where specified in this guide, *for less* discounts are available on top of reduced senior prices.

Students: Student concessions are available at many attractions and museums when acceptable ID, such as an ISIC card, is produced. Where specified in this guide, *for less* discounts are available on top of the normal student discount.

Gay: The Centre Gai et Lesbian *(3 rue Keller, 11th, ☎ 01 43 57 21 47)* is both an information centre and a meeting place.

Centre Gai et Lesbian

. . . Visitor Information . . .

SPORT

Call Allô-Sports (☎ 01 42 76 54 54) during business hours for general information about sports and sporting events in Paris.

There are several golf courses outside Paris

Athletics: There are open-air running tracks in the Bois de Boulogne and the Bois de Vincennes. The Paris Marathon happens every April.

Boating: Hire boats on the lakes in the Bois de Boulogne and the Bois de Vincennes.

Cycling: The Tour de France finishes in Paris every July and always attracts a large crowd of spectators.

Bicycles can be hired in the Bois de Boulogne.

Football: Parc des Princes (☎ 01 42 88 02 76) is the home of Paris's main football team, Paris St-Germain, and also hosts rugby matches.

Golf: All the golf courses are outside the périphérique, but the Fédération Française du Golf (☎ 01 44 17 63 00) will give you details of non-member clubs.

Parc des Princes

Horseracing: The famous Prix de l'Arc de Triomphe race is held at the Hippodrome de Longchamp (☎ 01 44 30 75 00) in the Bois de Boulogne.

Ice Skating: Weather permitting, there is skating on the Lac Supérieur in the Bois de Boulogne. The Patinoire de Boulogne (☎ 01 46 21 04 26) is an indoor rink just outside Paris.

Pétanque: This form of bowls is the most popular sport in Paris. Contact the Fédération Française de Pétanque et de Jeux Provençales (☎ 01 48 74 61 63) for details.

Boating in the Bois de Boulogne

Stade Roland Garros

Riding: You can go horseriding in the Bois de Boulogne or the Bois de Vincennes.

Swimming: Aquaboulevard (page 170) is an aquatic park which offers a discount to *for less* cardholders.

Tennis: The French Open tennis tournament is the Parisian equivalent of Wimbledon, held every year at the Stade Roland Garros (☎ 01 47 43 48 00).

. . . Visitor Information . . .

Working Out: There are plenty of branches of the well-equipped *Gymnase Club* in the city. Many hotels have their own gyms.

TAXES

If you reside outside the EU you may reclaim tax on goods purchased in France, the only condition being that you spend 1200F or more in one place. You need to fill in a form (available from shops) and present it along with the goods at the airport when you leave.

TELEPHONES

The area code for Paris is ☎ 01. Public telephone boxes in Paris do not take coins; you need to purchase a *télécarte* from *métro* stations, tabacs and post offices.

Alternatively, you can use your **for less** card as a telephone calling card by following the instructions on page 8.

Public telephone

TIPPING

Restaurants - service is included on the bill in restaurants, although it is customary to leave a further tip (*pourboire*) for good service.

Taxis - a tip of 15% is expected.

Theatres and Cinemas - always tip the usher.

Toilets - most public toilets have attendants and a tip of about 2F even as you enter is unavoidable.

TOILETS

Follow the 'WC' or 'Toilettes' sign. Toilets in hotels and large stores are marginally more pleasant than public ones.

Office de Tourisme on the Champs-Elysées

TOURIST INFORMATION

The main tourist office is in a prime spot at the end of the Champs-Elysées, at no.127, near the Arc de Triomphe (☎ 01 49 52 53 54). It is open every day from 9am-8pm. Someone on the staff should be able to speak English. There is recorded tourist information in English on ☎ 01 49 52 53 56.

Smaller branches of the tourist office are located at the main train stations: Austerlitz (☎ 01 45 84 91 70), Gare de l'Est (☎ 01 46 07 17 73), Gare du Nord (☎ 01 45 26 94 82), Gare de Lyon (☎ 01 43 43 33 24), Gare Montparnasse (☎ 01 43 22 19 19), and at the Eiffel Tower (☎ 01 45 51 22 15).

Office de Tourisme

. . . Visitor Information . . .

TRAVELLING IN PARIS

Métro - the Paris underground railway is fast, reliable and efficient, although changing trains sometimes involves a long walk from platform to platform. In order to catch the right train, you must know the final destination of the line you require.

The *métro* is also quite cheap, with a *carnet* of 10 tickets currently costing 48F. There are also travelcards which last for one, three or five days, costing from 100F. If you are in Paris for at least a week, you may save money by getting a *coupon hebdomadaire* for 72F. Lasting from Monday to Sunday, this entitles you to as many journeys as you can make at any time of the day. You will, however, need to get a photocard to go with it (ask at any ticket booth).

RER - the RER trains run into the suburbs, and are connected to the *métro* within the centre of the city. For longer journeys across the centre it is often quicker to take an RER line.

The métro

Buses - *métro* tickets can be used on buses. Night buses serve the outer reaches of Paris when the *métro* and daytime buses stop running.

Taxis - a white light on the roof means that a taxi is free. There are taxi ranks at railway stations and on main roads.

Car rental - driving in the centre of Paris is not recommended for visitors. It is difficult to follow directions and parking places are few.

TRAVELLING OUTSIDE PARIS

Trains - several places of interest outside Paris, including Disneyland and Versailles, are served by the RER (see above). The SNCF (French national railway) provides an efficient service to more far-flung places. The high-speed TGV trains serve main routes.

SNCF tickets must be stamped in the validation machines on the platform before you board, otherwise a fine may be incurred. For information about SNCF

Parisian taxi

INSIDER'S TIP

Don't put weekly or monthly métro *coupons* through the validating machines on buses - it renders them useless. Show them to the driver instead.

TGV sign

INSIDER'S TIP

For information about getting to and from the airports, see page 18

. . . Visitor Information

services, call ☎ 01 45 82 50 50.

Car rental - outside Paris, driving is a good way to see some of the French countryside at your own pace. International car rental firms such as Avis *(☎ 01 46 10 60 60)* and Hertz *(☎ 01 47 88 51 51)* have offices at the airports and in Paris itself.

USEFUL TELEPHONE NUMBERS

Emergencies - Police: ☎ 17, Fire Service: ☎ 18, Ambulance: ☎ 15.

Railway Information - ☎ 08 36 35 35 35.

Lost credit cards - American Express *(☎ 01 47 77 72 00)*, Diner's Club *(☎ 01 47 62 75 75)*, Mastercard *(☎ 01 45 67 84 84)*, Visa *(☎ 01 42 77 11 90)*.

Emergency Dentist - ☎ 01 43 37 51 00.

RATP - information about public transport in Paris is on ☎ 08 36 68 77 14.

Central Post Office - 52 rue du Louvre, 1st, ☎ 01 40 28 20 00.

Time - call ☎ 36 99 for the speaking clock.

Traffic Information - for information about motorways outside Paris, call ☎ 01 47 05 90 01.

Weather - for recorded information on weather in the Paris region, call ☎ 08 36 68 02 75. For country-wide and international forecasts, call ☎ 01 45 56 71 71.

Explore France by car

Central post office

WEIGHTS, MEASURES AND CLOTHING SIZES

Add 28 to British women's sizes to find the French size, and add 30 to American sizes (e.g. a British size 14 is 42 in France, and an American size 14 (British size 16) is 44).

Men's American sizes are the same in France. Add 12 to British sizes for suits and coats and between 21 and 27 to British shirt sizes the higher they go (i.e. add 21 to size 14, 22 to size 14.5, 23 to size 15 etc.).

Add 33 to women's and 34 to men's British shoe sizes, and add 31 to women's and 33 to men's American shoe sizes to find the French sizes.

Paris clothes shop

INSIDER'S TIP

To convert from Celsius to Fahrenheit, multiply the number by 9, divide by 5 and add 32.

To convert from Fahrenheit to Celsius, subtract 32, multiply by 5 and divide by 9.

Index of Discounters . . .

. . . Index of Discounters . . .

TOURS

. . . Index of Discounters . . .

SHOPS

Accessories	La Perlotte	104	LQ
Accessories	Richard Gampel	121	IT
Accessories	Richard Gampel	194	MO
Antiques	Sarah Boutique	108	LQ
Beauty Salon	Josiane Laure	65	LO
Beauty Salon	Josiane Laure	104	LQ
Beauty Shop/Perfume	Parfumerie Lamsel	106	LQ
China/Gifts	Paradis 13	87	MA
Clothing/Jewellery	L'Ibis Rouge	122	IT
Clothing/Tableware	Anne Marie Beretta	106	LQ
Ethnic Gifts	L'Ephemere	122	IT
Eyewear	Optic 2000	90	MA
Gifts	Calao	88	MA
Gifts/Jewellery	Pulcinella	66	LO
Gifts/Jewellery	Yvie	124	IT
Gifts/Home Furnishings	L'Atelier Bleu	172	PI
Gifts/Housewares	Creation Sylvanie	107	LQ
Gifts/Housewares	Marie-Liesse	123	IT
Gifts/Jewellery	Laquari	172	PI
Gifts/Teas	T'cha	107	LQ
Glassware	Unio	103	LQ
Hairdressing	Marianne Gray	104	LQ
Hairdressing	Richard	162	VI
Hats	Corinne Zaquine	122	IT
Home Furnishings/Gifts	L'Atelier Bleu	172	PI
Housewares/Gifts	Creation Sylvanie	107	LQ
Housewares/Gifts	Marie-Liesse	123	IT
Jewellery	Robert	66	LO
Jewellery	François Paultre	105	LQ
Jewellery	Synthetic	121	IT
Jewellery	Rosset-Gaulejac	123	IT
Jewellery	Caillou	148	MO
Jewellery	Caillou	181	MO
Jewellery/Clothing	L'Ibis Rouge	122	IT
Jewellery/Gifts	Pulcinella	66	LO
Jewellery/Gifts	Yvie	124	IT
Jewellery/Gifts	Laquari	172	PI
Leather Goods	Terre de Bruyère	120	IT
Leather Goods	La Diligence	147	MO
Leather Goods	Terre de Bruyere	148	MO
Lingerie	Nikita	108	LQ
Men's and Women's Clothing	L'Habilleur	89	MA
Men's and Women's Clothing	Café Coton	89	MA
Men's and Women's Clothing	Franck-Alexandre	90	MA
Men's and Women's Clothing	You and Me	121	IT
Men's Clothing	Café Coton	64	LO
Men's Clothing	Only You	123	IT
Men's Clothing	Café Coton	136	Œ
Oils	Huilerie Artisanale Leblanc	107	LQ
Perfume/Beauty Shop	Parfumerie Lamsel	106	LQ
Second-hand designer labels	7e Divine	124	IT

. . . Index of Discounters

SHOPS CONTINUED

Second-hand designer labels	Asphodele	66	LO
Second-hand designer labels	L'Eventail	136	Œ
Second-hand designer labels	Les Caprices de Sopjie	194	MO
Shoes	American and British Shoes	65	LO
Shoes	Show-Sur	88	MA
Shoes	Melbury	89	MA
Shoes	Mary Collins	90	MA
Shoes	Stege	105	LQ
Shoes	British Shoes	162	VI
Shoes	Melbury	182	MO
Tableware/Clothing	Anne Marie Beretta	106	LQ
Teas/Gifts	T'cha	107	LQ
Toys	Cerfvolissime	106	LQ
Toys	Le Monde en Marché	108	LQ
Toys	Le Preau de Ferdinand	148	MO
Wine Shop	Le Nectar de Bourbons	88	MA
Wine Shop	Les Plaisirs du Palais	147	MO
Women's Clothing	Divine	65	LO
Women's Clothing	Emaldi	103	LQ
Women's Clothing	Ane Kenssen	105	LQ
Women's Clothing	Etienne Brunel	124	IT
Women's Clothing	Perlyne	182	MO
Women's Clothing	Le Comptoir de la Mode	182	MO

PEFORMING ARTS

Au Duc des Lombards	211	Jazz
Cabaret la Boheme	210	Cabaret
Caveau da la Huchette	211	Jaz Nightclub
L'Abbe Constantin	210	Cabaret
Le Balle au Bond	209	Dinner Show
Le Canotier	210	Cabaret
Le Rive Gauche	211	Concert Hall
Le Saint	212	Club
Maxwell Café	212	Live Music Club
Opéra-Comique	208	Opéra
Point Virgule	209	Cafe-Théâtre
Slow Club	212	Jazz Club
Théâtre de la Bastille	208	Ballet and Dance
Théâtre de la Cite International	208	Dance, Comedy and Drama
Théâtre de Nesle	209	Théâtre

PHOTO CREDITS

The Publishers would like to thank the following people and organizations for permission to reproduce their photographs over which they retain copyright. Any omission from this list is unintentional and every effort will be made to include these in the next edition of this publication. Olivier Prevosto (principal photography), Photothèque des Musées de la Ville de Paris, Massimo Listri, L.S. Jaulmes, Christophe Walter, Karin Maucotel, Marc Dubroca, Musée de l'Armée, Caroline Rose, J.P. Lagiewski, Patricia Canino, M.C. Bordaz, Vittoria Rizzoli, J. Moatti, Musée de la Poupée, J. Manoukian, Michel Lamoureaux, Arnaud Legrain, F. Guy, L. Danière, A. Scuivan, Heliflash, Mairie de Toulouse, Dannie A. Launay, Disney, Bernard Maison, Office de Tourisme de Tours, Office de Tourisme de Lyon, Mairie de Dijon, Office de Tourisme de Reims, Office de Tourisme de Strasbourg, Gilles Rigoulet, P. Crapet, J.F. Benard, Office de Tourisme de Chantilly, Eurostar (U.K.) Ltd, Marcel Peeters, Nanteuil, Houel, Paristoric, J.P. Defail, Musée de l'Histoire de la Medecin, P. Pitrou, Domingo Dado, J.A. Brunelle, Promotrain, L'Atelier du Cuivre, Musée en Herbe, Parc Zoologique de Thoiry, France Miniature, J. Valle, André Chastel, Alain Courtois, J.L. Catherine, Office de Tourisme de Amiens

Index of Hotels

KEY TO ABBREVIATIONS

LO = Louvre and Opéra
MA = Le Marais and République
LQ = Latin Quarter
IT = Les Invalides and Tour Eiffel
CE = Champs-Elysées

PW = Paris West
MN = Montmartre and North-west Paris
MP = Montparnasse
★ = Hotel rating category (see page 32)
F = Hotel price category (see page 32)

Á l'Abbe Constantin (page 210)

No. of adults	1 2 3 4 5	Circle as appropriate - voucher valid for number of people who hold *for less* cards
No. of children	1 2 3 4 5	
No. of seniors	1 2 3 4 5	
No. of students	1 2 3 4 5	

T.G.I. Friday (page 61)

Ce coupon donne droit à 1 à 5 personnes à la réduction de 20% sur le montant total de l'addition (boissons comprises).

Au Duc des Lombards (page 211)

No. of paid admissions: 1 or 2 (please circle)

Voucher valid for number of people who hold
for less cards –
maximum 2 free admissions

Point Virgule (page 209)

No. of paid admissions: 1 or 2 (please circle)

Voucher valid for number of people who hold
for less cards –
maximum 2 free admissions

Institut du Monde Arabe (page 99)

No. of paid admissions: 1 or 2 (please circle)

Voucher valid for number of people who hold
for less cards –
maximum 2 free admissions

La Balle au Bond (page 209)

No. of adults	1 2 3 4 5	Circle as appropriate - voucher valid for number of people who hold *for less* cards
No. of children	1 2 3 4 5	
No. of seniors	1 2 3 4 5	
No. of students	1 2 3 4 5	

Ce coupon donne droit au titulaire de la carte **for less** aux réductions suivantes chez Á l'Abbe Constantin (page 210):

Adulte 20% de réduction Retraité 20% de réduction
Enfant 20% de réduction Etudiant 20% de réduction

Not valid in conjunction with any other offer. Voucher should be presented with bill before paying or discount cannot apply. Not redeemable for cash.

Ce coupon donne droit au titulaire de la carte **for less** à la réduction suivante chez Au Duc des Lombards (page 211):

2-pour-1 entrée: chaque entrée achetée vous donne droit á une entrée gratuite d'une valeur égale ou inférieure (jusqu'à 2 entrées gratuites)

Ce coupon donne droit au titulaire de la carte **for less** à la réduction suivante chez Point Virgule (page 209):

2-pour-1 entrée: chaque entrée achetée vous donne droit á une entrée gratuite d'une valeur égale ou inférieure (jusqu'à 2 entrées gratuites)

Ce coupon donne droit au titulaire de la carte **for less** à la réduction suivante chez Institut du Monde Arabe (page 99):

2-pour-1 entrée: chaque entrée achetée vous donne droit á une entrée gratuite d'une valeur égale ou inférieure (jusqu'à 2 entrées gratuites)

Ce coupon donne droit au titulaire de la carte **for less** aux réductions suivantes chez La Balle au Bond (page 209):

Adulte 50% de réduction Retraité 50% de réduction
Enfant 50% de réduction Etudiant 50% de réduction

Le Canotier (page 210)

No. of adults	1 2 3 4 5	Circle as appropriate - voucher valid for number of people who hold *for less* cards
No. of children	1 2 3 4 5	
No. of seniors	1 2 3 4 5	
No. of students	1 2 3 4 5	

Aquaboulevard (page 177)

No. of paid admissions: **1** or **2** (please circle)

Voucher valid for number of people who hold
for less cards -
maximum 2 free admissions

Musée Pasteur (page 177)

No. of paid admissions: **1** or **2** (please circle)

Voucher valid for number of people who hold
for less cards -
maximum 2 free admissions

Petit Train de la Défense (page 199)

No. of adults	1 2 3 4 5	Circle as appropriate - voucher valid for number of people who hold *for less* cards
No. of children	1 2 3 4 5	
No. of seniors	1 2 3 4 5	
No. of students	1 2 3 4 5	

Maxwell Café (page 212)

No. of adults	1 2 3 4 5	Circle as appropriate - voucher valid for number of people who hold *for less* cards
No. of children	1 2 3 4 5	
No. of seniors	1 2 3 4 5	
No. of students	1 2 3 4 5	

Ce coupon donne droit au titulaire de la carte **for less** aux réductions suivantes chez **Le Canotier** (page 210):

Adulte 20% de réduction Retraité 20% de réduction
Enfant 20% de réduction Etudiant 20% de réduction

Ce coupon donne droit au titulaire de la carte **for less** à la réduction suivante chez **Aquaboulevard** (page 177):

2-pour-1 entrée: chaque entrée achetée vous donne droit á une entrée gratuite d'une valeur égale ou inférieure (jusqu'à 2 entrées gratuites)

Ce coupon donne droit au titulaire de la carte **for less** à la réduction suivante chez **Musée Pasteur** (page 177):

2-pour-1 entrée: chaque entrée achetée vous donne droit á une entrée gratuite d'une valeur égale ou inférieure (jusqu'à 2 entrées gratuites)

Ce coupon donne droit au titulaire de la carte **for less** aux réductions suivantes chez **Le Petit Train de la Défense** (page 199):

Adulte 50% de réduction Retraité 50% de réduction
Enfant 50% de réduction Etudiant 50% de réduction

Ce coupon donne droit au titulaire de la carte **for less** aux réductions suivantes chez **Maxwell Café** (page 212):

Adulte 20% de réduction Retraité 20% de réduction
Enfant 20% de réduction Etudiant 20% de réduction

Château d'Auvers-sur-Oise (page 229)

No. of paid admissions: 1 or 2 (please circle)

Voucher valid for number of people who hold
for less cards –
maximum 2 free admissions

Château de Thoiry (page 230)

No. of paid admissions: 1 or 2 (please circle)

Voucher valid for number of people who hold
for less cards –
maximum 2 free admissions

France Miniature (page 230)

No. of adults	1 2 3 4 5	Circle as appropriate - voucher valid for number of people who hold *for less* cards
No. of children	1 2 3 4 5	
No. of seniors	1 2 3 4 5	
No. of students	1 2 3 4 5	

Château Vaux-le-Vicomte (page 230)

No. of paid admissions: 1 or 2 (please circle)

Voucher valid for number of people who hold
for less cards –
maximum 2 free admissions

Mutual of Omaha / Travelex (page 254)

Save 100% on transaction fees (commission free service) on foreign currency
and foreign currency travellers' check exchange at Mutual of Omaha / Travelex
branches listed on page 255.

Mutual of Omaha / Travelex (page 254)

Save 100% on transaction fees (commission free service) on foreign currency
and foreign currency travellers' check exchange at Mutual of Omaha / Travelex
branches listed on page 255.

Ce coupon donne droit au titulaire de la carte **for less** à la réduction suivante chez **Château d'Auvers-sur-Oise** (page 229):

2-pour-1 entrée: chaque entrée achetée vous donne droit á une entrée gratuite d'une valeur égale ou inférieure (jusqu'à 2 entrées gratuites)

Ce coupon donne droit au titulaire de la carte **for less** à la réduction suivante chez **Château de Thoiry** (page 230):

2-pour-1 entrée: chaque entrée achetée vous donne droit á une entrée gratuite d'une valeur égale ou inférieure (jusqu'à 2 entrées gratuites). Cette offre s'applique pour le promotion du Chateau, Jardins et Reserve Africain vendu ensemble uniquement.

Ce coupon donne droit au titulaire de la carte **for less** aux réductions suivantes chez **France Miniature** (page 230):

Adulte 50% de réduction   Retraité   50% de réduction
Enfant 50% de réduction   Etudiant 50% de réduction

Ce coupon donne droit au titulaire de la carte **for less** à la réduction suivante chez **Château Vaux-le-Vicomte** (page 230):

2-pour-1 entrée: chaque entrée achetée vous donne droit á une entrée gratuite d'une valeur égale ou inférieure (jusqu'à 2 entrées gratuites)

This voucher entitles the holder of a valid **for less** card to a savings of 100% off transaction fees (commissions) for foreign currency and foreign currency travelers' checks at the **Mutual of Omaha / Travelex** branches listed on page 254.

For official use only: Transaction value:_____
Cashier's use only: process through the **London for less** promotion
Cannot be combined with any other promotional offer.

This voucher entitles the holder of a valid **for less** card to a savings of 100% off transaction fees (commissions) for foreign currency and foreign currency travelers' checks at the **Mutual of Omaha / Travelex** branches listed on page 254.

For official use only: Transaction value:_____
Cashier's use only: process through the **London for less** promotion
Cannot be combined with any other promotional offer.

Oh!...Poivrier!

Ce coupon donne droit à 1 à 5 personnes à la
réduction de 20% sur le montant total de
l'addition (boissons comprises).

Oh!...Poivrier!

Ce coupon donne droit à 1 à 5 personnes à la
réduction de 20% sur le montant total de
l'addition (boissons comprises).

Oh!...Poivrier!

Ce coupon donne droit à 1 à 5 personnes à la
réduction de 20% sur le montant total de
l'addition (boissons comprises).

Oh!...Poivrier!

Ce coupon donne droit à 1 à 5 personnes à la
réduction de 20% sur le montant total de
l'addition (boissons comprises).

L'Amanguier

Ce coupon donne droit à 1 à 5 personnes à la
réduction de 20% sur le montant total de
l'addition (boissons comprises).

L'Amanguier

Ce coupon donne droit à 1 à 5 personnes à la
réduction de 20% sur le montant total de
l'addition (boissons comprises).

Not valid in conjunction with any other offer. Voucher
should be presented with bill before paying or discount
cannot apply. Not redeemable for cash.

Not valid in conjunction with any other offer. Voucher
should be presented with bill before paying or discount
cannot apply. Not redeemable for cash.

Not valid in conjunction with any other offer. Voucher
should be presented with bill before paying or discount
cannot apply. Not redeemable for cash.

Not valid in conjunction with any other offer. Voucher
should be presented with bill before paying or discount
cannot apply. Not redeemable for cash.

Not valid in conjunction with any other offer. Voucher
should be presented with bill before paying or discount
cannot apply. Not redeemable for cash.

Not valid in conjunction with any other offer. Voucher
should be presented with bill before paying or discount
cannot apply. Not redeemable for cash.

L'Amanguier

Ce coupon donne droit à 1 à 5 personnes à la réduction de 20% sur le montant total de l'addition (boissons comprises).

L'Amanguier

Ce coupon donne droit à 1 à 5 personnes à la réduction de 20% sur le montant total de l'addition (boissons comprises).

Poul' d'Or

Ce coupon donne droit à 1 à 5 personnes à la réduction de 20% sur le montant total de l'addition (boissons comprises).

Poul' d'Or

Ce coupon donne droit à 1 à 5 personnes à la réduction de 20% sur le montant total de l'addition (boissons comprises).

Poul' d'Or

Ce coupon donne droit à 1 à 5 personnes à la réduction de 20% sur le montant total de l'addition (boissons comprises).

Poul' d'Or

Ce coupon donne droit à 1 à 5 personnes à la réduction de 20% sur le montant total de l'addition, (boissons comprises).

Not valid in conjunction with any other offer. Voucher should be presented with bill before paying or discount cannot apply. Not redeemable for cash.

Not valid in conjunction with any other offer. Voucher should be presented with bill before paying or discount cannot apply. Not redeemable for cash.

Not valid in conjunction with any other offer. Voucher should be presented with bill before paying or discount cannot apply. Not redeemable for cash.

Not valid in conjunction with any other offer. Voucher should be presented with bill before paying or discount cannot apply. Not redeemable for cash.

Not valid in conjunction with any other offer. Voucher should be presented with bill before paying or discount cannot apply. Not redeemable for cash.

Not valid in conjunction with any other offer. Voucher should be presented with bill before paying or discount cannot apply. Not redeemable for cash.

Paris Airports Service (page 19)

Fare: Single   Circle before
                     or   boarding:
                   Return   voucher valid
                                     for either single
                                        or return

Paris Airports Service (page 19)

Fare: Single   Circle before
                     or   boarding:
                   Return   voucher valid
                                     for either single
                                        or return

Paris Airports Service (page 19)

Fare: Single   Circle before
                     or   boarding:
                   Return   voucher valid
                                     for either single
                                        or return

Paris Airports Service (page 19)

Fare: Single   Circle before
                     or   boarding:
                   Return   voucher valid
                                     for either single
                                        or return

Paris Airports Service (page 19)

Fare: Single   Circle before
                     or   boarding:
                   Return   voucher valid
                                     for either single
                                        or return

Paris Airports Service (page 19)

Fare: Single   Circle before
                     or   boarding:
                   Return   voucher valid
                                     for either single
                                        or return

Paris Airports Service (page 19)

This voucher entitles the holder of a valid **for less** card to a discount of 20% off a single fare and 20% off a return fare on the **Paris Airports Service** between central Paris and Orly or Charles de Gaulle (Roissy) Airports.

Paris Airports Service (page 19)

This voucher entitles the holder of a valid **for less** card to a discount of 20% off a single fare and 20% off a return fare on the **Paris Airports Service** between central Paris and Orly or Charles de Gaulle (Roissy) Airports.

Paris Airports Service (page 19)

This voucher entitles the holder of a valid **for less** card to a discount of 20% off a single fare and 20% off a return fare on the **Paris Airports Service** between central Paris and Orly or Charles de Gaulle (Roissy) Airports.

Paris Airports Service (page 19)

This voucher entitles the holder of a valid **for less** card to a discount of 20% off a single fare and 20% off a return fare on the **Paris Airports Service** between central Paris and Orly or Charles de Gaulle (Roissy) Airports.

Paris Airports Service (page 19)

This voucher entitles the holder of a valid **for less** card to a discount of 20% off a single fare and 20% off a return fare on the **Paris Airports Service** between central Paris and Orly or Charles de Gaulle (Roissy) Airports.

Paris Airports Service (page 19)

This voucher entitles the holder of a valid **for less** card to a discount of 20% off a single fare and 20% off a return fare on the Paris Airports Service between central Paris and Orly or Charles de Gaulle (Roissy) Airports.

L'Opentour (page 215)

20% discount on adult price

(27F off)

Present voucher to driver when purchasing ticket on bus

L'Opentour (page 215)

20% discount on adult price

(27F off)

Present voucher to driver when purchasing ticket on bus

L'Opentour (page 215)

20% discount on adult price

(27F off)

Present voucher to driver when purchasing ticket on bus

L'Opentour (page 215)

20% discount on adult price

(27F off)

Present voucher to driver when purchasing ticket on bus

L'Opentour (page 215)

20% discount on child price

(14F off)

Present voucher to driver when purchasing ticket on bus

L'Opentour (page 215)

20% discount on child price

(14F off)

Present voucher to driver when purchasing ticket on bus

L'Opentour (page 215)

This voucher entitles the holder of a valid **for less** card to a discount of 27F off an adult fare (135F) on the Paris L'Opentour open-top bus tour.

L'Opentour (page 215)

This voucher entitles the holder of a valid **for less** card to a discount of 27F off an adult fare (135F) on the Paris L'Opentour open-top bus tour.

L'Opentour (page 215)

This voucher entitles the holder of a valid **for less** card to a discount of 27F off an adult fare (135F) on the Paris L'Opentour open-top bus tour.

L'Opentour (page 215)

This voucher entitles the holder of a valid **for less** card to a discount of 27F off an adult fare (135F) on the Paris L'Opentour open-top bus tour.

L'Opentour (page 215)

This voucher entitles the holder of a valid **for less** card to a discount of 14F off a child fare (70F) on the Paris L'Opentour open-top bus tour.

L'Opentour (page 215)

This voucher entitles the holder of a valid **for less** card to a discount of 14F off a child fare (70F) on the Paris L'Opentour open-top bus tour.